ROYAL PALACES

Edited by M. MORELLI

BARNES & NOBLE

NEW YORK

ROYAL PALACES

EDITED BY
Marcello Morelli

EDITORIAL PROJECT
Valeria Manferto De Fabianis

EDITORIAL COORDINATION
Giulia Gaida
Alberto Bertolazzi
Bianca Filippone

TRANSLATION
C.T.M., Milan

GRAPHIC DESIGN
Clara Zanotti

NORTH AMERICAN EDITION
Managing editor JoAnn Padgett
Associate editor Elizabeth McNulty

1 Detail of the royal coat of arms on top of the entrance gate of Buckingham Palace in London.

2-3 View of the castle of Neuschwanstein, Germany.

4-5 Hall of Mirrors inside the palace of Versailles, France.

6 Decorative detail depicting the sun emblem, Louis XIV's symbol, at Versailles.

6-7 Main facade of Buckingham Palace, the royal residence in London.

7 bottom Detail of a decoration on the gates of Versailles.

The publisher would like to thank the following people and institutions for their kind cooperation in the realization of this book: Soprintendenza per i Beni Ambientali ed Architettonici del Piemonte, the staff of the Royal Palace of Turin; Giuseppe Fragalà, President of the association Amici di Palazzo Reale, and Sonia Bigando; La Liste Civile du Roi et Les Archives Royaux du Palais Royal de Bruxelles; the Press Office of Het Loo Palace; Stiftung Preussische Schlösser und Gärten Berlin-Brandenburg; Dr. Jolán Bak, Director of the Castle of Esterháza; Dr. Peter Kristiansen, Curator of Rosenborg; Dr. Göran Alm, Deputy Chief of Information of the Royal Palace of Stockholm; Dr. Thomas Thiis-Evensen, the Royal Palace of Oslo and NORTRA.

ISBN-13: 978-0-7607-8375-7
ISBN-10: 0-7607-8375-6
Library of Congress Cataloging in Publication Data available
Printed and bound in Thailand
3 5 7 9 10 8 6 4 2

Introduction

8 top *The walls of Windsor Castle, England, in the foreground, with St. George's Chapel behind.*

8-9 *Facade of the new palace of the castle of Sans Souci in Potsdam, Germany.*

9 top left *Detail of a statue adorning the* parterre d'eau *in the gardens of Versailles, France.*

9 center right *Staircase of the Ambassadors inside the Winter Palace, or Hermitage, in St. Petersburg, Russia.*

9 bottom *The Fountain of Ceres in the gardens of the Royal Palace at Caserta in Italy.*

The complex universe of the great historical residences of the world can be approached in many different ways. It is possible to study them from the point of view of the structures creating their graceful forms, or of the design of the architectural decoration adorning their fabric; the furnishings embellishing their salons and galleries may be appreciated; the collections of art that often make the historic residences into picture galleries and museums may be admired; their history may be studied through a series of events that took place hundreds of years ago—although, by some mysterious spell, these events are still alive and real within the walls of castles and palaces or on the trim walks of the ancient parks and gardens with their elegant symmetry. But there is another way of looking at these residences built by a whole host of architects, artists and craftsmen, furnished and decorated as splendid expressions of the taste of different periods and countries. In fact, because they were destined to be the residences of princes and lords, places for pleasure and recreation, and visible symbols of the power and importance of those who built them or lived in them, they represent, above all, the most direct and immediate expression of the personality and psychology of their owners. With regard to Versailles, the statesman and writer the Duc de Saint-Simon wrote in his *Mémoires* that the frequent banquets and the promenades at Versailles with close friends, were the means that the king used to distinguish or mortify people, choosing those who were to participate on each occasion, in order to make sure that each of them was attentive and constant in pleasing him. (The king at the time was Louis XIII: Versailles was still a small castle on the site of which Louis XIV was later to build his splendid palace.)

Thus—and, in this case, the testimony of the writer is invaluable—the residence was only one of the elements serving to make the courtiers aware of the importance of being pleasing to the sovereign. The latter would then show his appreciation with an invitation to one of the many banquets taking place at Versailles or with another request to accompany him to that residence. And, during the Sun King's reign, at Versailles everything was aimed at making the power and prestige of the monarch clearly visible—and, in many ways, tangible. Hence power was expressed by the splendid salons and imposing hall of mirrors, the pictures, tapestries and sculptures, and the gardens, fountains and other water features. Another example of this tendency is illustrated by the numerous castles built by Louis II of Bavaria, which expressed the tragic king's irresistible yearning in their style—the boldness of some of the architectural elements, such as the numerous spires and pinnacles, the upward thrust of the buildings in a desperate attempt to stretch out toward the unreachable. He yearned for a remote world, one that was no longer human or earthly but existed only in his terribly disturbed imagination. And who would deny that the gloomy and imposing royal palace and monastery of the Escorial was a close reflection of the tormented mind of Philip II, who was dramatically torn between the ascetic rigor of his religious faith and his ambition to rule the entire continent of Europe?

Furthermore, in the massive yet elegant structure of the Red Fort in India one cannot fail to see the most direct and coherent expression of the desire of Akbar the Great and Shah Jahan—the enlightened Mogul emperors who ruled India in the 16th and 17th centuries—to

display their power and invincibility before both their enemies and their loyal subjects. Thus they created an architectural complex combining robust walls and deep moats—which if required for defense could be filled with the waters of the River Jamuna—with the exuberant beauty of pavilions and gardens intended for the use of the powerful and wise sovereigns.

Naturally, it would be easy to get carried away with these examples. The Royal Palace at Caserta in Italy was built for the Bourbon King Charles III, who, in the mid 18th century commissioned the architect Luigi Vanvitelli (and after the latter's death, his son Carlo) to design and construct a building emulating the splendor of Versailles. And, in effect, the Bourbon palace is the epitome of an era in which the power of the sovereigns was expressed in part by the wonder, surprise and fascination elicited in loyal subjects and worldly-wise courtiers alike by the palaces in which the sovereigns lived and from which they governed.

But today we visit palaces, castles and villas and wander through the rooms and galleries with the detached attitude of the museum visitor who is ready to register in his or her mind the most significant images of these places and the furnishings and works of art they contain. In these circumstances we should not forget that a historical residence has been (and in many cases still is), first and foremost, a home—in other words, a place in which men and women, be they kings and queens, landowners or peasants, princes or artists, men of god or rich merchants, have lived, and

experienced the pleasures and pains of human existence. And we should also remember that the walls, furnishings, paintings and frescoes that we admire or study have been silent witnesses of triumphs and tragedies, love affairs, revenge and betrayal; of difficult decisions, of the applause of jubilant crowds or the invective of the rebellious populace. Yes, a historic residence is above all this: a home. And only when this first aspect has been fully appreciated can it become a museum—a place, that is, to visit and observe.

For this reason, these residences cannot, and must not, be considered merely as museums—that is, buildings where valuable works of art and objects of particular interest are preserved, catalogued and displayed— because these works and objects have been collected over the years by people who,

independently of their social and political roles, tracked them down, collected, acquired and commissioned them, allowing them to reflect their tastes, inclinations, interests and passions. This is true of the mighty fortresses of military commanders with their modest collections, just as it is of the splendid villas of country gentlemen and the great art collections built up over the centuries by the Hapsburgs in Austria and Spain, the Romanovs in Russia, the Valois and then the Bourbons in France, the House of Orange in the Netherlands, the Electors of Saxony in Germany and the Tudors in Britain. And if we analyze the historical process that led to the formation of these collections, now of inestimable value, we will realize that they reflect—as Sir Oliver Millar, former Surveyor of the Queen's Pictures and Director of the Royal Collection notes—their discernment and

Introduction
Introduction

10 top The Throne Room, castle of Neuschwanstein, Germany.

10 bottom Sundial of the palace of Wilanów, Poland.

10-11 Exterior view of the Royal Palace of Queluz, Portugal.

VII

IV

prejudices, their good and bad taste, their friendships and enmities and hostility, their loves and hates, foibles and obsessions. Millar's observation regarded the collection of over 5,000 paintings and drawings—with works by such artists as Titian, Bruegel, Hans Holbein the Younger, Frans Hals, Vermeer, Rubens, Rembrandt, Lucas Cranach and many more besides—largely kept in the Queen's Gallery at Buckingham Palace and built up by the kings and queens on the English (and then British) throne, from the Tudors to Elizabeth II.

However, as I have already pointed out, these magnificent palaces, despite the splendor of their architecture and the elegance of their lines, were built in many cases not to flaunt the wealth of their owner, but rather as an expression of their social position. To become a member of the upper classes and to have an important place in the social scale, it was not enough to have accumulated wealth: it was necessary to have a concrete manifestation of what a person or a family counted for in the community. And the palace, with its architecture, the splendid gardens that often surrounded it and the sumptuousness of the salons and galleries inside it, was the best means of concretely representing the social position, the importance and the lineage of the individual who had built it. As the German sociologist and historian Norbert Elias pointed out in his book *La Société de Cour*:

"Those who have an elevated social position are obliged to possess a residence and make sure it has a pleasant appearance. What, from the point of view of the economic morality of the bourgeoisie would only be a waste of money...is, in

11 top Patio de los Leones inside the Alhambra, Granada, Spain.

reality, the expression of the ethos of the upper classes."

In other words, sumptuous palaces, villas and castles have been built over the centuries so that the people could admire them and thereby become aware of the distance separating themselves from the lord—whether he be a feudatory lord, a local prince, or the sovereign. The palaces served as tools to help the people come to terms with the social differences that were heavily underlined by the explicit manifestation of wealth and power, as if these were a definitive and reassuring justification for their own lower social position.

12 View of the Winter Palace in St. Petersburg.

12-13 foreground Karskoe Selo in St. Petersburg.

The term "palace" derives from the Latin *palatium*, which denoted the imperial residence on the Palatine Hill in Rome, and was later applied to any royal residence. In the Middle Ages, palace architecture was given great impetus by the emergence, on the one hand, of the temporal power of the Church (resulting in the papal palaces of Avignon in France, and in Orvieto and Viterbo in Italy) and, on the other, of new types of government that stimulated the quest for totally new architectural forms, such as, for example, the Doge's Palace in Venice, with its seemingly weightless structure and its plan that remained unchanged for centuries. Although in the 13th and 14th centuries the princely palaces continued to develop, with complex layouts and often more than one block, municipal buildings also began to appear. And during the 15th century—rightly considered to be one of the most important periods in architecture, particularly in Italy—splendid Renaissance palaces were constructed. This especially in Tuscany and, above all, in Florence, where

Michelangelo's design for Palazzo Riccardi, that of Brunelleschi for Palazzo Pitti, that of Alberti for Palazzo Rucellai, and many others offer outstanding examples of private aristocratic residences in the Renaissance.

A particularly important characteristic of this period is the fact that the palaces were not only intended to be the residences of those who ruled the various republics—hence buildings that could be described as "public"— but also that, for the first time, they began to be constructed by the emergent families of the sociopolitical groups that were now coming to the fore. Thus, at this time, the concept of the palace as a private residence of single families or citizens originated. Generally they were of noble birth, and while they did not hold specific posts in the government of the city, by building they intended to assert their status with regard to the rest of the population, so as to distinguish themselves and promote their public images.

While many of the palaces constructed in the 15th century still looked like castles (an

Introduction

Introduction

13 top *The north side of the Knights' Hall (formerly called Long Hall) at Rosenborg, Denmark.*

13 center *background* *Facade of the castle of Schönbrunn in Vienna, Austria.*

14 top left The Channel of Paradise in the Rang Mahal of the Red Fort in Delhi, India.

14 right Sacred emblem of the Chakri dynasty inside the Throne Room of the Chakri Maha Prasad, Royal Palace of Bangkok, Thailand.

14 center Bronze lion inside the Forbidden City in Beijing, China.

15 left Mythological figure at the entrance of the Temple of the Royal Palace in Bangkok.

15 right Detail of an inscription inside Topkapi Palace in Istanbul, Turkey.

16-17 Decorative motifs of the Temple Wat Phra Keo in the Royal Palace of Bangkok.

outstanding example is the Ducal Palace at Urbino), this aspect completely disappeared in the 16th century to make way for the more spectacular architecture of the great palaces, outstanding examples of which are to be found in Rome (the Palazzo Farnese and the Michelangelo-style Palazzo dei Conservatori). However, this did not happen in other European countries, where the Gothic tradition continued to hold sway for some time. In France, the Louvre (built in the mid-16th century) is the first example of a palace constructed according to what were to become the canons of modern architecture, especially with regard to its innovative layout.

From the early 17th century onward, in civil architecture all over Europe, a process of renewal was underway in which the Baroque style played a major role, leading to a new approach to the design of princely palaces. Thus the facades were extended, the design of the courtyards was changed, and the old quadrilateral layout evolved into more complex forms. The palaces were now surrounded by parks and gardens designed by those who were to become the most outstanding landscape architects, not only of this period, but of all times. One such visionary was André Le Nôtre, who created the gardens at Versailles, which then became a model for countless other aristocratic residences all over Europe.

In the following centuries increasing importance was given to the way the spaces were used, with an attempt being made to give them a more precise function, without, however, reducing the specific weight of the artistic and the decorative features of the buildings. Although the chief aim was to make the palace a symbol of the social, and often political, standing of its inhabitants, a new requirement was felt: that of having rooms which in addition to being sumptuous were also comfortable and, as we would say today, "usable."

Of all the elements of the historical residences that contribute to making each of them unique, there is one that must be highlighted for its decisive role. I am referring here to the gardens, which, like the proscenium for an imaginary theatre stage, frame the buildings, enhancing them with the splendor of the plants that grow in them and with the regularity and symmetry of their layouts, their fountains, nymphaea, stables, green outdoor "rooms" and the shady bowers and imposing waterworks that soar upward in myriads of iridescent drops of water. In fact, the parks, gardens and surrounding estates do not merely embellish the appearance of the villas, castles and palaces, but are an inseparable element of their structures, forming part of their lines and development just as much as the marbles, capitals, columns, courtyards and porticos, or the many other elements that may be found in the harmonious and orderly representation of beauty. Moreover, in England in the 18th century, the garden was an important factor in the growth of a new aesthetic category, that of the picturesque. This category was largely derived from gardens, partly as a result of the contribution of painting and, more generally, of

the composite sociocultural situation of the period, thanks, above all, to the creation—or rather the discovery—of what was to become landscape gardening. On the other hand, would it be possible, for example, to imagine Versailles without its 1,730 acres of park or its 200,000 trees, or the 210,000 flowering plants that are bedded out every year, or the 50 fountains and 620 water jets? Or the Portuguese castle of Queluz without its splendid park? And again, what would the Alhambra of Granada be like without its pools and the play of thousands of jets of water sparkling with the colors of the rainbow? And let us not forget the marvelous Japanese gardens—the famous "stone garden" of Ryo-an-ji, or those in the villas of Katsura and Shugaku-in, or at the palace of Kyoto-gosho—nor the oldest royal garden in the world, the Chinese Beihai park on the western side of the Forbidden City, or the more modern Mogul garden in the official residence (the Rashtrapati Bhavan) of the President of India. Palaces and gardens of every age and nation are the elements of cultural expression that often mingle and integrate to form a harmonious set of meanings. Those who ordered their creation and passed on their beauty and art to posterity have left precious and irreplaceable testaments to what constituted beauty in past ages and distant lands.

Courts of Europe

Designed by famous architects and decorated by artists of genius, the magnificent palaces of royal European dynasties were both architectural masterpieces and extraordinary centers of power. It was in these palaces that the fates of countries were decided, great projects planned, murky plots laid and love and crimes intertwined in a setting of mystery and beauty. What follows is a trip through Europe and its history; the splendors and grandeur of the architectural jewels presented have survived but bear witness to the vicissitudes and ordeals of the history they have lived through. They are dazzling buildings that, far from being simply intellectual exercises in engineering, have evolved and been renewed throughout the ages in the most varied architectural and stylistic schemes while retaining (like organisms equipped with biological memory) the genes of their original beauty. It is no coincidence that the most beautiful palaces are the result of harmonized work that involved a concerted effort, given that, due to the size and complexity of the structures, their design and its realization—even where these are normally associated with the name of a single artist—were, in fact, the result of the skills and creativity of many.

This characteristic is especially evident in the two Italian royal palaces of Turin and Caserta.

The first building is the splendid result of more than 200 years of alterations with two very famous contributors who worked among others: Guarino Guarini, creator of the chapel of the Shroud, and Filippo Juvarra, who designed the unusual Scissors Stairway. The second building was begun by Luigi Vanvitelli and continued by his son Carlo, but only completed a century later. Vanvitelli's original magnificent layout of the palace has been retained, but the alterations the building has undergone, in part during the 19th century, are apparent in the interiors.

A perfect example of harmonious design is the chateau at Fontainebleau: in the mid-16th century, Francis I commissioned Le Breton to enlarge it; the architect called on the services of numerous Italian artists who were able to embellish the walls and ceilings of the castle with elegant decorations. And these stuccoes, frescoes and oil paintings thus contributed to the diffusion of the modes of the Florentine Renaissance in France thanks to the work of such artists as Rosso Fiorentino, Primaticcio, Nicolò dell'Abate and Benvenuto Cellini.

Numerous architects worked at Versailles, where the hunting lodge built in 1624 by Louis XIII was, in successive periods, gradually expanded: they included Louis Le Vau, the royal architect, who played a leading role in the development of French architecture in the 17th century; André Le Nôtre, who planned the splendid gardens of the future palace; Jules Hardouin-Mansart, Louis XIV's architect, who built the Grand Trianon; Jacques-Ange Gabriel, who designed the delightful Petit Trianon; and many others.

In Vienna, work on the imperial palace of Schönbrunn, designed by Johann Bernhard Fischer von Erlach, began in 1696, and it was subsequently expanded by Nikolaus von Pacassi in 1744. Meanwhile a Dutchman by the name of Steckoven, together with the Austrian Johann Ferdinand von Hohenberg, designed the gardens in the second half of the 18th century.

In London, Buckingham Palace, the residence of the British royal family, had been purchased by George III in 1762 and was converted into a royal palace by John Nash. After Nash's dismissal due to the excessive cost of the work, he was replaced in 1831 by Edward Blore. But it was only in 1913, when Aston Webb added the existing facade of

18 top Facade of the castle of Sans Souci, Potsdam, Germany.

18 bottom background Main entrance of the castle of Eszterháza near the Lake of Neusiedl, Hungary.

18-19 Basin of Apollo in the gardens of Versailles.

19 center left Patio de los Leones in the Alhambra in Granada.

19 top right Detail of a fresco in the Golden Age Room in the Royal Palace of Caserta.

19 bottom The White Sea in the Royal Palace in Stockholm, Sweden.

Portland stone, that the building was finally completed.

And when visiting the Alhambra, an outstanding example of Arab art with its complex and exquisite calligraphic architecture, how can we think that it was the work of just one artist? It could not have been just a single architect who, from the anonymous gravity of the ochre walls, was able to conjure the lightness of its internal structures and the graceful interlacing of thousands of decorative motifs.

There is yet another building, the architectural splendors of which are described in this book, that was constructed and decorated by numerous artists: the monumental royal palace and monastery of the Escorial. Philip II decided to build this

complex to commemorate the victory of San Quintino, which, together with other battles, allowed Spain to dominate Europe. Begun by Juan de Toledo in 1563, it was continued by Giambattista Castello, called "il Bergamasco," who was responsible, in particular, for the splendid staircase leading from the church to the palace, and by Juan de Herrera, who built the wonderful library, and then by Antonio Villacastin.... But many other artists and architects contributed in various ways to making this one of the outstanding buildings of Europe. They included Leone and Pompeo Leoni, who designed the tombs of Philip II and Charles V, and the Roman Giovanni Battista Crescenzi, who, in 1564, built the royal crypt.

Thus, as is evident from this brief outline, the description of the historical residences of

Europe as a "concerted effort" seems to be justifiable due to the multiplicity of the artists, often from different countries, who with their varied skills contributed to the design and construction of the buildings and the creation of the decoration and the innumerable artifacts embellishing them, thus allowing the places to become museums as well as homes. This happened in two different ways, both of which were essential for the diffusion of European culture and art: through the work of architects, decorators, painters, sculptors and furniture-makers who sought to satisfy the needs of those who, having admired their talents, engaged their services; and through the schools of art they created all over the world, which helped to form a host of followers and connoisseurs. This is why, very often, as one travels around Europe visiting palaces, castles and villas of diverse periods one seems to find something familiar in them. It is the effect of a common expression of the spirit resulting from the overlapping of artistic experiences and the migration of artistic talents that even during past centuries made Europe a large and single nation. One might go as far as to say that the building of these palaces was the most important cause of the diffusion of styles and artistic trends beyond the national boundaries within which they evolved.

Thus we can consider, for example, what happened to allow the diffusion of Baroque all over Europe. This style, born in Rome as a result of the crisis of 16th-century classicism, was taken to France by Italian artists who went there to work, or by French artists who visited Italy. From France it spread to Belgium and then Holland, Spain and Portugal, where it found very special expression without losing its links to Italian tradition. Free circulation of art in Europe, on one hand, produced an internationalization of styles and, on the other, encouraged the development of individual artists and their clients who were able

to influence architectural decisions with taste and competency. It is worth stressing once more that the residences, especially those in the "Old Europe" (or Western Europe) bear the indelible mark of the characters of those who commissioned them and who, during the construction of a sumptuous palace, imposing castle or elegant villa, added what nowadays we would call (with a term that smacks of psychology and psychoanalysis) the "imprint" of their personalities. And it is perhaps the careful search for this stamp, left on the residences of those who built them and lived in them, that serves as a stimulus for the imaginary journey that this book permits us to undertake.

20 top View of the Alcázar in Segovia, Spain.

20-21 Northern facade of the Great Palace of the Kremlin in Moscow, with detail on the left from the Terem Palace. In the background on the left are the cupolas of the Terem Church and the cathedral of the Dormition; on the right is the Belltower of Ivan the Great.

21 left External view of the main entrance of the castle of Schönbrunn, Vienna

21 top right Library of the Monasterio del Escorial, near Madrid, Spain.

21 bottom center Winged figure on the Victoria Monument in front of Buckingham Palace.

22 top *This painting by Horace Vernet (1789-1863), displayed in the entrance to the Galleria Sabauda, shows Carlo Alberto, king of Sardinia, receiving the homage of a garrison.*

22-23 *The facade of the Royal Palace is the backdrop to the castle square. The Royal Palace stood at the center of operations in its time, now the site of Turin's major monuments: here stand the Palazzo Madama, the royal c hurch of San Lorenzo, the palace of the dukes of Chiablese, the Chapel of the Shroud, the cathedral, the royal Armory and the Library, the palaces of the royal Secretariats, the gardens, and the Court Archive and the Theatre; in the past, the Mint and the Riding School stood here too. The Museum of Antiquities is housed in the orangeries near the excavated ancient Roman theatre, the remains of the ancient walls and, slightly to the northwest, the turreted entrance to the Roman city, the Palatine Gates.*

22 bottom left and 23 top right *Allegorical images are found throughout the gardens of the Royal Palace. The 17th century statues of the months; the seasons by Ladatte; and the fountain by Martinez (a nephew of Juvarra) stand in the elegant setting of the avenues that the visitor can still enjoy today.*

22 bottom right *The elegant arabesques of the railings that open onto the palace, and that stand in front of Abbondio Sangiorgio's statues of the Dioscuri, were designed by Pelagio Palagi for King Carlo Alberto.*

The Royal Palace of Turin

RESIDENCE OF DUKES AND KINGS

The Royal Palace of Turin is filled with the traces of those who built, decorated and lived in it. The prestigious and priceless collection of portraits of the Savoy family is an indication of the culture and open-mindedness of the princes and princesses who were both art collectors and patrons of artists. The walls offer them to us like tangible reminders of a past that still lingers in all its magnificence. It is the women in this collection who are the key to understanding the pictures. Each lady brought an echo of the court that she left behind when she married and came to lead an elegant life in the palace of Turin (a palace that competed for prestige with the royal residences of France and the Empire) and the delights that surround the city. In the 17th and 18th centuries—the period of the Piedmont Baroque—the splendor of the royal palaces grew as commissions from the Savoys flooded forth to a host of artists.

When Duke Emanuele Filiberto (1528–80), the imperial commander who won the battle of St. Quentin, made Turin the capital of his territories, he did not consider the old castle—built on one of the four Roman gates—to be suitable as a center of power. He moved into the bishop's palace, which was not only larger but receptive to alteration. Situated in the city's operational center, the palace allowed him to oversee two entrances to the city, the Pretoria and the Palatine Gates. This palace, called the Palazzo Vecchio and also known as the Palazzo di San Giovanni, had been the seat of the French viceroys during the struggles between France and Spain, and was now enlarged and decorated with the paintings and sculptures that the dukes began to collect. The ancestors of the House of Savoy lined the galleries with symbols of their power painted against background scenes of territories conquered and castles won, often with an image of the holy Protector at their side.

In keeping with the eclecticism of the Mannerist age, Emanuele Filiberto, like many other Italian princes, kept animal, botanical and mineral items in his galleries; for example, he had different types of marble from the various quarries of Piedmont. Like a *wunderkammer*, the Large Gallery held collections of medals, weapons and antiquities under Carlo Emanuele I. who also organized a library and an observatory with all kinds of books, mathematical instruments and codices. To

23 bottom The Dutch engraving from the Theatrum Sabaudiae *shows the Ducal Palace and the garden. Designed perhaps by Carlo Morello, the ducal garden must have been orderly and well looked after. It stretched onto the Green Bastion, which, with its watchtower, defended the east. Partly a product of the imagination of the designers of the Theater, this is the only picture of the original layout at the time of Emanuele Filiberto, a layout later developed by Carlo Emanuele I and his successors.*

23 top Vittorio Emanuele II, here depicted on horseback, was the first king of Italy. He succeeded his father, Carlo Alberto, and gained the name of "Gentleman King" because he favored the enlightened policy of Cavour that would unite Italy and free it from Austrian domination.

24-25 The Alcove Room still has almost all the decorations designed by Carlo Morello in 1662-63. The 18th-century furnishings and doorways are by Sebastiano Ricci, the marble fireplaces are 19th-century. The many portraits and the collection of Oriental vases are of particular interest.

24 bottom This detail of the decoration designed by Pelagio Palagi for the Audience Room shows the Savoy shield at the center of a triumphal crown with elegant ribbons. It is surrounded by palmette decorations that were typical of Neoclassical taste.

celebrate the marriages of his daughters—the Infanta Margherita wed Francesco Gonzaga, duke of Mantova, and the Infanta Isabella wed Alfonso d'Este, duke of Modena—he built a ring of porches topped by an open gallery around the castle square.

Vittorio Amedeo I (1587–1637) made a splendid marriage to Christiana of France and thus was able to embellish his court. To enlarge the Palazzo di San Giovanni, he demolished several houses belonging to clerics and began new construction in 1637. But building was not completed because of his early death and the ensuing struggles. Though somewhat restricted, the San Giovanni residence was filled with works of art; there were paintings by Titian, the Caraccis, Guido Reni, Perugino and others. But the masterpieces were sometimes stolen:

Madame Reale, the royal widow, paid a hefty ransom for the return of four works by Raphael. She preferred to live in the old castle, which was called Palazzo Madama in her honor. The richness of the decoration in both residences is well-documented; the walls were covered with velvet and Chinese silks; other tapestries were made from damask or silk with gold trimmings.

The rooms of the Palazzo Vecchio had imaginative names derived either from their use (the Princesses' Room, the Provinces' Room, the Parade Room, the Drawing Studio) or by their decoration (the City Room, the Jerusalem Room). A cannon foundry (where bronze statues were also cast), a powder magazine, a small hospital and various stables were annexed to the building. There were also a riding school, gardens with avenues and views,

The building of the Ducal Palace was a direct consequence of Emanuele Filiberto's choice of Turin to be his capital city in February 1563, upon which Turin acquired a new strategic role as a center of power. Between 1583 and 1584, Carlo Emanuele I announced a competition open to any "worthy men" who came to Turin from all over Italy; these included Pellegrino Tibaldi, Francesco Orologi and Ascanio Vittozzi. It was Vittozzi who was asked to fit out the square in front of the Castle and to design the Ducal Palace, and in that same year, 1584, the foundations were laid. A wooden model made by the carpenters Beltramo and Enchier showed the castle to have two floors above ground with flat pilaster strips and diamond-shaped ashlar facing. Various people were involved in the expansion of the Palazzo Vecchio. Amedeo di Castellamonte is usually considered to have been the superintendent of works although his name was not documented.

Under the direction of the cultured courtier Emanuele Tesauro, inspirer of mythological themes, insignia and exploits, the following

25 top The Dining Room was created from the king's summer bedroom and the dressing room, which Pelagio Palagi combined for Carlo Alberto. The ceiling painting by Gonin depicts the life of Umberto Biancamano. The wallhangings were made in Turin from drawings by Beaumont. Savoyard princesses are shown in the 18th-century panels above the doors.

25 bottom The King's Throne Room is perhaps the oldest room in the palace, and was built within the walls of the ancient Bishop's Palace. The ceiling painting by Jean Miel with the Latin motto Multis melior pax una triumphis *provided the original name, Room of Peace. which was changed only after 1830. The gilded wood ornamentation of the ceiling above the 19th century decorations was created by Botto di Savigliano around 1662.*

and a *trincotto,* a field for playing the ballgame that predated tennis. Although construction of the Palazzo Novo Grande had begun, the rooms of the Palazzo Vecchio di San Giovanni were repeatedly repaired. In 1656 it was still worthy of receiving Queen Christina of Sweden. She was welcomed in magnificent rooms with a four-poster bed and canopy, tapestries, silk embroidery, and velvet with gold and silver figures of flowers, birds and arabesques.

In the following century these rooms were used to accommodate ambassadors, until both the rooms and the theater were destroyed by a fire. The fire was an inauspicious end for Piedmont's most beautiful rooms and the glory of the old palace. The new palace, however, was being prepared as the chief and most magnificent residence of the king.

craftsmen worked: Giovenale Boetto was in charge of drawings for the painters; Quirico Castelli from Lugano and the Bottoses made gilded wood marquetry; Bernardino Quadri was director of marblework; and Jean Miel, Claude Dauphin, Bartolomeo Caravoglia, Giovan Andrea Casella, Francesco Cairo, and Antonio and Giovanni Fea from Chieri did painting. The ruler's apartments were on the main floor, most importantly those for Carlo Emanuele II (1634–75) and his wife Francesca d'Orléans, known as the "Dove of Love" for her fragile grace. The Rooms of the Virtues, Victories, Peace, Enigmas and Sleep were decorated with wallhangings, magnificent furniture, engraved and gilded alcoves, mirrors and glass. The Room of Dignities and the Room of Gentlemen Archers displayed the Duke's motto *Ad ortum solis ab hesperio cubili* to indicate that the "dignities" were derived both from the East (the *perpetuo vicariato imperiale*) and from the West (the *perpetuo elettorato*). In the Throne Room, also known as the Room of the Triumph

of the Graces, allegories with the characteristics of a perfect princess—beauty, modesty, good humor and gentleness—were displayed around Jean Miel's painting on the gilded ceiling. The virtues of France's fleur-de-lys were praised on the ceiling and in the decoration of Francesca d'Orléans' alcove: from the putti holding up her virtues to King Clovis receiving a shield decorated with the flower from angels. The Green Study was Carlo Emanuele II's reception room. It was also called the Room of Time, since the gilded ceiling carried allegorical paintings of day, night, the year and eternity.

Carlo Emanuele II's heir, Vittorio Amedeo II (1666–1732), was born of the duke's second marriage, to Giovanna Battista di Savoia Nemours. Vittorio Amedeo wanted a summer apartment looking onto the court and a winter apartment overlooking the garden and the Daniel Gallery (named for the Viennese painter Daniel Seiter, who painted the extraordinarily inventive ceiling amid the gilded plasterwork).

Construction of the Chapel of the Shroud by

The Royal Palace

Residence of Dukes and Kings

of Turin

26 top left *The Scissor Stairs were designed by Filippo Juvarra on the occasion of the marriage in 1722 of Vittorio Amedeo II's son, the future Carlo Emanuele III.*

26 center left *A graceful Madonna with Child and Saints in the roundel in the Queen's Private Chapel has been attributed to Carlo Maratta (1625-1713).*

26 bottom left *The Ballroom is a sumptuous reception room. It was designed by Palagi between 1835 and 1842.*

26 top right and bottom right *The Daniel Gallery (top) takes its name from Daniel Seiter, who painted the fresco* Apotheosis of a Hero *(bottom) in which Jupiter announces to Vittorio Amedeo the glories of his ancestry.*

27 *In 1997, a fire that broke out on the main stairway (now restored) seriously damaged paintings and stuccowork, the telamons made from* papier mâché, *the ceiling fresco showing Carlo Alberto, and the large historical canvases painted by Ferri, Gastaldi, Gamba and Bertini.*

Guarino Guarini of Turin was completed in 1684; it is attached to the west wing of the royal palace. Bernardino Quadri also worked on it, and Antonio Bertola designed the altar. The king could pass through the Shroud Gallery to reach the Chapel holding the Shroud, the Savoy family's most treasured possession (it was only recently given to the Vatican by Umberto II).

Once he became king of Sicily, Vittorio Amedeo II requested the presence of the Sicilian abbot, Filippo Juvarra, at court. Architect and descendant of a line of silversmiths, Juvarra had trained in Rome, where he had worked for Cardinal Ottoboni. He arrived in Turin in 1714. During the greatest period of Piedmontese art, he coordinated a group of famous artists who embellished the palace with sculptures, beautiful furnishings, and pictures, including Francesco Beaumont's series of superb frescoes. Juvarra was responsible for the creation of a new staircase design known as "scissor stairs," and for the design and provision of the lacquers in the Chinese Study.

The royal palace grew: Carlo Emanuele III, king of Sardinia (1701–73), raised a garden terrace so that he could build two apartments below, one for special archives and one for foreign princes (called the Apartment of Modern Paintings). In 1738 a new gallery linked the Swiss Salon to the Battle Gallery. The gallery that led to the Chapel of the Shroud opened into the Swiss Salon, a majestic room decorated with

a cycle of frescoes that celebrated the Saxon origins of the House of Savoy (painted by Antonio and Giovanni Fea, 1660–61). As the Savoy dynasty rose to be a European power, nobler origins were required (tradition had showed the Savoys descending simply from Bosone, count of Provence). The consort of Vittorio Amedeo I, Madama Reale Cristina, daughter of Henri IV of France, wanted the historian Guichenon to trace the roots of the House of Savoy back to the Saxon figures of Signeard, Widukind, Otto I, Bernard, and Frederick, whose stories decorate the Salon.

But the most important work in this room is the canvas of the Battle of St. Quentin painted by Palma the Younger (1582–85) for Carlo Emanuele I in remembrance of his father Emanuele Filiberto, the "Ironhead" duke.

Meanwhile, the Regia Chapel had been built, using some space from the one dedicated to Blessed Amedeo IX. Teams of painters had been used for the elegant decorations.

Later, during Carlo Emanuele III's reign, the architect Benedetto Alfieri (from the Cortemilia branch of the family, which also produced the poet Vittorio) succeeded Juvarra. He contributed to the Daniel Gallery, designed the Queen's Boudoir and decorated the Queen's Chapel (formerly the Miniature Room). Outstanding painters during this period were Guglielmi and De Mura.

Style tended toward Neoclassicism under Vittorio Amedeo III (1726–96) and the furnishings became increasingly rich under the direction of Pietro Piffetti and Luigi Prinotto, master cabinetmakers. Sculptures by Francesco Ladatte and tapestries and wallhangings produced by Demignot in Turin on the models of Beaumont and Gobelins were added to the lovely rooms. Using his experience as a cabinetmaker, Giuseppe Maria Bonzanigo decorated and furnished many palace rooms.

After the French occupation in 1799 and the Restoration, work on the palace resumed in the reign of Carlo Alberto (1799–1849). It was directed, from 1832, by Pelagio Palagi, "painter in charge of the decoration of the royal palaces." He renovated the Salon of the Swiss Guards, the Room of the Cuirassiers, the Throne and King's Room and the Audience and Council Room. Four rooms on the second floor were modernized for the wedding of Vittorio Emanuele II (1820–78) to Maria Adelaide of Austria. One of these, the Ballroom, was created by combining the Princesses' Room with the Room of Harmony, and was decorated in pure Neoclassical style. Domenico Ferri was brought in to design the new staircase during Vittorio Emanuele II's reign and, under his successor, Umberto I (1844–1900), the architect Stramucci decorated the Dining Room and the Queen's Throne Room.

Most subsequent modernization was merely functional until, with the ratification of the Republican Constitution on 2 June 1946, the

palace became a national museum of the life and works of the court of Savoy.

The gardens of the palace alone deserve attention. A paradise of leisure and magnificence, the palace's Baroque garden represented the concept of absolutism. Set atop the bastions of Turin, it was a spectacular spot for strolling or idling. The creation of the park was an elaborate and costly affair: a decree by Emanuele Filiberto names the considerable sum of "five thousand sixty-eight lire and eleven soldi." Parts of the fountain remain: a cyclops and perhaps the statues of the months of the year. Almost intact is an element which seems to have been designed by Vittozzi: the Garittone, also known as the Bastion of the

Angels. Its name was changed to Bastion of the Angels when Carlo Emanuele II had it redecorated in shades of green for his sick consort who loved to stand on it and look over the surrounding plains. It was decorated with a painted pergola, and cupids carried symbolic objects expressing the Duke's sadness. Further work on the garden was done at the end of the century: a payment was made to Du Parc in 1698. In 1754, the 85-year-old gardener for the Princes of Condé, Le Nôtre, lavished his creative talent on the park.

The orangeries now house the Turin Museum of Antiquities, which was created around the first archaeological collections of the House of Savoy.

28-29 Under Daniel Seiter's frescoed ceiling depicting the Four Seasons in the last room in the Queen's Apartments is a wallhanging showing the Tales of Don Quixote. A richly inlaid floor, gilded rocaille decorations and elegant furnishings complete the exquisitely feminine room.

The Royal Palace of Caserta

IMAGE OF AN ENLIGHTENED REIGN

Italy

CASERTA

On 20 January 1752, his 36th birthday, Charles III, the Bourbon king of Naples, laid the first stone of the royal residence that, in size and magnificence, would rival the great European palaces like Versailles in Paris and Buen Retiro in Madrid. The ceremony took place in a lovely setting at the foot of a gentle hill overlooking a wide, fertile countryside that stretched to the sea just a few miles from Naples. Squadrons of cavalry and infantry in full dress uniform lined the perimeter of the planned building, while long-range cannons manned by artillery troops were arranged at the corners. In the center the king and queen were attended in a wooden pavilion with the Papal nuncio, who was there to bless the laying of the first stone. In an unnatural silence, the king placed an octagonal marble box containing medallions with the royal portraits into a prepared hole; on top he laid a square marble slab with crosses at the corners, spread a little mortar over it with a silver trowel and finally placed the foundation stone. The architect of the palace, Luigi Vanvitelli, immediately laid on top of that a second stone inscribed with a phrase in Latin that read "May the Royal Palace, the Papal Seat and the Royal seed [i.e. Royal power] last till this stone sees the sun again."

The considerations behind the enlightened king's decision to build the palace are an indication of his farsightedness. He wished to move the royal court and government away from its dangerous proximity to the sea: in 1742 the English fleet arrayed in the bay of Naples had threatened to bombard the city. The king also wished to create jobs for the large

30 center The painting by S. Fergola (1799-1874) depicts the 1846 equestrian tournament in front of the Royal Palace. The building had already been used as a royal residence for some decades and its construction was almost complete, as it had been decided that the central dome and corner towers in the original design were to be omitted.

30 bottom The group of Astraea, goddess of justice, between Hercules and the personification of the provinces of the Kingdom of Naples (V. Villareale 1813), made of gilded stucco, dominates the large room decorated in Neoclassical style during French rule in Naples.

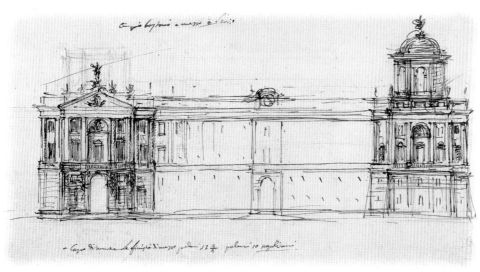

30-31 The palace's immense park is marked by rows of large pools that gradually drop lower. They are decorated with statuary and flanked by open expanses of grass and square flowerbeds.

31 top A large exhedra with the main balcony is framed between four Ionic pilasters in the upper part of the facade.

31 bottom Luigi Vanvitelli's sketch shows the approach to the palace in the project presented to the king on 7 December 1751. The left side of the facade is shown and we can see the indecision of the architect on whether to complete the corners with towers or simple classical pediments.

32 top In the 18th century, the large European courts wanted royal residences away from the cities and many architects designed buildings of extraordinary size and monumentality. Such was the case of M. Gioffredo's design for the palace at Caserta, a design that was never built and which seems in part inspired by Vanvitelli's ideas.

32-33 The visitor arriving from Naples sees first the mass of the building (822 x 202 x 133 feet) with its facade well balanced horizontally and vertically and the harmonious proportions of the windows that suggest the five floors above ground.

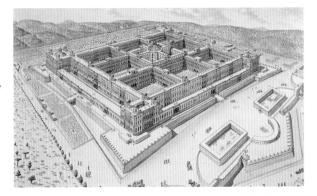

number of decorators, craftsmen and workers who filled Naples in the mid-18th century. And, no less important, this countryside was rich with the woods, birds and animals that were so appreciated by the court, for whom hunting was a primary entertainment. Charles's idea was to build a single, self-sufficient structure, capable of accommodating all the forces required for government of the kingdom, and which would also act as the center around which a new capital could be built. To put this concept into practice, he sent to Rome for the indefatigable architect Luigi Vanvitelli, who had already distinguished himself as a painter, hydraulic engineer, designer and town planner. Indeed, Vanvitelli's versatility was his greatest talent, and this versatility was to characterize the whole project. The palace's compositional logic featured "a stereometric severity in the architectural composition and sophistication of the core points of the palace" (De Seta). These core points were, for example, the large central vestibule, the vestibule on the floor of the royal apartments,

the great stairway, the royal chapel, the court theater and the garden. On 7 December 1751, Luigi Vanvitelli officially presented "The Declaration of the Plans for the Royal Palace" to the court. This contained a written introduction (in which, among other things, the architect praised the king's choice of site) as well as fourteen large drawings that showed the features of the palace in detail. The plans were so enthusiastically received by the king and queen that, just a month later, the laying of the foundation stone took place. The area became a large worksite directed with a firm hand and great skill by Vanvitelli. The massive equipment and huge number of workers made a great impression on visitors who travelled from Naples to admire the "great construction." Sightseers doing their Grand Tour (the journey made by wealthy European aristocrats and the children of aristocratic families to study literature and arts in Italy) all described in their diaries the strong impression made on them when visiting the site. This is hardly surprising given that Luigi Niccolini, the court archivist,

REGVM . NEAPOLITANORVM . SERIES .

recorded that between 1755 and 1763 the following numbers of people worked on the site: three directors of works, 14 administrators, 300 master masons, 1810 workers, 200 women, 166 prisoners condemned to forced labor, 245 Turkish slaves, 160 Christian slaves and 438 guards. In addition, for the supply and transportation of materials the workers used numerous elephants, camels and other beasts of burden. Undoubtedly, the visitors witnessed a very busy, animated and complex spectacle.

The works proceeded at a good rate. In June 1752, all the foundations were dug and construction of the walls was begun. The following year was occupied by the construction of the Caroline Aqueduct, which carried water from the Tifatini mountains to the palace and then on to Naples. On 7 May 1762, water arrived at the "grande fabrica," bringing to life an important part of the scenery of the Palace. In 1756 the two floors

built below ground were finished and the first 53 rooms on the ground floor were already covered; but in the same year Ferdinand IV of Spain died and Charles III was obliged to leave the Kingdom of the Two Sicilies to succeed him. He left on 7 October 1759. This development was uncomfortable for Vanvitelli to whom the loss of the king meant not only the disruption of a guaranteed and constant flow of funds but also the disappearance of an attentive client who was knowledgeable about architecture. Nonetheless, the works continued after Charles' departure; as Charles' successor to the throne, Ferdinand IV, was only eight years old, the kingdom was under the guidance of the Prime Minister, Bernardo Tanucci.

Construction of the Court Theater was begun in 1760 and two years later the marble personally chosen for the decorations by Queen Maria Amalia arrived. By the end of

34 top The arrival of water at the palace on 7 May 1762 aroused great enthusiasm. The moment was immortalized by A. Joli in this painting of 1769 showing the inauguration of the waterfall.

34-35 The pool of the Aeolus fountain is fed by a waterfall from a series of arches in the form of caves from which winged cupids exit, symbolizing the 28

winds. The center was supposed to be crowned by Juno on a carriage pulled by peacocks but this was never completed.

34 bottom left The fountain shows Ceres holding the coat of arms of Sicily and flanked by statues personifying the Anapo and Limeto rivers in Sicily. It was sculpted by Gaetano Salomone in Carrara marble in 1783 and 1784.

34 bottom right The fountain of the myth of Diana (here showing the group of Actaeon) was produced by a group of Neoclassical sculptors including Solari, Persico, Brunelli and Violani in 1785 and 1789.

35 top The artificial waterfall is fed by an aqueduct designed by Vanvitelli that takes its water from the Tifatini mountains. Besides supplying the fountains, it provides water to the palace and then continues to Naples.

35 center The fountain of Venus and Adonis was also produced by Salamone in 1784 and 1785. The goddess in the center is trying to dissuade Adonis from hunting the boar that will be the cause of his death.

35 bottom The fountain of Diana and Actaeon is elliptical and gets its water from the artificial waterfall. The goddess, surrounded by nymphs on the right, is angry at having been trailed by Actaeon.

1763, the western facade was practically complete.

Over the next three years work was greatly slowed by the famine that affected Naples in 1764. But work renewed with vigor in 1767, after Vesuvius erupted on 22 October and Ferdinand IV decided to transfer the royal family from Portici, on the volcano's slope, to the safety of Caserta.

The Court Theater was inaugurated in 1769 but this was the only part of the palace that Vanvitelli was to see completed, as he died on 1 March 1773. Management of construction passed to his son Carlo who, though he followed his father's project carefully, did not see it fully completed.

The Royal Chapel was consecrated on Christmas Day 1784 and the first royal apartment (known as the "old" apartment), corresponding to the southern facade, was finished in 1790 with all its decorations. The work in the park was also approaching completion, including the English Garden, which was laid out between 1785 and 1830. When in 1845 decoration of the "new" royal apartment was finished, the palace was complete as we see it today.

The royal family lived at Caserta until 1860, when the property passed to the Savoy family with the conquest of Italy. It was ceded to the Italian State in 1919 and was transformed into a museum and a public park. On the night of 24 September 1943, a bomb from an Allied plane struck the Chapel, destroying most of its decorations. Today, the complex of the Caserta palace and its park is one of the most important tourist attractions in the region of Campania; each year more than a million visitors admire what is perhaps one of the largest and best preserved houses representing the passage from Mannerism to Neoclassicism.

The palace appears in all its majesty when viewed from the west: the enormous avenue that connects it to Naples, and which acts as the axis of perspective for the palace and park, is the reference point for the entire complex. The building itself is rectangular with four identical courtyards shaped by the

perimeter wings and the two sections of the building that cross in the center. The sides measure 274 by 218 yards and the height of the building above ground is 133 feet. Luigi Vanvitelli's plans included four large square towers at the corners of the palace rising two stories higher than the facades as well as a large center dome on a tall drum, but unfortunately these were never built. These features would have emphasized the vertical thrust of the building and the dome would have offered a centripetal element. The external facades are characterized by a lower register of ashlar above which an upper

register is marked by composite-style pilaster strips. The pilaster strips frame two orders of windows, one at the level corresponding to the royal apartments and the other at the level corresponding to the noble apartments. The facades are surmounted by a cornice with quadrangular windows and topped by a balustrade which Vanvitelli designed a long series of statues.

The facade has three light tetrastyle avant-corps with composite-style half-columns and a tympanum that, in the original plan, was to hold a statue of Charles III. The arched entrance to the Great Portico stands in the

36-37 The marble-covered main staircase is perpendicular to the axis of the octagon that acts as the center of the building. It rises from the floor of the lower vestibule to the royal apartments. The middle flight gives a view of great elegance thanks to the three arches that lead into the upper vestibule.

37 bottom The lovely apartment of Queen Maria Carolina has four rooms. The third, the bathroom, contains this fresco with nymphs pouring water.

center of the facade, and the entrances to the courtyards to the sides. The whole construction has seven floors: two are below ground and are used as storerooms, workshops and kitchens. The ground and the first floors were used by the court; the second floor was a service area; the third floor housed the royal apartments (the king's apartments facing north and the queen's south); on the fourth floor were grouped the lodgings of the high court dignitaries; while the last, or fifth, accommodated other members of the royal family and members of court. Each floor has 34 windows on the long sides and 31 on the short. In addition to the massive main stairway, there are 26 other internal stairways to the different floors which all told contain 1,217 rooms!

A wide octagonal vestibule in the center of the internal structure of the palace opens onto the four courtyards and onto the main stairway to the upper floors. A sumptuous upper vestibule, also octagonal, lies above the lower one and leads to the Palatine Chapel, the royal apartments, the Throne Room and the Library. The Court Theater was reached from the two northern courtyards. The expanse of the park opens

38 top This painting by G. Cammarano (1820) with Vesuvius in the background shows King Francesco I and his family around the bust of Ferdinando IV.

38 center The Theatre was only included in Vanvitelli's design on the express wish of the king. It was built in the shape of a

horseshoe with 42 boxes on three richly decorated rows. Ferdinando IV was a great lover of the theatre and appointed choirmaster Giovanni Paisiello, who performed his first works here.

38-39 The Mars Room was decorated during French rule in Naples and shows all the Neoclassical influences of the Imperial style. The architectural order is Ionic and the panels in between the gilded pilasters contain bas-reliefs of Mars and war by French artists.

at the end of the Great Portico. The gallery crossing the palace is a long, covered path with poor light and many shadows and it further amplifies the brightness of the park in the distance. The view is of a long chain of pools flashing oval reflections of statues and fountains based mostly on mythological figures such as Aeolus and Hera, Ceres, Venus and Adonis, Diana and Actaeon. The view to the east is of the waterfall that originates in the grotto atop the hill of the Caroline Aqueduct. Also to the east, but south of the line of fountains, lies the English Garden, planted with exotic trees

and containing the romantic Bath of Venus. It is surrounded by artificial ruins that show how Charles III wove together the construction at Caserta and the excavations at Pompeii and Herculaneum, which he also oversaw. In his *Voyage Pittoresque, Age of Enlightenment* Abbot Richard de Saint-Non wrote, "the palace alone is worth a visit to Italy."

39 bottom left The Palatine Library occupies three adjacent rooms. It was set up on the wishes of Queen Maria Carolina as though to give the image of a cultured court and to counter the negative gossip about the court.

39 bottom right The Astraea Room is similar in form to the Mars Room and was decorated by Valerio Monreale (1813). The style is evidence of the ascendance of French decor.

40-41 *The Spring Room was used by the king for audiences. It was decorated by A. Dominici with cupids and festoons and featured views of ports of the kingdom by J. F. Hackert along the walls. Today those pictures rest on top of San Leucio silk.*

40 bottom left *The large canvases of the walls of the Alexander Room include one by G. Maldarelli showing the handover of the Kingdom of Naples to Ferdinando IV Bourbon.*

40 bottom right The Golden Age Room exemplifies the taste of a court still linked to the themes and styles of 18th-century Baroque but it also demonstrates the capabilities of the Neapolitan craftsmen who put their experience of decorating the town and country houses of the nobles to good use at Caserta.

41 top right The Rooms of the Seasons take their names from the ceiling frescoes. They were reception rooms for the first royal apartment that was built in the southwestern block of the palace. This is the Autumn Room in which Dominici painted the meeting between Bacchus and Arianna, and Funaro painted the festoons and tendrils.

41 center This detail from the ceiling fresco of the Spring Room painted by Dominici shows a concertino in the open air with red-cheeked ladies and laughing cupids beneath plaited garlands.

41 center right M. Rossi's fresco represents the Marriage of Alexander and Roxanne. It occupies the short side of the large ceiling in the Alexander Room (the third antechamber used by guests without titles).

The work is of great visual impact and stylistically shows the influence of the Venetian school that decorated many royal residences throughout the 18th century.

41 bottom right The Summer Room was painted by F. Fischetti in 1777 and 1778 with the myth of Persephone who presents herself to Ceres after leaving the underworld. The room is finely decorated with dadoes in white and gold wood on the walls and painted tiles on the floor. The fossil wood table decorated with agate was made by the scientist Gerolamo Segato.

The Royal Palace of Versailles

THE GREAT LOVE OF LOUIS XIV

42 top Louis XIV portrayed in full dress in a 17th-century painting kept in the palace museum. It was he, the Sun King, who conceived Versailles as an emblem of the absolute monarchy.

42 top left This decoration, a detail taken from the palace railings, reproduces the coat of arms of the Capetian reigning dynasty.

42 bottom left The image shows a painting by Pierre Patel. In 1668 the painter represented Versailles with the circular court conceived by Le Vau, which was later enclosed in Jules Hardouin-Mansart's subsequent project.

The object of the Sun King's passion was not some artful courtier, nor a noble lady or even some secret child born out of wedlock: it was Versailles, the palace he built himself and the symbol of the monarchy at its peak. But before Versailles was constructed, it was the pleasure of the hunt, the woods wrapped in early morning mist and a bag filled with game that inspired Louis' love for the place where his father, Louis XIII, had built a hunting lodge in 1624 in a marshy area of ponds, woods and reed-beds and where he, the Dauphin, had learned to hunt deer even as a child. "I will never understand," wrote the Duke of Saint-Simon, author of the celebrated *Mémoires*, "why the King left Saint Germain-en-Laye (Louis' place of birth and home to a royal palace where the King stayed after the death of his mother, Anne of Austria, in 1666), surrounded by forests, streams and meadows, for Versailles, the saddest and most unwelcoming place on earth: without views,

water or land and boasting only treacherous sands and marsh." The modest hunting pavilion stood on a small hill near the Val de Galie, not far from Paris, between the valley of the Seine to the north and the valley of the Brièvre to the south. The building was enlarged between 1631 and 1634 by Philibert Le Roy and was to become the "petit château de cartes" in bricks and stones at the heart of the immense palace that was slowly raised around it over the following years. The outline of that original nucleus can still be made out in the facade of the Marble Court, which has remained almost intact.

At the beginning, Louis XIV used the little lodge as a secret refuge for his amorous trysts with the lovely Louise de la Vallière and built a fairy tale park around it. And the setting in which the unforgettable "Fête des plaisirs de l'île enchantée" took place in honor of Louis' favorite, attended also by Molière, was truly magical. In 1660, after a few months of

43 top *The Latona Basin, shown here on the far side of the parterres d'eau (pools), is reached via a wide stairway. Amid the many fountains in the gardens of Versailles, it is not difficult to imagine the nobles and courtiers who spent hours in pleasant idleness walking here at the time of Louis XIV.*

43 bottom *The gardens are not only a splendid example of landscape gardening: the wide vistas culminate in settings populated by statues of nymphs, gods, sphinxes and Titans as planned by Le Nôtre, the great garden designer who realized the Renaissance ideals of the Italian garden in great splendor at Versailles.*

42 bottom right *The architect Jules Hardouin-Mansart, shown here, made a decisive contribution to the completion of Versailles. Born in Paris in 1646, he was Louis XIV's favorite architect and was appointed general superintendent of the Bâtiments du Roi by the king himself. Mansart was the best interpreter of Louis's cultural policies aimed at exalting the sovereign, the only true expression of an absolute state.*

42-43 *This aerial view of Versailles shows one of the most glorious and perfect examples of 17th-century French art in all its magnificence. The palace is also France's second most visited museum after the Louvre, welcoming about four million visitors each year.*

44 top The Basin of Apollo is set on the main axis (almost two miles long) of the garden. The octagonal pool lies at the far end of a long grassy expanse with the wonderful sculpture by Jean-Baptiste Tuby at its center. The group represents the Sun God in his chariot as he is about to begin his journey across the sky.

44-45 Two parterres d'eau *were built in front of the central section of the palace. The pools are decorated with superb allegorical bronzes of rivers. The large pools perform an important decorative effect: besides providing the dynamism of fountains, they also function as mirrors, elongating perception of the architectural components.*

44 bottom left The Marble Court takes its name from its marble slab pavement. The palace is the heart of the huge complex of Versailles and these buildings, in particular, are the nucleus of the whole site, though their original appearance has since been altered.

marriage to the Spanish Infanta, Maria Teresa, not wishing to demolish the hunting lodge that had been so dear to his father, the young Louis XIV decided to transform it into a more grandiose affair. He already had the model he wished to imitate in mind—the magnificent palace of Vaux-le-Vicomte that his Finance Minister, Fouquet, had built a few miles from Paris. Consequently, he bade the same architects work for him; they were Louis Le Vau, the painter and decorator Charles Le Brun, and the landscape designer André Le Nôtre. Le Vau built the first Orangerie and began the Ménagerie. In 1668, he began the project to enlarge the lodge on the garden side. In 1672, he worked on the Apartement des Bains and the Escalier des Ambassadeurs. In 1678, Jules Hardouin-Mansart, the king's principal architect, drew up the plans to enlarge what was turning more and more into a palace from *A Thousand and One Nights.* The terrace that overlooked the gardens was removed to make way for the magnificent Hall of Mirrors, the Galerie des Glaces. The man responsible for the finances, Colbert, attempted to convince the king that Versailles was too costly for the country's coffers, but in

as a symbol of civilization and pleasure, the seat from which the king radiated his power and where the destiny of Europe was decided for over a century. From that moment, the sumptuous chateau thirteen miles from Paris became the most extraordinary "ville royale" in the world. Ten thousand courtiers (five thousand of them nobles) sat down to dine there every day. They surrounded the king and served him with dignity and honors and he, in his turn, opened the doors of his apartments to them and offered them dances, games and "divertissements."

The building continued for the whole of his reign but the cost in human life to build Versailles must not be forgotten. Thousands of the 30,000 who worked on the site died of cold, hunger and disease in the failed attempt to deviate the waters of the river Eure to pass by Versailles along a 43-mile network of canals. The small village of Versailles, which had been no more than a handful of country houses in 1661, was in 1713 the "ville nouvelle" of 45,000 inhabitants where no building was allowed to be higher than the palace (a rule still enforced) and connected to Paris by an incessant traffic of horses, carriages

45 top Attention to detail characterizes all the works at Versailles. The three designers who began the realization of the Sun King's dream were the architect Louis Le Vau, the painter and decorator Charles Le Brun and the garden designer Le Nôtre. The three artists had only just completed Fouquet's palace at Vaux-le-Vicomte, which had aroused Louis XIV's envy.

45 bottom This portrait by Jean-Baptiste Martin (1659-1735) shows Louis XIV on horseback. The palace of his dreams stands in the background, already completed.

44 bottom right The facade of the Princes' Wing overlooking the gardens is tinged with warm colors in the light of the approaching dusk and is reflected in the waters of the parterre d'eau onto which it faces.

vain (the cost in 1684 came to nearly eight million francs). In reply, the Sun King organized an absurdly expensive celebration that was officially in honor of the Peace of Aix-la-Chappelle but in fact had the purpose of rendering homage to Louis' new favorite, Madame de Montespan.

In 1682, Louis XIV chose Versailles as the fixed residence of the sovereign, his court and the government. Day by day, Versailles became the superb Baroque palace known to the world

and carts going to and fro.

Strict rules governed Versailles: the princes, the ministers and high dignitaries lived in the north and south wings overlooking the gardens, while courtiers' apartments faced the village. The royal apartments were situated on the first floor of the central body of the palace, the king's to the north and the queen's to the south. They were reached by two marble stairways, the Escalier des Ambassadeurs (no longer in existence) and the queen's stairs.

There was also a small manual written by the king himself in 1689 entitled *Manière de montrer le jardin de Versailles* (the original is held in the Bibliothèque Nationale of Paris) in which the king gave suggestions in 25 paragraphs on how best to visit the terrestrial paradise of which he was the supreme artificer and architect.

A lover of tall trees, the king personally selected pines, poplars and plane trees which he had brought from every part of France, Flanders and even Italy. He loved flowers just as much, particularly those with a strong perfume, and the gardener Le Bouteux was constantly in search of rare essences to satisfy

the king's wishes. Although there is no portrait that shows him against a background of Versailles' avenues, it easy to imagine Louis dressed in his brocade and lace suit, his hat placed on his magnificently bewigged head as he relishes the fountains, flower beds and pools of water for which gondolas were even brought from Venice. Right up to the end of his reign, the park was Louis' permanent preoccupation and delight and he found in Le Nôtre (1613–1700), the son of Louis XIII's gardener, a pupil of the painter Simon Vouet imbued with Roman culture, the perfect collaborator and interpreter of his most fanciful projects. Le Nôtre designed not a

The Great Love of Louis XIV

garden for the king but a Baroque city filled with surprises so that the king's fervent imagination was free to indulge itself in creating the most beautiful celebrations on earth. To create a city out of the surroundings, the architect modeled nature like a theater stage; he used effects of all kinds and planted long curtains of trees and copses in every corner. Mythological statues, pools, fountains and mazes were dotted throughout the grounds. He supplied water to the pool called the Grand Canal and created a miniature fleet of warships for naval battles, a favorite pastime of the king and nobles. The "gardens of logic and intelligence," as they were called, not only had to represent the highest expression of landscape architecture, but also reflect the scientific rigor invoked by the theories of mathematician René Descartes, the initiator of modern rationalism and inspiration to 17th-century thought.

The gardens were an ideal setting for love affairs, court intrigues, romantic walks and

47 bottom center The king's personal taste, and his desire to amaze those who came to the palace to pay homage to him, are reflected in the Salon of Mars, also in the Grands Apartements, with its gilt, painted ceiling and ruby-colored damask on the walls. The room was used for giving balls and concerts.

47 top right The Salon of Diana is a trove of pictorial decoration, with frescoes on the large lunettes of the ceiling, marble busts and inlays on the walls. The recurring themes are hunting and sailing, both activities that were connected with the goddess. This room too is in the Grands Apartements, the part of the palace that Louis XIV soon abandoned to receptions in favor of building other royal apartments.

46-47 The Salon of Abundance is one of the more familiar and intimate rooms in the king's apartments. The furnishing is lavish with pictorial details, portraits of kings in Baroque frames, busts of philosophers, decorations and antique furniture contributing to the whole.

46 bottom left The Salon of Venus, also in the Grands Apartements, is dedicated to the goddess. The ceiling is completely decorated with scenes from mythology while marble niches in the walls contain statues of other ancient heroes.

47 bottom right This detail of the magnificent fresco painted by François Lemoyne in 1733-36 in the Salon of Hercules shows the Apotheosis of Hercules. The room joins the older section of the palace with the new wing designed by the architect Hardouin-Mansart.

secret appointments. They were aligned east-west so that the king could gaze into infinity from his chambers as he looked past the Basin of Apollo. They stretched down a central axis for over two miles in a straight line from the palace, first along the Grand Canal and then fanning off into other intersecting avenues which led onto other prospects.

The garden statuary was begun in 1661 by a team of the best 50 sculptors that France could produce, including Girardon, Coysevox, Le Hongre and all the members of the Académie under the direction of Charles Le Brun, the king's principal painter, first, and then Jules Hardouin-Mansart. Models of the statues were first created in plaster and temporarily set in the avenues. The decision,

naturally, lay with the king on whether to have them cast in bronze in the foundry of the Keller brothers (who produced his war cannons) or to have them sculpted in the pink marble of Languedoc or the green marble of the Pyrenees. The gardens formed a sort of Olympus where the many mythological statues and figures depicting titans and giants in the fountains could be seen as locked in eternal struggle. Such ideas inspired Louis who liked to identify members of his court in the cast of mythological characters. One day, however, the king found that these figures were too severe and that they needed to be "lightened" with dancing youths and cupids. This prompted the building of the Avenue of Water where threesomes of young boys and girls

The Great Love of Louis XIV

48 center left The Salon of War is decorated with a medallion by Coysevox showing the Sun King defeating his enemies.

48 bottom left The Salon of Peace takes its name from the fact that the king liked to be portrayed by Lemoyne as a peacemaker in Europe.

48 top right The Opéra Royal was designed during Louis XIV's reign but completed by Louis XV. Its perfect proportions could hold a thousand spectators and be transformed into a ballroom by raising the floor to the level of the stage.

48 center right The Bull's Eye Salon gets its name from the oval window in the gilded stucco plastering.

48 bottom right The ceiling of the Hall of Mirrors, decorated by Le Brun, illustrates important episodes from Louis XIV's life. Louis is represented in the paintings as an ancient hero.

49 The royal Chapel was designed by Jules Hardouin-Mansart and was the magnificent setting for all court religious ceremonies. The upper of the two floors was reserved for members of the royal family.

seem to dance in step while water splashes over them like a silver veil. The collection of over three hundred statues, not including the baths, busts, marble vases and bronze statues, form the most important open air museum in the world today. To make a visit to the gardens even more spectacular, concerts of Baroque music blended their notes with the incessant plash and burble of water from the fountains, night and day. The present day plays of water still have an important role at Versailles: on certain Sundays from May to September, they attract 20,000 visitors per day who marvel at the jets of water and nighttime celebrations on Neptune's pool which evoke the times of the

Sun King. Neptune sprays 44 jets of water from his mouth to a height of 75 feet. In the grotto of Thetis, a hydraulic clock imitates bird song and the four horses of Apollo ride across the water as though they had just emerged from the depths of the earth. Many scenes and settings from Louis' time have since disappeared, but they live on in the pictures kept in Versailles Museum—for example, the Royal Island that Louis replaced with the romantic English garden.

It was not easy to supply the water needed for the park. In 1665 there was only a single pump which was able to provide 22,000 cubic feet of water a day. A decade later, a masterpiece of hydraulic engineering was built which

50-51 *The Hall of Battles is almost 370 feet long. It was built for Louis-Philippe to celebrate France's great military victories. In order to build it, four apartments destined for members of the royal family had to be eliminated. The wall paintings show kings and famous generals on the battlefield.*

was able to supply more than eight times that amount.

Not all the Sun King's reign was golden nor were all the days spent in the great palace happy. At the end of Louis' life, the terrible winter of 1709 brought famine and a polar cold to Versailles. In the park there were hungry wolves. The Dauphin, the last survivor of six illegitimate children, died in 1711. In 1714, the same fate met the Duke of Berry, Louis' last grandchild. Only a great-grandson remained when the king of Versailles died, exhausted from gout, at a quarter past eight on 1 September 1714.

Once king, his great-grandson Louis XV

Adam, Bouchardon and Lemoyne which can still be seen. His heir Louis XVI drew up plans for restructuring the whole palace but he hardly had time to plant new trees in the large park and to see the Hameau de la Reine completed in 1783 before the Etats-Générales met at Versailles on 5 May 1789. Although the atmosphere was not relaxed, it was hoped that a peaceful resolution to the troubles could be found, but events moved quickly and the French Revolution was underway. On the dramatic night of 6 October, the king descended a secret passage in the palace and met Marie-Antoinette who had hurriedly left her own apartment. She had been the

(1710–1774) quickly abandoned Versailles for Vincennes, but in 1722 he changed his mind and brought his court and government back to the palace where he was born. He completed the works begun by Louis XIV and also created some of his own, such as the Salon of Hercules, the Opéra, and the Petit Trianon, though at the expense of the Apartement des Bains and the Escalier des Ambassadeurs, which were knocked down. He also modernized the apartments of the king, queen and princes in the taste of the day, and his architect, Gabriel, modified the design of Neptune's pool and placed sculptures by

youngest and most cosseted of the fifteen children of Emperor Frederick I and Maria Theresa of Austria (portrayed at Versailles in the famous painting by Elisabeth-Louise Vigée-Lebrun) and been engaged to the 12-year-old Louis XVI when she was just 10 years old herself. She had found herself living in the most luxurious palace in Europe, married to a king who preferred hunting to her company. Perhaps this was one reason why she began to spend enormous fortunes and became hated by the common, hungry people. Caught, she and her husband were made prisoners of the Revolution, locked up in Les Tuileries, then

52-53 The queen's guards' room is another example of the ostentatious decoration by craftsmen and architects that reached the height of grandeur at Versailles. The fundamental elements of this room are the marbles, the engraved metal bas-reliefs and vaulted ceiling entirely decorated with frescoes by Noël Coypel inspired by mythology.

52 bottom left The king's bedchamber, restored to its original splendor, was the heart of the palace. The paintings on the walls are nearly all those chosen personally by the Sun King, who died here in 1715.

52 bottom right The Clock Cabinet is part of the Petits Apartements and faces onto the Marble Court. The brightly lit room with pure gold plasterwork owes its name to the beautiful 18th-century astronomical clock.

The Great Love of Louis XIV

53 bottom The queen's bedchamber is a masterpiece of modern restoration work. Everything in it, and in particular the fabrics and materials of the four-poster bed, are the result of a long and careful reconstruction by a silk factory in Lyons based on drawings and original fragments of cloth. This is the main room in the Grands Apartements and certainly the one with the most eventful history: here 19 children of royal blood were born and two queens and two princesses of France died. Marie Antoinette was in this room on 6 October 1789 when the revolutionaries surrounded Versailles.

53 top left The photograph shows a jewelry casket, made by the goldsmith Schwerdfeger, in the queen's bedchamber.

53 top right The members of the royal family are shown as gods of Olympus in this painting by Jean Nocret. The Sun King, like Zeus, sits on the right with his wife and is surrounded by his children.

guillotined in Place de la Concorde.

Before the Revolution, the grounds at Versailles stretched out of sight in every direction. They covered 8,000 hectares and were enclosed by a wall 25 miles long in which there were 24 monumental entrances, of which only five remain. Of this immense area, a part of the Little Park, the whole of the Great Park reserved for hunting and the villages enclosed by the wall all disappeared. The overall size was reduced to 1,730 acres: small compared to its original state but enormous nonetheless.

It took more than half a century to build Versailles as the Sun King wanted it, and then it took many other years and kings to bring it to the magnificence enjoyed today by all those who pass through its golden gates to delight in its many marvels. During and after the Revolution, Versailles was looted. Jewelry, paintings and valuable ornaments were taken to the Louvre, books and medals to the Bibliothèque Nationale and the furniture that was not destroyed or burned was sold at auction.

Its empty rooms were used to house an institute for natural history, a library, a music conservatory and a special museum for the

54 top The Grand Trianon is a single story building with a portico facing onto the garden. The facades are lined with white and pink marble.

54 center The Temple of Love in the park of the Petit Trianon was designed in 1778 by Richard Mique for Marie Antoinette. A copy of

Bouchardon's statue Cupid Cutting His Bow from the Club of Hercules stands in the center. The original is kept in the Louvre.

The Great Love of Louis XIV

Ecole de France. In 1830, Louis-Philippe saved the palace from ruin and decided to transform it into a museum dedicated to all the glories of France. The restoration of the building started after the First World War thanks to the intervention of the American magnate, Rockefeller. This work was continued after 1952 by the French government.

Inside the golden gate, within that "royal beauty unique in the world," as Versailles was described by the marquise de Sévigné, within the maze of mirrors, immense staircases, silk-lined rooms, damask drapes and gigantic chandeliers, splendor and grandeur reign once again. There is the Cour des Ministres with the equestrian statue of Louis XIV and the commemoration of the first ballooning experiments (1783–84) by Montgolfier and Pilâtre de Rozier. Then there is the Cour Royale where the carriages of the royal family and their ministers arrived, and the Marble Court showing the traces of Louis XIII's original hunting lodge.

The western face of the palace measures 630 yards long. Inside there is a succession of rooms with portraits of kings, queens, favorites and other famous people; the large apartment of the Sun King, for whose bedroom a silk factory in Lyons has recently spent two years remaking the original precious silks; the bedchamber of Marie-Antoinette, one of the most evocative rooms, which saw the birth of 19 babies of royal blood (including Louis XV and Louis XVII) and the deaths of two queens and two princesses. Here too is the throne room where the Sun King Louis would sit, solemn and distant, on his ten-foot-high throne standing on a gold carpet. Then there is the Hall of Mirrors, Versailles' most theatrical visual effect, created by Mansart between 1678 and 1686. It is decorated with paintings by Le Brun, marble busts and gilded torches. Seventeen mercury mirror panels are illuminated by the light from 17 windows and reflect pieces of furniture made from solid silver lined up against the wall; these are replacements, for the originals were melted down to pay war debts.

54 bottom left The Petit Trianon was designed in 1768 by Gabriel and formed the heart of the gardens. In the center stood a small square castle with perfect Neoclassical proportions. Louis XV spent long hours here with his favorite, the Comtesse Du Barry.

54-55 *The Grand Trianon was Louis XIV's place of relaxation; he came here with only his family and very few servants. The building was loved even more by Marie Antoinette and it was she who laid out the gardens as they are today.*

55 top *This picture, kept in the Castle, shows the Grand Trianon in the 17th century, characterized by life at court.*

55 bottom *Marie Antoinette's Hameau stood on the bank of a small lake in the park of the Petit Trianon. It was an artificial rural village in the sumptuous gardens of Versailles where the queen liked to play the unfamiliar role of a peasant woman in the company of her family and courtiers.*

The Hall of Mirrors was used every day: courtiers would pass through its glittering length each morning on their way to Mass.

Beyond this are the queen's apartments, the room of the queen's guard, the Coronation Room, the apartment of the Dauphine and Dauphin, and the Opéra. This masterpiece by the architect Gabriel was built in 1770 in less than a year for the marriage of Louis XVI to Marie-Antoinette of Austria.

Then, of course, there is the park and the gardens in which so many other treasures are to be found, for example, the Grand Trianon originally designed in 1668 by Le Vau for "le bon plaisir du roi." Louis XIV often said "I built Versailles for the Court, Marly for my friends and the Trianon for me." The Grand Trianon amazed even his contemporaries; it was "un rêve de céramique" built in white

The Royal Palace of
Versailles

The Great Love of Louis XIV

and blue porcelain tiles. It was also a refuge where the king and queen were able to be alone together. Today the porcelain has gone but the replacement white and pink marble, part of a later project by Jules Hardouin-Mansart, has returned the Trianon to all its former glory. In 1763 Louis XV asked Gabriel to build him a new pavilion large enough to live in. The result was the Petit Trianon, built in 1768; it was the last residence of Madame de Pompadour, the

king's celebrated, scheming lover. Louis XVI gave the Petit Trianon to Marie Antoinette who later had the Hameau de la Reine built beside a small artificial lake not far away. The Hameau was a rustic hamlet built to celebrate the fashion of a return to nature as propounded by Rousseau. It was not long before the revolution reduced Versailles to not much more than a dazzling memory.

57 bottom left Five Empire crystal chandeliers illuminate 24 paintings by Cotelle in the Hall of the Grand Trianon.

57 bottom right The Green Salon takes its name from the color of the upholstery. It is one of the most richly decorated rooms in the Grand Trianon.

The Castle of Chambord

A TALE OF STONE

Neither the castles of Blois and Amboise nor the royal residences where he stayed with all due pomp and circumstance were enough to appease Francis I's dreams of grandeur. At the age of 23, back from the successes of his first military campaigns, this king had only one thought: to build the largest and most spectacular castle the world had ever seen, or rather the largest and most extraordinary hunting lodge, as this would be the building's primary function. He rode through the Loire valley and boarded a boat at Gien with a retinue of horses and courtiers in search of the ideal location. He

58 top right This 19th-century engraving shows Francis I with his sister, Marguerite de Navarre. The work is housed in the castle of Chambord.

58 bottom left This view of Chambord was painted on a Sèvres vase in 1824. The vase was ordered by King Charles X for one of the rooms in the castle.

58-59 More than any other, the chateau at Chambord symbolizes the Loire. The dream of Francis I took 30 years to build. When he

returned from confinement in Madrid, the king wanted to build a palace that exceeded all the other royal residences along the Loire in beauty and magnificence and, on 6 September 1519, he signed the edict for its construction. Unfortunately only a few of the documents relating to the huge project have survived. The chateau fully answered the king's ideal: the facade is 416 feet long and boasts lots of spires, turrets, skylights, towers and lookouts facing onto the canal dug from the river Cosson.

admired the roofs of the castle of Sully, drifted by La Bussière and passed the feudal citadel of Beaugency before coming to an immense forest in the deserted Sologne which promised memorable days of hunting. He disembarked and explored along the river Cosson near the ancient path that passed between the valleys of the Loire and the Cher. Here, he decided, where the counts of Blois already had a small hunting lodge dating from the 12th century, he would build the largest construction of the Renaissance. The boggy terrain argued against any type of building but the wish of the king prevailed. Some felt that Francis had different reasons for choosing this area: because the Blois, France's capital during the reign of Louis XII, was nearby; because he was attached to his first wife, Claudia of France, and to the castle where he was born. More spitefully, others said it was because the Countess of Thoury, with whom the king was madly in love, lived nearby.

Starting in 1519, up to 1,800 workers, carpenters, builders, master masons and superintendents began the task of transforming the gray slate and the white stone of Bourré into a magnificent castle of 440 rooms, 80 stairways, 365 windows, 300 fireplaces and a petrified forest of towers, turrets and pinnacles covered with blue enamel and painted on the tips with gold leaf that shone in the sun. The castle was to be surrounded by a rectangular park of 13,591 acres filled with deer and boar and enclosed by a wall 20 miles long. In fact, the wall begun at the end of Francis I's reign (1542) was completed only under Gaston d'Orléans in 1645. Originally the king thought he would divert a short stretch of the river Loire, but contented himself with the Cosson instead. Avid for novelty, glory and splendor, the king wished to surpass the magnificence of the residences of all his predecessors. He spent an immense fortune attempting to realize his utopian folly by calling in the greatest artists of the time: the author of the project may have been Leonardo da Vinci or Domenico da

59 top left This Parisian arras from the end of the 16th century portrays Francis I as he sets out to hunt. The king's passion for hunting was the deciding factor in the choice of site for the chateau—in the center of forests and marshes filled with wildlife.

59 top right The genius of Leonardo da Vinci also contributed to the chateau's bold architecture. Sketches by him of a double ramp staircase have been found.

initials are sculpted upside down, particularly on the second floor, so that someone looking down from heaven could not fail to notice. Francis I, king of France, wanted God to read his name.

Monarchic absolutism is evident in every stone of Chambord. The volumes of the rooms are superbly rational and emphasize the complex architecture that has been turned to the service of power. Yet how is it possible to accept the idea that Francis I found it necessary to build the largest castle of his time simply as a hunting lodge in which he would spend no more than 27 days in the course of his reign? Was it to suggest to Charles V of Spain and Henry VIII of England that the French monarchy could impress all of Europe?

Probably designed by Leonardo da Vinci, the initial project was based on the shape of a Greek cross which had until then been the prerogative of Italian churches. Repeated on each floor, the symmetry of the apartments is

Cortona (known as Boccadoro), the pupil of Giuliano da Sangallo. No one knows for sure who the designer really was but almost certainly, when Leonardo died at Amboise in 1519 in the arms of Francis I after designing the castle of Romorantin on the banks of the river Sauldre, that project was abandoned and all attention was transferred to Chambord. And there is no doubt that the monumental double spiral stairway of the castle, which had

60 top left The abbreviation "FRF" (François, roi de France) is the building's indelible and obvious royal seal. The decorative feature occurs frequently at Chambord.

separate ascending and descending flights of steps so that two people could go up or down at the same time without meeting, was the fruit of Leonardo's genius. A giant fleur-de-lys, the king's heraldic symbol, stood out above the main stairway; that symbol was sometimes linked with the abbreviation FRF (François, Roi de France) and with the symbol of the salamander which was present on fireplaces, over doors and on turrets throughout the castle and which carried Francis' motto "Nutrisco et Extingo"—I nourish [myself with warmth, prosperity and spirituality] and I banish [evil, war, famine and sickness]. Sometimes Francis'

perfect: four towers, four square apartments and a large hall in the form of a cross. The four gateways face the cardinal points of the compass, which was an allusion to the gates of the heavenly city of Jerusalem.

At the beginning, Francis conceived of the project of draining the land and digging a deep moat to surround the castle. This was an operation that cost as much as it took to build the entire construction. His ideal itinerary would take visitors to climb the Renaissance stairway, visit the rooms and go out onto the terraces near the pinnacles and turrets to look at the immensity of the park. This was the

60 top right and 61 bottom These pictures show the elegance and attention to detail on the Italian terrace on the top floor. Only by walking around it can one appreciate the immensity of Chambord and the richness of its decoration.

60 bottom The aerial photograph of Chambord demonstrates its vast scale. Built in a park of 22 square miles, the castle initially was considered no more than a hunting lodge. With its enormous enclosure wall and central tower surrounded by four round towers, the palace expresses the strength and power of the French monarchy at its peak.

60-61 Another aerial view of the chateau that Francis I preferred to all others and which he called "mon chez moi" (my home). The castle was begun in 1519 and completed five years after the king's death in 1547. His son, Henry II, completed the chapel wing. Despite its grandeur, the chateau was rarely lived in by the kings of France.

A Tale of Stone

62 top left The François Sommer Room is on the second floor. It is decorated with numerous hunting trophies and wallhangings from the mid-17th century.

62 center left The wallhangings in this room date from the end of the 16th century and show Francis I while hunting.

62 bottom left Louis XIV's bedchamber was installed in 1681. This room also accommodated the Dukes of Orleans for short periods and, for 8 years from 1725 until 1733, Stanislas Leczcinski, the exiled Polish king.

62 right Two stairways close the corners of the external wings. Their airy architectural lightness is evidence of the influence of the Italian Renaissance in the design and use of materials.

62-63 The amazing crossed double-spiral stairway rises in the center of the castle; it has one flight of steps for going up and the other for going down. The vault is richly decorated with the king's initials and the image of a salamander.

63 top The base of the central stairway is 26 feet wide. It rises as far as the lantern that crowns the imposing construction.

megalomaniac dream of Francis in all its splendor. His vision of himself was that his arm was strong enough to hold up even the heaviest of swords, his shoulders could bear the strongest of armor, his build was that of a fearless knight in arms, but he also had a mind capable of conceiving the most extravagant and magnificent castle: a mirage from afar, a labyrinth inside.

The apartments were laid out in the four towers. The square windows in elegant frames were positioned to allow views of the hunting parties as they set out for and came back from the forest, and were clearly influenced by the Italian Renaissance. The interiors are characterized by colossal fireplaces and the fittings and furnishings are typically French. Although it was never long inhabited and was in fact abandoned when Francis returned from the Loire to live in Paris, the castle represented the expression of monarchic absolutism. It impressed Louis XIV, who elected Chambord as the ideal residence for festivals and parades on his accession and it no doubt inspired him in his dreams of Versailles. It is said that Molière also found inspiration in its rooms for his play "Le Bourgeois Gentilhomme." After Louis XIV, the castle was rarely inhabited but it maintained its symbolic function of representing what an absolute power could achieve in terms of useless construction based solely on the whim and imagination of a ruler. During the 17th century, the Dukes d'Orléans put up there for brief periods, and from 1725 to 1733 it was home to Stanislas Leczcinski, the Polish king in exile.

The castle was stripped of everything during the French Revolution and bought by Marshal Berthier, then by the Duke of Bordeaux (future Count of Chambord). On 5 July 1871 after spending just four days at

64 left The first antechamber in Louis XIV's apartment is entirely lined with portraits of the kings, queens and aristocrats who were guests at the palace.

64 top right There are few traces of Charles X at Chambord. He ascended the French throne in 1824 but his policies attracted the hostility of all social classes until the Parliament declared the end of the Bourbon dynasty. He was then obliged to seek refuge in England.

64 bottom right Louis XIV (1638-1715), the Sun King, is shown here in military uniform. He greatly loved Chambord but only stayed there a few times in order to hunt and to enjoy the lively life of the court away from the capital.

Chambord, the count, legitimate heir to the French crown, renounced his right to become Henry V. Five carriages prepared for a triumphal entry to Paris were unable to leave Chambord, and he pronounced his loyalty to the Third Republic in a manifesto. The fact that the immense and empty building had been uninhabited for long periods, or rather had only been lived in for twenty years overall in the course of its secular existence, meant that not one of its temporary inhabitants felt the need or any pleasure in the thought of adapting the castle to his own needs, the destiny of nearly all Loire valley chateaux. Chambord was purchased by the French state in 1932.

Having been built from start to finish on the basis of the an original design, Chambord still maintains exceptional unity which is rare for a building of this importance and proportion. Francis I's passion for the chase is evident in the series of superb tapestries in the castle rooms showing scenes of the king hunting. Louis XIV continued the royal passion for the sport and turned it into a spectacular ceremony. In the museum of hunting and animal art on the second floor of the castle are works of art, costumes, pictures by Snyders, Boel and Desportes and tapestries showing the legends and mythology of the chase and tracing the history of hunting over the centuries. In 1947

64-65 Although the palace is only partly furnished, some rooms are lined with marvelous portraits of kings, queens and favorites, like this one of Marie Leszczinska, Queen of France, who married Louis XV in 1725.

the castle became a national reserve for local fauna, in particular red and roe deer, boar and foxes. Under the impetus of President Georges Pompidou, private hunts were organized, but these have now been abolished. Since 1981, Chambord has been registered as part of the Unesco World Heritage; after Chenonceau it is the most visited chateau in France and is the treasure of the Loire valley. The 800,000 visitors it receives annually easily lose themselves in the vastness of the park and the labyrinthine castle where they have access to 80

bedrooms, the carriage room, the apartments and the royal chapel on the first floor, to the hunting museum on the second floor and to the terraces. These are magical places where the visitor is surrounded by a forest of turrets, pinnacles, chimney stacks, pillars and skylights. One of the first visitors to be enchanted by this marvelous sight was Charles V of Spain who stopped at Chambord in 1539 while crossing France to reach Ghent. Needless to say, Francis' pride and joy at this visit were boundless.

Today Chambord is not only a hymn in praise of grandeur. One part of the immense park that surrounds the chateau is open to the public, who can walk undisturbed along paths through the forest, ride horses on marked tracks and admire the animals that wander free. A carefully devised program aimed at letting the public discover nature is open to all; it includes canoeing on the Cosson, photographic safaris, outings at dawn to admire the animals, special trips in autumn to witness the deer mating season, excursions in horse-drawn carriages and candlelit nocturnal tours of the lesser known parts of the castle. There are countless ways to awaken the ghosts of a stone world in all its historic glory.

65 bottom left In this 17th-century portrait, Henry IV (1553-1610) is wearing a cloak decorated with the fleur-de-lys. The king only stayed at Chambord for short hunting periods, preferring the chateau at Fontainebleau.

65 bottom right Louis XIII, depicted here, succeeded his father, Henry IV, to the throne and gave Chambord to his brother, Gaston d'Orléans, who often stayed at the castle for long periods.

66 top left View of the castle from the basin touching the Grand Parterre, the French garden that still bears traces of the original 17th-century design by Le Vau and Le Nôtre. The 17th-century garden in turn replaced a previous garden commissioned by Francis I. The shoreline is decorated with a modern copy of the statue of Tibre (now housed in the Louvre). The copy was executed to replace the original, which was torn down during the Revolution. The building appearing in this image, with the Italianate superimposed open gallery, houses the ballroom with its large windows.

66 top right The fountain of Diana, built under Henry IV, celebrates the myth of the hunter-goddess and was designed by the engineer Francini. The fountain is in the old Queen's Garden, facing the Gallery of the Deers, on the side of the southern structure bordering the town of Fontainebleau.

66-67 This bird's eye view shows the complex of Fontainebleau, favorite residence of Francis I, which was also used by nearly all the Kings of France for longer or shorter periods, from the reign of Louis VII in 1137 up to the fall of the Second Empire in 1870.

The Castle of Fontainebleau

JEWEL BOX OF ART AND HISTORY

The impetus for the construction of the Fontainebleau castle was, as at Chambord, hunting and the megalomania of Francis I. Having returned from his forced stay in Madrid, he abandoned the Loire for Fontainebleau, which he preferred to any other castle. The reason for this was the 17,000 hectares of forest where it was possible to catch "red and black beasts" (his words).

Only one tower remained of the original 12th-century castle which stood in the Oval Courtyard. The tower was the probable location of the bedchamber of the king or, rather, of the kings, as Philippe Auguste and St. Louis had lived here and Philippe le Beau was born here in 1262 and died here in 1314. Almost eight centuries of French history was affected by this chateau—from 1137, the year of the coronation of Louis VII, to the fall of the Second Empire in 1870.

Francis I (1494–1547), the creator of the castle at Chambord, was constantly searching for the pleasure that only construction and hunting were able to give him, and it was he who ordered the total demolition of the former castle at Fontainebleau in 1528. The castle had fallen into abandon with the exception of the medieval central tower. He built a part of the Porte Dorée, the ballroom, the chapel of Saint-Saturnin and the gallery known as the Gallery of Francis I. He called in the Italian artists Rosso Fiorentino, Primaticcio, Nicolò dell'Abate and Vignola, typical representatives of the 16th-century Mannerism that gave rise to what was later called the First School of Fontainebleau. Part of their splendid work can still be seen in the Gallery of Francis I, in the ballroom and in the bedchamber of the Duchesse d'Etampes (the king's favorite) where the frescoes that remain after many restorations tell the story of Alexander and Roxanne. Francis filled the rooms and salons

67 top The right wing, known as queen's mother's wing, faces west. The 16th-century structure was designed by Philibert Delorme to house the apartments of Henry II.

67 bottom This 17th-century engraving signed by Matthaus Merian portrays the general view of the castle at that time.

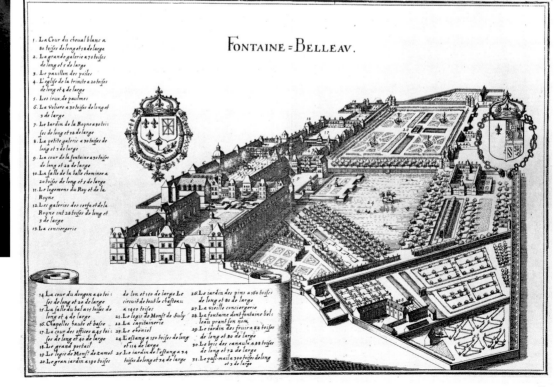

FONTAINE = BELLEAV.

68 top The Gallery of Francis I overlooks the Courtyard of the Fountain, the inner courtyard to the right of the main entrance. Construction commenced in 1528. The ground floor features a series of wide arches that support a long terrace. This gallery used to link the royal apartments with the Cour du Cheval Blanc.

68 center The Oval Courtyard is the oldest part of the castle. The royal apartments branch out from around the central keep, named after St. Louis, that dates back to the 12th century. In the background to the right can be seen a glimpse of the Porte Dauphine.

68 bottom The Porte Dorée was commissioned by Francis I in a bid to astound King Charles V with its imposing architectural beauty. The foreign monarch who visited Fontainebleau in 1539 passed under the Renaissance arch that was sumptuously decorated in his honor.

with art masterpieces, jewelry, pieces made from gold and silver, weapons and tapestries, and most of all with works of art by Italian artists who he had admired on his military trips over the Alps (he conquered the Duchy of Milan but lost it again at the Battle of Pavia in 1525). Architects including Serlio, painters including Primaticcio and Andrea del Sarto, sculptors including Cellini, and interior designers and decorators in the Renaissance style who the king had noted were called to France to embellish his residences. This followed the pattern set years earlier with Leonardo da Vinci

who had gone to Francis at Amboise, carrying such paintings as the *Mona Lisa* and the *Virgin of the Rocks*, and died there in 1519. It is not difficult to imagine Francis' pride and the amazement of Charles V when the Spanish king was received (in a celebration in his honor commemorated by the poet Ronsard) in the two chateaux symbolizing Francis' power: Chambord and Fontainebleau.

The kings of France in the 16th century had so many chateaux that it was normal practice for them to move from one to another dragging in their wake the thousands of people that made

68-69 The Cour du Cheval Blanc is also known as the Courtyard of Farewells, commemorating the leavetaking ceremony at the foot of the staircase in honor of Napoleon

when he left Fontainebleau for the Island of Elba in 1814. The imposing horseshoe-shaped staircase was commissioned by Francis I and was completed between 1544 and 1565.

The Castle of

69 top left The Porte Dauphine is also known as the Baptistery Door in memory of the fact that it served as a backdrop to the baptism of Louis XIII, when the newborn crown prince was presented in the midst of great festivities in the Oval Courtyard on 14 September 1606.

69 top right The North Wing of the Cour du Cheval Blanc, also called the Ministers' Wing, was built around 1530 and is today the main entrance to the castle.

up the court and carts loaded with furniture, tapestries, rugs, silverware and furnishings for the new residence. Once the stay was over, all was packed back into the chests and the empty rooms returned to silence, perhaps for years.

The successors to Francis I also contributed huge sums to decorate and embellish Fontainebleau, which had become one of the French royalty's favorite palaces. Henry II (1519–1559) was in part responsible for the new decoration of the ballroom that Catherine de' Medici, his wife, used as a setting for her phantasmagorical celebrations inspired by the refined Renaissance she had seen in Florence and never forgotten. Under Henry IV (1553–1610), the palace became more of a king's house and the home of many dauphins; one of them was the future Louis XIII, born in 1601 and baptized in 1606 in the Oval Courtyard in a ceremony of such magnificence and pomp it has passed into history. Radical restorations of Fontainebleau were undertaken by Henry IV: he added wings, remodeled the garden and called in new artists such as Dubreuil, Dubois and Fréminet to decorate the interiors. On Henry's death, Louis XIII continued the works begun by his father but began to prefer, for hunting purposes, a small lodge in the middle of the plains southwest of Paris. This lodge was to become the nucleus of the palace of Versailles under Louis XIV, who did the same as his father had done: he regularly visited Fontainebleau during the hunting season from September to November and had the apartment of the Porte Dorée fitted out for Madame de Maintenon (1635–1719), but he already had his grand dream for Versailles in his heart.

The need to find new accommodation for the court forced Louis XV to build the south wing of the Cour du Cheval Blanc designed by

Fontainebleau

Jewel Box of Art and History

70 top The gallery named after Francis I was built during his reign and holds a spectacular series of paintings; it is also decorated with stuccowork, inlaid woodwork and elaborately decorated ceilings. It was decorated by a varied group of Italian, French and Flemish painters coordinated by the Florentine artist Rosso Fiorentino (1494-1540) who was called to work for the king in 1530. The Gallery of Francis I was completed between 1534 and 1537.

71 top left This fresco portrays an elephant draped with hangings decorated with the fleur-de-lys, the symbol of Francis I. The animal symbolizes power extending to the farthest corners of the earth.

71 bottom Framed by a splendid oval in gilded stucco work, the *Nymph of Fontainebleau* is a 19th-century work that was added, together with the Danae by Primaticcio, to complete the series of 12 frescoes by Rosso Fiorentino.

70-71 When sunlight filters in through the windows and highlights the colors of the decorations, the fine detail of the frescoes and the subtle inlay work in the panels of the boiserie, the effect is fascinating. The Gallery of Francis I is 197 feet long and 20 feet wide. It lies in the wing of the residence that was built in 1528 to link the royal apartments with the chapel of the Trinitarian convent founded close to the castle by St. Louis.

70 bottom left The unique decoration of the walls of the gallery is highlighted here by stuccoes and frescoes that cover the upper area , where human figures and floral motifs are mixed together.

70 bottom right and 71 top right The magnificent fresco by Rosso Fiorentino portraying the death of Adonis stands out from among the numerous Renaissance paintings. The subject matter of the frescoes of the gallery was mainly taken from mythology and served to illustrate the good governance of the king, an enlightened prince.

72-73 *The Gallery of Diana was transformed into a library in the mid-1800s under Napoleon III. It houses 16,000 volumes. The globe belonged to Napoleon I.*

72 bottom *The Francis I Salon features a lacunar ceiling and a fireplace that both date back to the 16th century, when this served as a bedroom for the queen, the second wife of*

Francis I. It was later transformed into a banquet hall and music room. The magnificent tapestries, gold artifacts and furniture date back to the mid-1800s.

73 top left *The magnificent fireplace in the Francis I Salon bears the signature of Primaticcio (1504-1570), the artist from Bologna called to serve at the court by Francis I.*

73 bottom left *This detail clearly shows the rich decoration of the altar of the chapel, which according to the inscription was built in 1633. The work was executed by the sculptor Francesco Bordoni. The altarpiece was painted by Jean Dubois in 1642.*

After the first ritual autumn stay at Fontainebleau for hunting, Louis XVI also decided to make changes to the chateau. He redecorated the queen's apartments with arabesque trompe-l'oeils, and had a wonderful cylindrical secrétaire and a small worktable made, both of ivory and gilded bronze.

The Revolution emptied the chateau of its furniture but it was saved from further devastation, so Napoleon (1769–1821) only had to refurnish it from top to bottom when he chose it as one of his best-loved residences.

Napoleon decorated with great care and paid special attention when the Pope came to crown Napoleon emperor in 1804. The old kings' bedchamber was adapted as a Throne Room (the original decoration is still intact) and he made the royal apartments more welcoming and friendly. The apartment belonging to Empress Josephine naturally became that of Marie-Louise after the divorce in 1809. The Inner Apartment was used by Napoleon himself between military campaigns. The Throne Room is the most spectacular

73 bottom right The chapel of the Trinity was the backdrop to important events such as the marriage of Louis XV (in 1725) and the baptism of the future Napoleon III (in 1810). The 16th-century building stands on the foundations of an old convent. The decorations are from the 16th and the early 17th century, such as the paintings on the ceiling on the theme of the redemption of man, ordered by Henry IV from the artist Martin Fréminet in 1608. The center of the vault portrays Christ at the Last Judgment.

Gabriel in 1738; but this led to the sacrilege of knocking down the original wing containing frescoes of the Story of Ulysses by Primaticcio. Louis was also obliged to renew the arrangement and furnishings of his own apartments by creating the King's Stairs, doubling the size of the Gallery of Francis I leading out onto the garden of Diana, fitting out the new Council Hall and lining the king's and the queen's bedchambers with boiserie. These last were entrusted to Jean-Baptiste Pierre and Carl Van Loo, while the frescoes were the work of the famous Boucher.

Throughout his reign, Louis XV continued to make alterations to what today are known as the Petits Apartements. The king had abolished the pompous ceremonies adopted by his predecessor at table; there were fewer dishes and formality was reduced to the essential. His day at Fontainebleau passed with unchanging rhythms: a quick breakfast, dressing for the hunt, the outing with his dogs and buglers, a return to the palace two hours later and a visit to the queen and their children. At 5:30 PM he turned his attention to work, then at 8 PM was dinner, but without either his family or the music of the 12 violinists that his father had so loved. After dinner he would visit the apartments of Madame de Pompadour where she would attend him with trusted and entertaining friends.

73 top right The Louis XIII Room takes its name from the heir of Henry IV and son of Maria de' Medici. The large 18th-century paintings are by Ambroise Dubois.

74 top left After the death of
Francis I, his son Henry II
continued in his father's footsteps
as patron of the arts. He further
decorated the rooms of the
residence, commissioning the
works from the architect
Philibert Delorme and once
again calling in Primaticcio and
Nicolò dell'Abate from Italy to
decorate the walls of the
ballroom, shown here.

74 bottom left Apollo and the
Muses on Parnassus is the title
of this fresco in the ballroom,
based on a drawing by
Primaticcio and executed in
1550 by a group of artists
working under Nicolò
dell'Abate.

74 top right The magnificent
painted and inlaid caisson
ceiling was originally supposed
to be barrel-vaulted, but the
architect Delorme suggested the
design we admire today, which
was inspired by the Italian
Renaissance.

74-75 The ballroom is shown
here in all its majesty. The
decorations commissioned by
Henry II to render this part of the
residence sumptuous and
memorable are clearly visible.
This room is 98 feet long and the
windows overlook the parterres
on one side and the Oval
Courtyard on the other. A tribune
for musicians was designed
above the entrance door. Many
narratives from the period
describe the extravagant feasts
held against the backdrop of this
fantastic decor.

75 top The fireplace lies in the
middle of the rear wall of the
ballroom. Monumental and
richly decorated, it was designed
by Delorme, who also flanked the
work with two bronze statues of
satyrs designed by Primaticcio.
The statues were destroyed
during the revolution and
reconstructed in 1966. The letter
H for Henry is highlighted at the
center of the decoration, together
with another letter than can be
read both as a C (for Catherine
de' Medici, his wife) or a D (for
Diane de Poitiers, the King's
famous favorite).

room in the apartment, with silks and brocades enriched with precious decorations of gold bees and other Neoclassical symbols.

The purple Abdication Room also has the original decorations from 1808. Over the fireplace hangs a Sèvres porcelain pendulum clock in the form of a column with the hours marked by winged figures of Victory, and there is a guéridon on which Napoleon is said to have signed his surrender on 6 April 1814. The great general left Fontainebleau for Elba after signing the document that decreed his defeat in this unusual salon and then saluting the guard at the entrance to the chateau. He

took with him the memory of what he had called "the true residence of kings, the best furnished and most happily situated ancient house in Europe."

Today the museum dedicated to Napoleon in the house brings his epic career to life through small objects that were part of the daily life that he shared with his brothers and sisters, the monarchs of half of Europe. His successors, Louis-Philippe (1773–1850) and Napoleon III (1808–1873), were also greatly attached to Fontainebleau and made significant restorations to the majestic palace. To the modern visitor, the magnificence of

Fontainebleau seems like a perfect work where pure gold is the great interpreter of the magnificence in every corner, symbolic of the chateau's standing through eight centuries of history.

Here, as at Versailles, a wrought-iron gate and early-19th-century gilded decorations lead into the Cour du Cheval Blanc, the main entrance to the castle. The rooms, salons, galleries, staircases, brocades, silks, paintings and statues then usher us into a world of memories where dates no longer serve a purpose. It is enough to gaze and wonder at the course of so many centuries of history.

76 top The warm hues of the woodwork of the Dish Room, seen here, features inlays and geometrical motifs that highlight the precious collection of French porcelain.

76 bottom The walls of the large reception room in the apartments of the queen's mother are completely covered with tapestries. A magnificent 19th-century crystal chandelier hangs from the ceiling of wood and gold.

76-77 The Playroom of Mary Antoinette was also known as the Queen's Grand Cabinet since she gave audiences and organized concerts here. It was Louis XVI who started the renovation and updating work that was to be completed under the First Empire. The row of tabourets was reserved for the ladies who could sit comfortably on them without crumpling their crinoline dresses.

77 bottom left Detail of a piece of porcelain from the royal ceramics works at Sèvres. The piece is part of the collection of porcelain housed in the Dish Room of the apartments of the queen's mother.

77 bottom right A fresco portraying Alexander taming the horse Bucephalus, in an oval frame above one of the doors of the Chamber of the Duchesse d'Etampes. The monumental proportions of the room are highlighted by twenty statues in stucco designed by Primaticcio.

Jewel Box of Art and History

The Castle of Fontainebleau

78-79 The present form of the Throne Room was commissioned by Napoleon I, who transformed what was previously the King's Bedchamber, adopting this imposing and sumptuous decoration. The furniture is from various periods and is ennobled by the gold-plated woodwork executed by Verberckt in 1752. The splendid portrait of Louis XIII above the door is a work from the school of Philippe de Champaigne.

Jewel Box of Art and History

78 bottom The first Emperor's Bedchamber is located in the Small Apartments. All the furniture in these rooms are the original pieces commissioned by the Emperor before he decided on richer furnishings for the rooms on the upper floor.

79 top A view of one of the rooms of the inner Small Apartments where Napoleon I lived during the brief periods of peace that interspersed his famous military campaigns. Located on the first floor, these apartments were more soberly decorated than the rooms used for official functions and receptions.

79 bottom The bedchamber of Napoleon I was one of the six rooms making up the Emperor's private apartments, all of which were furnished with highly prized Empire-style furniture. This room was used by Napoleon I in 1808 and 1809.

80 top left and bottom The Alcazaba, the Arab citadel housing the palatial complex (alcazár) of the Alhambra, still appears as a massive fortress, surrounded by strong walls and defended by eight (originally 24) towers. As is common in Arab architecture, the walls close the area off from the outside but allow light to filter inward in various ways.

80 top right From the top of the walls of the Alcazaba—which owes its current shape to restoration work during various periods and to 16th-century extensions—Granada can be seen. The city was extended and enriched after the Arab conquest. Built at a height and isolated, the Alhambra served not only during war: it was also a symbol of power.

The Alhambra

THE RED FORTRESS
OF GRANADA

Few palace complexes have aroused such feeling and so symbolized a civilization as has the Alhambra in Granada. But to identify the Alhambra simply as a monument of Islamic art risks side-lining the Spanish historical and cultural context in which the Arab civilization found a cradle that allowed it to develop to a level of intellectual elegance and refinement unknown elsewhere. For over eight centuries from 711, when the Arab invasion defeated the languishing Roman-Barbarian kingdom of the Visigoths, until 3 January 1492 (year 897 of the Hegira calendar), when Granada capitulated to

cultures they represented, as emphasized by Américo Castro in his controversial but brilliant interpretation of the history of Spain. The Christians were often soldiers and animal farmers, the Muslims craftsmen and planters, and the Jews intellectuals and scholars.

This balance was maintained for a long time, even during the Reconquest, when the Christian kingdoms in the north of the country reappropriated the southern territory in that had been in Arab hands. Military reoccupation of Al-Andalus (the Arab name for the Iberian peninsula, "Land of the Vandals," referred to the territory not reconquered) was motivated

81 top left The miniature, from The Order of the Golden Fleece of the 15th century, shows Emperor Charles V, or Charles I of Spain. The Emperor, grandchild of the Ferdinand and Isabella, commissioned a Renaissance palace to be built within the Arab walls of the Alhambra.

80-81 As evening falls, the Alhambra seems to shine in a warm reddish glow, the color from which it takes its name. The mountain crests of the Sierra Nevada can be seen in the background. The belfry of the church of Santa María and the classical motifs of the Palace of Charles V emblematically highlight the Christian alterations brought to the structure.

Catholic forces, the Muslims had a defining presence in the southern Iberian Peninsula. This gave the Spanish Middle Ages a blend of the three cultures—Christian, Islamic and Jewish—that had never been encountered anywhere else. The three great monotheist religions lived together in reciprocal respect for a long time in a manner much less belligerent than one might imagine. In this system, economic functions were divided almost in a caste-like manner between the

more by political and economic than religious reasons. Consider, for example, the characterization of the Muslims and justification of war against them in the epic national poem from the 12th century, *Cantar de mío Cid*. After 1212, when the battle of Las Navas de Tolosa was won by the Christians, Islam was increasingly forced into subjection to the Christian kings. The Muslim kings became tributaries and only the complex local situation enabled the long twilight reprieve

81 bottom Isabella and Ferdinand, the Catholic Monarchs who finalized the reconquest of Spain by taking Granada, are portrayed here against the backdrop of the Alhambra in a painting by Carlos Luis Ribera y Fieve dating to 1890 now kept at the Cathedral of Burgos.

82 top left This picture shows a layout of azulejos magnificently contrasting with a finely crafted door left slightly ajar in the Patio de los Arrayanes. The Muslims were highly skilled craftsmen, masters in the art of working on wood, leather, metal and ceramics.

82-83 The southern side of the Patio de los Arrayanes affords a view of the windows that probably once hid the harem, above the first floor, together with a splendid arched gallery. Here, as in a large number of other places in the Alhambra, screens of perforated wood discreetly let the sunlight in.

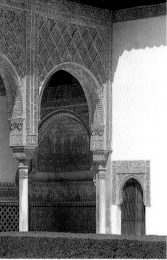

languid and almost decadent swansong of a civilization that, if it did not foresee its end, could no longer reasonably hope for a renaissance.

The city, under the rule of the Nasrid dynasty from 1237, ambiguously leaned toward both the Christian world and the Muslim world of north Africa, which competed to hold the city. So as not to be crushed between the two, Granada's alliances were complex and contradictory. Economic prosperity was based on trade—especially of silk—with Christians, and also made possible by the immigration of Muslims from reconquered areas. At Malaga and Almeria, both important ports of the kingdom, there were flourishing colonies of Italian merchants. On the other hand, the paintings in the *Sala de los Reyes* at the Alhambra that show Arab figures and knightly scenes were by 14th century Christian artists; this represents a collaboration of Christian infidels and limited devotion (typical of upper-class Muslims), since representation of the human figure was prohibited in Islamic art.

83 bottom left and top right In the Patio de los Arrayanes the seemingly endless Arab taste for decoration is evident. The potentially infinite repetition of the same geometric motif above the arch is an example.

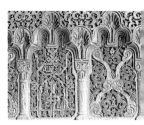

83 bottom right These arches, supported by the typical Granada columns, are in the Patio de los Arrayanes. Islamic architecture always made ample use of arches and, in Spain, used even the characteristic horseshoe arch from Visigothic architecture, later abandoned in favor of more richly decorated arches.

82 bottom The north side of the Patio de los Arrayanes is dominated by the high Torre de Comares. The side towers and the platform roofing below are modern. The central arch of the gallery is higher than the others, revealing the following arcade behind, which leads to the inside.

83 top left In Arabic architecture the smaller elements serve as an essential part of the whole, without however losing their own importance. Every detail expresses an incredible ability to create beauty from poor materials.

allowed to the kingdom of Granada. A noted Arabist, Francesco Gabrieli, wrote that "the long survival of this furthermost belt of Arab civilization on Spanish soil unfolded with the events taking place in Christian Spain, with the cessation of its efforts for the Reconquest which its rulers felt was practically completed, and with the rivalries and crises that racked the various Spanish states in the 14th and 15th centuries, above all that of Castile, which had led the war against the Arabs.... Consequently, twenty or so Nasrid sultans were able to succeed to the Granada throne during the 13th, 14th and 15th centuries and, between political intrigues and guerrilla activity, write the last glorious page of Andalusian Arabism in its flourishing culture and splendid architectural achievements." The balance was lost when Ferdinand I of Aragon and Isabella of Castile united their kingdoms in 1479 and made religious unity one of the cementing elements in the new kingdom of Spain. In 1492 they not only conquered Granada but forced the Jews to choose between conversion and expulsion.

The Alhambra is therefore not an expression of political brilliance, as its splendor would have us believe, but the

84 top left Detail of the Patio de los Leones, showing the frequent use of muqarnas on arches, creating a pleasant effect of escape.

84 center left General view of the Patio de los Leones, clearly highlighting the reason for which it is known as the jewel of Arab art in Spain. The rectangular courtyard measures 31 by 17 yards. The galleries that surround it, with 128 columns in white marble, are more than six yards high. In the heavily jagged perimeter of the courtyard stands out the pavilion at its center.

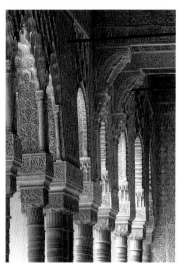

84 bottom left This bird's eye view of the Patio de los Leones highlights the ideal structure of the courtyard with the four water canals coming from four corresponding rooms at the cardinal points. The patio has been thoroughly repaired: the two jutting pavilions were restored and the roofs of the galleries were totally renovated.

84 center This detail of the patio as seen from inside one of the rooms shows the symmetrical alternation of double and single slim columns.

84 top right Light is the real focal point of the Patio de los Leones, an architectural structure conceived not only to capture light but to modulate it, from maximum brightness to deep darkness. The creation of Man dialogues with the joys of creation and assumes different tones as the stars created by Allah move in their orbits.

84 center right The series of columns and arches reveals that their decoration changes from arch to arch and capital to capital, despite the apparent monotony.

84 bottom right At the center of the Patio de los Leones stands the famous twelve-sided fountain surrounded by 12 summarily sculpted lions from which the courtyard takes its name.

85 This foreshortened view from the inside of the patio shows the variety and abundance of the profuse decorations that totally cover the walls of the Alhambra. The eye cannot find any empty space.

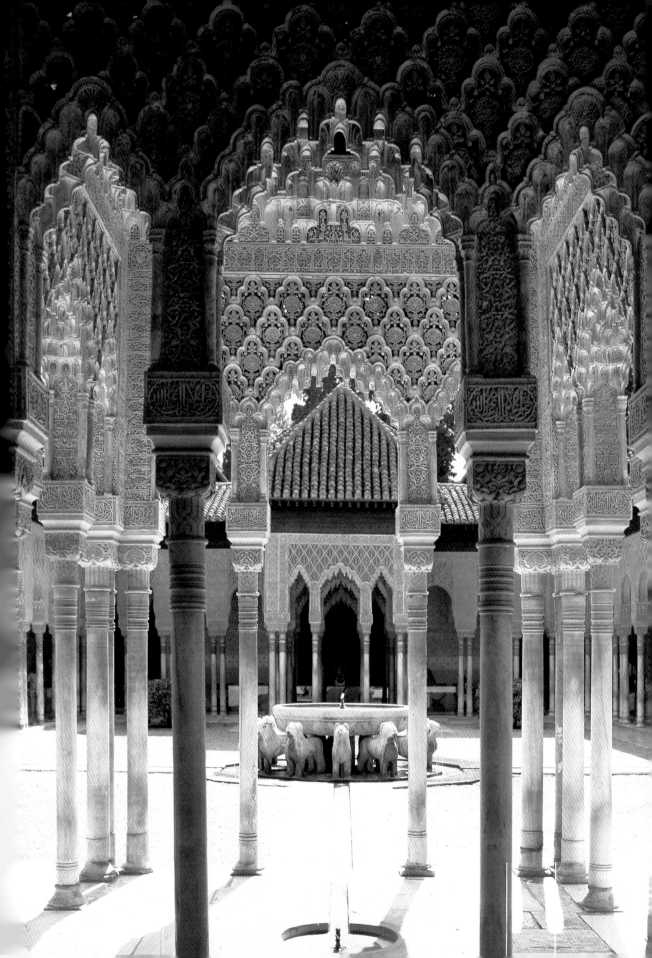

The Red Fortress
of Granada

The Alhambra

86 top left *The central avant-corps of the west facade of Charles V's palace has two orders of columns inside which roundels and gables help to emphasize the symmetry of the building.*

86 top right The southern facade of the Palace of Charles V shows the classical models typical of the Italian Renaissance, which inspired the architect Pedro Machuca during the decisive period he spent in Rome. This influence is clearly visible in the reference to the structural scheme of a Roman triumphal arch on the second level. Construction of the palace started in 1526 and, although work continued until the early 1600s, it was never completed.

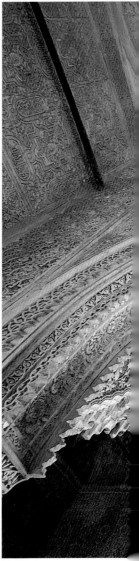

The most emblematic of the many individuals who enriched the intellectual life of the city was Ibn al-Khatib, a historian and poet and powerful minister, who was assassinated in Fez, where he had gone into refuge. As Gabrieli wrote, he "seemed in truth to personify the qualities and flaws of the dying Spanish Arabism: a wide and refined culture, a deep affection for his homeland, a lively sense of Islamic tradition together with a restlessness for intrigue, ambition, political lightness and an improvident dispersion of forces in internecine contests when threatened by the growing Christian menace."

It is against this cultural background that the Alhambra is to be admired, although many difficulties tend to obscure its historical reading.

On the left bank of the river Darro, at a height of 2,570 feet atop the Sabica hill in a position that dominated the whole of the plain, there already stood a castle in the mid-9th century, but it was only used in moments of danger and fell into ruin. The castle was built with the reddish ferrous clay of the hill and was therefore called al-Hamra or the Red Castle. The name passed to the new castle built on the ruins of the first by Mohammed I,

founder of the Nasrid dynasty. Since then, the Alhambra has not ceased to be a living architectural organism, the object of continuous works of expansion and embellishment that are not always easy to date. Yusuf I (1333–54) gave it a monumental appearance by erecting various gates and towers, still in existence, and the Sala de los Embajadores (Throne Room). During the reign of Mohammed V (1354–91), in which the king spent two years in Morocco in exile and returned only thanks to the help of Pedro I of Castile, the most famous sections were built, such as the outstandingly elegant

86 bottom The marble facade of the Palace of Charles V is decorated with bas-reliefs depicting heroic exploits. Even the small details reflect the Italian Renaissance architectural models on which the design of the palace was based.

86-87 The paintings on leather in the three alcoves of the Sala de los Reyes (Room of the Kings) were executed by Christian artists. The central painting shows ten Arab figures who were traditionally considered the ten kings of Granada. This foreshortened view provides an excellent glimpse of the muqarnas of the vault which, like other vaults at the Alhambra, is "in the form of a half orange" (hemispheric), a shape closely linked with Islamic architectural tradition. The role of the small upper windows and the typical layout of the stucco decorations, in well defined panels, are noteworthy.

87 top This detail shows a decorative motif on the entrance gate to the Palace of Charles V.

87 bottom The inner courtyard of the Palace of Charles V is widely acclaimed as one of the masterpieces of Spanish Renaissance architecture. The courtyard features two levels and has a diameter of 34 yards. The lower level of Doric columns was completed in 1568, while the upper level with its Ionic columns was completed in 1616.

The Red Fortress of Granada
The Alhambra

88 top left This foreshortening of the Sala de las dos Hermanas exalts the smooth passage from the inside to the outside that is a typical feature of the organization of space within the Alhambra. The calligraphy (seen on the horizontal band at the foot of the third arch to the left) incorporates strong aesthetic values; in decorative terms, it blends with the geometrical and floral motifs.

oratorio of the *mexuar* (the audience room), particularly striking for its *mihrab*, the Patio de Arrayanes and the Patio de los Leones with their respective buildings. It is probable that no more important sections were built after Mohammed V and the building became neglected because of the internal political situation. Immediately after the Reconquest, extraordinary maintenance work financed by the Crown was required, which resulted in complete reconstruction of some areas such as

the Cuarto Dorado, which was redecorated in the 16th century.

Varying degrees of maintenance work were carried out until the beginning of the 17th century. Between 1718 and 1829, the Alhambra was abandoned; restoration and excavation works (becoming more scientific) were undertaken again with vigor only from the mid-19th century. In the meantime, new Christian buildings were constructed within the enclosure wall of the complex: there were the monastery of San Francisco (1495), the palace of Charles V (one of the most lovely examples of Spanish Renaissance architecture, begun in 1527), and the church of Santa María la Real, begun in 1581 on land previously occupied by the Royal Mosque which, once consecrated as a church, was so precarious that it continued to stand for only a few decades before having to be demolished.

Such an intricate and complex architectural history prevents the possibility of ever knowing the Alhambra in its original splendor, especially as a large part of the painted decorations and the chromatic effects

of the decorative elements have been lost. (The only important exception is the tall base of *azulejos*—colored tiles—on many walls.) Likewise, the furniture and interior objects have disappeared except for a very few, such as the 14th-century Alhambra vase (or gazelle vase). However, it should be remembered that only continuous restoration, however alien to the philosophy of the modern day, has allowed the Alhambra to stand today.

The Alhambra places great importance on water and light, always an important factor in Islamic architecture. The alternation of

88 bottom left The Sala de los Embajadores (Room of the Ambassadors) is the largest and highest room in the Alhambra. Its length (12 yards) and height (20 yards) lend it a grandiose and solemn atmosphere. Space is vertically organized in two levels, the first featuring eight balconied

windows that offer splendid panoramas, and the second featuring twenty small windows at the top of the structure. All available wall space is covered by decorations in stucco that create a pleasant chromatic contrast with the ceiling in cedar; the ceiling repeats the star, one of the

geometrical motifs on the walls.

88 right This detail of the stucco decoration of the Sala de los Embajadores underlines the strength of the relief and the skillful alternation of stylized motifs (only the flower can be distinguished).

88-89 *This picture shows the magnificent ceiling with* muqarnas *of the Sala de las dos Hermanas. To better appreciate the "explosion" effect, viewers must bear in mind that the* muqarnas *were originally polychromatic and gilded.*

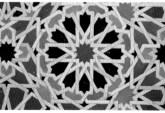

89 bottom *Azulejos are also present in the Sala de los Embajadores. This detail exemplifies the colors recurrently used in the Alhambra and a decorative motif, the star, that is found in various sizes all over the Arabic fortress.*

Ajimeces. The decoration—which as usual combines geometrical and stylized floral motifs—is exceedingly rich.

90 center left The Mirador (observation point) de Daraxa overlooks the gardens from a particularly spectacular viewpoint: windows open on three sides and the fourth side leads to the Sala de los

90 bottom left Water was essential to daily living at the Alhambra. This necessity explains the existence of the various artificial lakes designed to collect water, known to this day by their Arab name, acequias.

shadow and light, interior and exterior, is not dramatic: tall, concealed windows or grilled stucco screens let sunlight into the most shaded of recesses, and the covered porticoes are no less defined as transit space than the internal divisions of the larger rooms which often correspond to the windows (for example, in the Sala de los Embajadores). Water runs throughout and, with the lost wall decorations that carried brightly colored floral designs, helps us to anticipate the joys of Islamic paradise and its pavilions on earth.

The Alhambra
The Red Fortress of Granada

90 top right This foreshortened view of the Generalife gardens shows some blooming roses, a main attraction. Built in the 13th century and decorated during the first half of the 14th century, the Generalife was the country residence of the kings of Granada.

90 center right This image of the Generalife shows the Andalusian-style garden seen today. It must however be borne in mind that during the Moorish occupation, this area was mainly used for

agriculture, as was logical in the case of the villa "outside the walls."

90 bottom right The Daraxa Garden, a quiet and peaceful trapezoidal corner of the Alhambra, is all that remains of the inner park of the palace. The fountain was set here only in 1626.

91 The Patio de la Acequia is one of the Generalife's main attractions. About 55 yards long and nearly 14 yards wide, it owes its name to its long central tank.

"And those that believe and have done good will be received in Paradise, among Tall Rooms, below which rivers will run and there they will stay for eternity: how lovely is the reward for he that acts righteously!" (XXIX, 58 of the Koran; also XXXIX, 20).

Religious symbolism is apparent in the Patio de los Leones where the four rivulets from the fountains represent the four rivers of the Koranic Paradise (LV, 60 and 66). These collect in the central fountain decorated with twelve lions once considered to have been produced in the 10–11th centuries, though they probably date from the time of Mohammed V. In the same highly symbolic spirit, the ceiling of the Sala de los Embajadores reproduces the domes of the seven heavens.

In the inscriptions on the windows and the vault, the *sura* of the kingdom is cited from the Koran: "He that created seven heavens one on top of the other and you cannot distinguish any inequality in the creation of the Compassionate. Look up: do you see cracks?" (LXVIII, 3). These allude to

the power of the ruler but also to the power of God who commands over everything. The ceiling, as always in Islamic architecture, has a powerful abstract meaning and is directed toward the absolute. Analogously, the passage between suites of rooms on the vertical plane is tempered by courts. This is architecture that refutes spatial constriction in both the vertical and horizontal planes although it limits itself within a defined space (the perimeter walls are high and without large openings).

Light is collected in wide internal courts and refracted in different degrees of intensity to the interiors. Arches and columns are

The Red Fortress of Granada

The Alhambra

instrumental in achieving the effect; the Patio de los Leones has arches that are intentionally different in their design and typical Granada columns with a concave base, *collarinos* on the body of the column and varied capitals.

The use of abstract decorative elements offers an important service to this general aesthetic conception. Some examples are arabesques, calligraphic inscriptions chosen to suit the area which they decorate (amorous verses in the Patio de los Leones but epic or warlike inscriptions in the Sala de los Embajadores), *azulejos*, the more complex *muqarnas* (honeycomb patterns that represent the eighth heaven where Allah resides) of the Sala de las dos Doncellas or the Sala de los Abencerrajes, and of course the marvellous lacy stuccoes that recede into the distance.

It should be clear, however, that the architectural sense of the Alhambra also comes from its setting. Not only for those of us who can interpret it under the influence of Romanticism (*The Tales of the Alhambra* by Washington Irving, for example, and *Les Aventures du dernier Abencérage* by Chateaubriand), but also for its original residents, who were able to view from their palace not only the Albaicín, the Arab quarter outside the city walls that still retains its Arab layout, but also the Generalife (then an agricultural area) and the beautiful profile of the Sierra Nevada. Urban areas bordering untouched nature and rural spaces displaying the hand of man were the essential features of the Arab vision of the ideal countryside, which was closer to realization in the splendid Granada of the Nasrid dynasty than anywhere else at any time.

92 top left and center The Patio de la Acequia is seen here from the old residence. Myrtle, oranges, flowers and fountains of water all contribute to create a very special atmosphere.

92 bottom left Because of their harmony, the fountains in this foreshortened view of the Generalife recall the words of the Koran which recount of how every living thing was created from water.

92 top right This patio at the entrance of the Generalife has a water tank with a graceful geometric form featuring multiple lobes. While the abundance of water was essential to the Alhambra, especially in the case of siege, at the Generalife it served mainly to irrigate agricultural land.

92-93 This view of the Alhambra from the Generalife gardens, with the white houses of the Albaicín shimmering in the distance to the right, shows the most panoramic point of the palace and highlights the jagged layout of the towers from which the last king Abu 'Abd Allah (Boabdil for the Christians) could contemplate the fall of the last bulwark of Islam on Spanish soil.

93 bottom The Italian-inspired shapes of the box hedges of the Generalife contrast with those of the Alhambra and the Albaicín. No matter how wonderful they may seem, the Generalife gardens reflect neither the plant species nor the layout and structural choices adopted in the Arab gardens proper. Even in this aspect, the Alhambra documents the way in which European exoticism received Islamic influences in various periods.

MADRID

Spain

The Escorial

THE HOUSE OF THE "REY PRUDENTE"

94 top right The portrait of Philip II by Titian, housed at the Palatine Gallery in Florence, shows the Spanish king in the bloom of his youth. Titian Vecellio (1490?-1576) worked extensively for both Charles V and Philip II, leaving us memorable pictures of these two kings.

No building can aspire to being the complete expression of a monarchy more than the Escorial: it was conceived as such and was considered as such by its contemporaries and their descendants. Aesthetic appreciation of the building is influenced by one's opinion of that monarchy, whether ideologically appreciative or ideologically critical.

Built as a thanksgiving offering about 30 miles from Madrid for the victory in the Battle of San Quintino (10 August 1557), the grid-shaped ground plan of the monastery of San Lorenzo del Escorial on the Sierra de Guadarrama commemorates the peculiar martyrdom (by roasting on a grill) of St. Laurence, whose feast day falls on 10 August. The construction was also partly a mandate from Charles V who, at his death in 1558, ordered his son to build a pantheon for the Hapsburgs of Spain.

Getting the project under way was not easy. The choice of site was a problem and was handed to a commission of technicians to solve. It fell on the village of Escorial for its proximity to Madrid, the new capital of the kingdom, and for its abundance of water and local building materials. The choice of architect was also difficult: at first, use of an Italian architect was considered; the possibility of Michelangelo was discarded as he was by then an old man. Eventually Juan Bautista de Toledo was selected; he was patronized by the ex-viceroy of Naples, Pedro de Toledo, and he had also had experience in Italy. The general design of the building was defined in 1562 and work began on 23 April 1563, the same year in which the Council of Trent ended. By this time the Renaissance distinction had been drawn between the architect and the construction's executor, two roles which were filled by the same person during the Middle Ages. In this

94 top left *The main facade of the Escorial features three monumental facades. The central facade was built using stone blocks so huge that they had to be transported on custom-designed carts pulled by forty pairs of bulls. The stone statue of St. Laurence, above the door, is over four yards high.*

95 top right *On the vault of the ante-choir Luca Giordano painted exotic scenes from the life of Solomon. Here, as in the other frescoes, light opens the sky to the eternal regions beyond.*

94 bottom *Considered the eighth wonder of the world even as it was being built, the Escorial has been celebrated by Spanish poets, described by foreign travelers and portrayed in numerous drawings and pictures, including the old watercolor engraving, with its Latin legend, reproduced here.*

94-95 *This splendid view with the main facade in the foreground clearly shows the complexity of the imposing structure—note especially how the basilica rises from the central structure—as well as the natural landscape of the Sierra de Guadarrama.*

95 top left *This view of the right lateral facade highlights the structure's architectural expression by emphasizing the geometrical distribution of the windows and the monumental features of the whole, especially the side towers. The grey roof is of slate quarried close to the monastery.*

96 left The facade of the basilica of the Escorial is dominated by the statues of the six kings of Judah sculpted by Juan Bautista Monegro, who also executed the statue of St. Laurence on the facade of the Escorial. The stone and marble statues feature scepters and crowns in gold-plated bronze.

vein, Juan Bautista de Toledo was assisted by able helpers, and he completed the lovely southern facade and the first floor of the Patio of the Evangelists. Juan de Herrera (ca. 1530–1597) was Juan Bautista de Toledo's assistant, and he took complete charge after the death of the maestro in 1567, becoming the king's favorite architect. (He was indeed to become responsible for other important constructions such as the palace of Aranjuez and the Alcazar in Toledo.) Herrera completed the remaining facades and designed the imposing basilica (1575–82). Building took

more than 20 years and finally ended on 13 September 1584. The project had notable economic fallout for the surrounding villages, which considerably increased their populations.

Philip II the Prudent, a great centralizer, did not see the Escorial palace as a monument to his family nor to the Spanish monarchy in general. He had a strong cultural background and an intense spirituality in the vein of the Counter-Reformation which allowed him to imagine the absolute expression of an idea inherent in the domination and construction of space that architecture enables. Confrontation

with the historical trends that ran counter to what the Catholic monarchy represented—the Reformation, Protestant mercantilism, anti-absolutism—prompted the king to shape the building as an expression of the vision of the world that the Spanish Hapsburgs were trying to affirm. This was an ideal model, often distant from the motley and subtle social and cultural reality (as the classic monograph by Fernand Braudel on Philip II constantly suggests) but strongly felt and generously pursued. Classic models on the one hand, and Solomon's Temple on the other, were borne in mind; it is debated

96 top left The basilica, the religious heart of the Escorial, overlooks the Patio de los Reyes. Two towers flank the imposing facade. A passage under six huge Doric columns leads to an arched vestibule with a balcony that supports the statues of the six kings of Judah.

The 104-yard-high dome rises above the tympanum top.

96 top right The large Patio de los Evangelistas by Juan Bautista de Toledo is the part of the Escorial that shows most clearly the influence of the Italian Renaissance.

The Escorial

The House of the "Rey Prudente"

whether or not the temple, the archetypal biblical construction, was actually considered but, in any case, the parallel was created by contemporaries, starting with Padre Sigüenza who dedicated a chapter to it in his *Historia primitiva y exacta del monasterio del Escorial*, written on the basis of his direct knowledge of the vicissitudes of the building work. "The idea was to create a perfect architecture, a holy building that sacralized, from a Christian point of view, some of the untouchable dogmas of the aesthetics of Vitruvius, fundamental in the culture of Renaissance artists" writes Checa Cremades. The aesthetic design of the Escorial stands out for its originality in comparison to previous architecture and its independence of Italian models. It was used taken as an example even as late as the 20th century. As Padre Sigüenza and documents of the period testified, the king oversaw, discussed and approved every detail of the work in progress.

To say that the Escorial is imposing is to do it an injustice, both because sheer figures are more eloquent (the perimeter measures 225 by 175 yards) and because a purely quantitative

perception of what was called the eighth wonder of the world does not express its true worth. Imposing, yes, but also austere, solid, solitary, certainly sad and a thousand miles from the idea of Spanish art as excess or unrestrained embellishment (the Italian Baroque is incommensurably better at uniting these characteristics). Even the vaults of the church have little in common with Roman tradition. The traditional models that were proposed (especially that of the Roman baths) certainly seem more appropriate to express its grandiose sobriety of forms.

96-97 The vault preceding the Capilla Mayor features the Passage of the Virgin. Note how the figures are placed according to the structure to be decorated.

97 top The large fresco by Luca Giordano on the basilica's vault next to the choir portrays the Last Judgment. The Italian Baroque painter worked at the Escorial in 1692-93 and demonstrated his

great talent as a skilful decorator of large surfaces. He remained in Spain until 1702.

97 bottom This fresco by Luca Giordano inside the basilica portrays the militant Church—the hierarchical community of believers on earth—in harmony with the triumphant Church, the community of souls who already enjoy closeness with God.

The House of the "Rey Prudente"

However, what strikes one first is the mass of grey granite and the play on perspective between the main facade and the secondary facades; the symmetry of the windows and the dormers; the power of the two towers at either end of main facade, and the slightly raised central section. The whole presents a series of solid and empty spaces on two levels, animated not by the material but by the movement. Nor is there much in common with either Renaissance decorative taste (which in Spain tended to make a triumphal arch of the entrance) or with Baroque gateways which—often in contrast with bare facades—were to be typical of the Spanish 17th century.

The soaring church dome with its pure lines is one of the most important of the 16th century in the Iberian peninsula. Access to the church is granted via the Patio de los Reyes (not without a certain transparent ideological value). The patio was an intimate space for faith in an age when ascetics and mystics flourished in Spain, but it was also a space protected by the power of the sovereign. Also of great importance in the appraisal of the monument is the dialectic between the wide and narrow courtyards, almost an expression of a multiplicity rationally and ideologically assembled in units. The Italian elements (suggested by Francesco Paciotto for the church, and perhaps also by Vignola's original design for the church of Il Gesù in Rome) were always interpreted by Herrera, who did not allow a single element to escape the general, inflexible rules of the whole. The result is an interplay not just of spaces but also of tones: the monumentality of the Patio de los Reyes (so called for the statues of the six Old Testament kings who contributed to the construction and adornment of the Temple in Jerusalem) is a modification by Herrera of an original design by Paciotto that contrasts with the Patio of the Evangelists by Juan Bautista de Toledo, which displays a certain Italian style not without Iberian inflexibility.

But to understand the Escorial, one should study more than the architecture. The place contains thousands of works of art which, in many cases, were produced especially for the building or were brought there by the wishes of

Philip II or his heirs. For example, the important sculptures by the Milanese Leone Leoni and his son Pompeo Leoni; the Italians had already had many commissions from Charles V and were asked to produce the bronze statues that adorn the larger retable and also the funerary statues for Charles V and Philip II placed within de Herrera's classical church.

Moreover, the building has a twofold nature. First, it is a monastery that was originally entrusted to Hieronymites: they were chosen

100 (detail) and 101 center The splendid wooden door leading to the Throne Room dates back to 1567. The impression of depth created by the columns is especially noteworthy. The work of a German school, it features geometric and architectural motifs created through a skilful combination of various types of wood.

101 left The bedroom of Isabella Clara Eugenia, daughter of Philip II, features the same simplicity that marks the rooms in which Philip II himself lived.

101 top right The Throne Room is noteworthy for its relative simplicity. The Flemish tapestries and the high paneling in azulejos (colored majolica tiles) covering all the walls dates back to the 16th century and marks the austere court style of the Habsburgs.

because they lived in Charles V's last refuge—the monastery of Yuste in Extremadura—and also because they dedicated much time to worship and so would guarantee solemnity. Later the Hieronymites were replaced by Augustinians who still occupy the monastery today. Second, the Escorial was also a royal palace, of which a quarter is occupied by private apartments. Initially, Philip II had wanted the Escorial to be his Yuste but from 1571 it became one of his main residences. The king passed the summer months there as well as spending long periods during the principal liturgical celebrations. The dual nature of the building clearly explains the extensiveness of the various picture, book and other collections as an expression of the humanistic spirit of the king and as defiance against the ravages of time.

Originating from all over Europe and often sent as gifts to the king, the enormous number of holy relics at the Escorial is an important sign of the religiousness of Philip II and the age in which he lived. There was even talk of a plan to transfer the holy body of St. James the Greater from Compostela, the destination of one of the most famous pilgrimages in Europe.

The picture gallery at the Escorial can be thought of as almost a parallel to the Prado which, in fact, exhibits many works from that royal monastery. Great Spanish and foreign painters who suited the Hapsburg taste such as El Greco, Velásquez, Tintoretto and Bosch are represented by important works. Some were expressly commissioned; for instance, *The Martyrdom of St. Laurence* by Titian (which was not liked by the king and was not displayed in the basilica), *The Martyrdom of St. Maurice* by El Greco (also not liked) and *The Dream of Philip II,* also by El Greco, showing the king at prayer. Others were farsighted purchases (the canvases by Ribera today in the Escorial and in the Prado

MDLXVII

Escorial

102 center The Bourbon apartments are noteworthy especially because of its extraordinary collection of more than 300 tapestries. These were woven partly in Flanders and partly at the famous Real Fábrica de Tapices of Madrid, which produces carpets to this day.

102 bottom The Hall of Battles is a 60-yard-long gallery. One wall features a representation by various Italian artists (1587) of John II's victory over the Arabs at Higueruela in 1431. The other wall, divided into panels, depicts the battle of San Quintino and some of Philip II's other major victories.

were bought by Velásquez in Naples expressly for the building and for the royal palace). Valuable works of art were sent from private individuals and from all the European courts, such as Cellini's famous *Christ*, given by the Grand Duke of Tuscany in 1586. Decorators and fresco painters (often Italian like Luca Cambiaso, Pellegrino Tibaldi and Luca Giordano) covered the walls with frescoes through the centuries. Philip II commissioned Italian painters (Niccolò Granello, Lazzaro Tavarone, Fabrizio Castello and Orazio Cambiaso) to reproduce the Battle of Higueruela (1431) in which John II of Castile defeated the Arabs. The lively depiction, which covers the entire wall of one gallery, must have pleased the king, who also had his victory at San Quintino painted.

The Library offers double interest for the visitor and scholar. The salon is impressive on one hand for its functionality (the positioning of the windows was clearly purposefully done) and for the majesty, beauty and sumptuousness of the frescoes painted by Pellegrino Tibaldi, who during his stay at the Escorial in 1586–93 depicted the seven liberal arts on the domed ceiling and theology above the entrance. On the other hand, the collection of codices and printed books is priceless and is consulted by scholars from around the world every day. The nucleus of the Library contained 4,000 books from Philip II's personal collection but was augmented by the libraries of Diego Hurtado de Mendoza, poet and ambassador to Venice and Rome, of the historian Jerónimo Zurita and of the great Biblicist Arias Montano, whom Philip charged with cataloguing the Escorial Library and with looking after the famous *Royal Bible* printed in Antwerp by Christophe Plantin. The Library is less important for the number of its works (40,000 printed books and 5,000 manuscripts) than for their rarity: it includes handwritten works by St. Teresa of Avila, important Greek codices and a unique collection of Arab manuscripts which formed the Library of the Sultan of Morocco, Muley Zidan, which Philip II sent to the Escorial after a war-raid on his palace in 1611.

The Library allows us to understand what the king read, while the austerity of his existence and the effort he poured into the execution of his duties are witnessed by the small and modest rooms he occupied: they are almost monk-like, with humble furniture, simple tiled floors, *azulejos* (colored tiles) from Talavera rising midway up the walls, and white plastered surfaces. His many work tools and books, engravings and paintings, are proof of an intellectual curiosity that was never satisfied.

The Escorial is a monument not just to an age but also to a man; this connotation was so strong that the building was not tolerated after the end of his dynasty. When the Bourbons were recognized as monarchs of Spain in 1713, the rooms of the Escorial must have seemed to have outlived their purpose. During the 18th century, part of the palace was transformed and is today adorned by an extraordinary collection of tapestries decorated with scenes based on cartoons by Goya. A pavilion for banquets and reunions, the Casita de el Príncipe, was also built (1772) with lovely 18th-century decor by the architect Juan de Villanova like that of the Casita de Arriba.

102-103 The Library is a large
rectangular hall about 11 yards
high. Scholars consulting the books
kept here use a smaller reading
room maintained by the
Augustinian Fathers who still live
in the complex. The showcases
house certain particularly precious
or curious volumes.

103 top The Salas Capitulares,
frescoed by 16th-century artists,
house a rich collection of paintings
and decorative art. The renovation
and conservation work on the
Escorial in the 1960s and 1970s
have led to the redesigning of
exhibition space and the
reorganization of the art works.

Portugal

LISBON

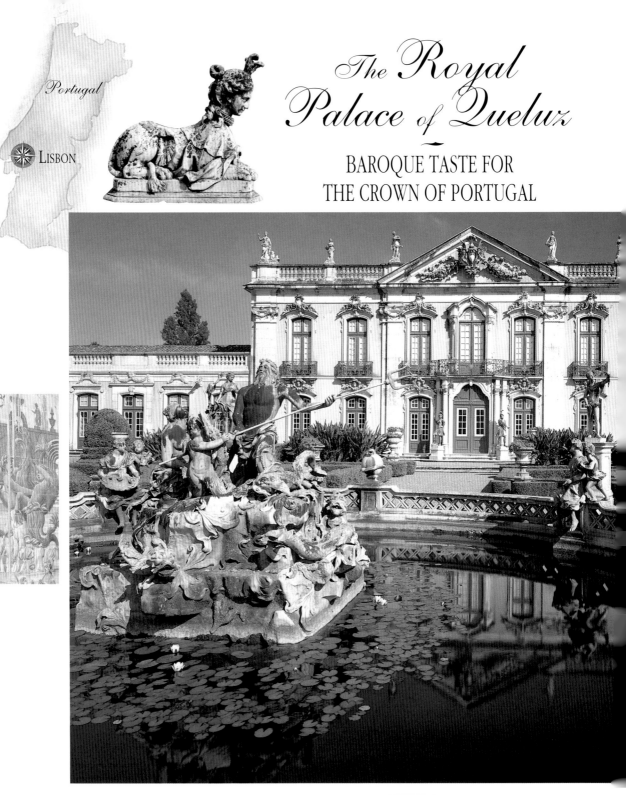

The Royal Palace of Queluz

BAROQUE TASTE FOR THE CROWN OF PORTUGAL

104 top An 18th-century sphinx in the garden of Queluz guards the secret of the perfect harmony of its natural surroundings.

104 left The Azulejos Corridor in the Queluz palace is lined with mythological scenes, fountains and gardens.

The Royal Palace of Queluz, the Portuguese Versailles, stands about six miles from Lisbon and is one of the most important examples of 18th-century architecture in the country. The choice of site, close to the capital but in the healthy countryside, is immediately symbolic. The 18th-century art of harmonious *savoir-vivre* and the ideal of a secluded summer holiday near the city, with less rigid etiquette and a simpler and more amusing social life than in the capital, is magnificently expressed at Queluz, more so than at other, similar European houses. Evidence of this is the gentle alternation of private rooms (bedchambers, intimate conversation rooms) with public rooms (the throne room, the music room, the chapel). The taste expressed by the building is no longer the Spanish Baroque but, in reaction to the almost out-of-date style, French Classicism. This does not however exclude a degree of national character which can be seen both in the details and the overall structure.

The building stands on the former property of Cristovão de Moura, the Spanish-loving Marquis of Castelo Rodrigo, which was confiscated after 1640 when restoration of the Portuguese Bragança dynasty put an end to sixty years of domination by Portugal's powerful neighbor, Spain. The property was absorbed by the Casa do Infantado, the personal inheritance of the king's second-born. Then what was only a rather modest country house was turned into a palace by the Infante Don Pietro (1717–1786), the second son of John V and brother of Joseph I.

Queluz is one of those sites that took a long time to build simply because of its massiveness. The work began in 1747 with Mateus Vicente de Oliveira and was completed after 1790. The Frenchman Jean Baptiste Robillon was drafted in to direct the project; he completed the west wing in 1760 and took charge of decoration of the sculpture room and renovation of the throne room. What is remarkable is the number of painters, stucco molders, sculptors and engravers who worked on the building. As many of them were Portuguese (though in many cases they had worked abroad), we may wonder how the national taste and artistic culture were adapted to the European Rococo style for which the palace is so renowned.

The problem was of great cultural importance across the whole Iberian peninsula in the 18th century and not only in the field of art: the age of Enlightenment forced Spain and

104-105 The large fountain in the hanging garden is strategically placed in front of the main facade of the Royal Palace. Its dramatic quality is assured but it is of an almost intimate and private nature. The facade faces the interior of the complex and the pleasant, familiar scenery of the garden.

104 bottom left In line with the vogue of the late 18th century, both interiors and exteriors at Queluz are painted in pale colors. Pink predominates, prompting José Saramago, the Portuguese winner of the Nobel Prize for literature, to describe the palace as a "sugar-coated almond."

104 bottom right The grand Lions Staircase designed by Robillon is one of the palace's most attractive features. As an 18th-century architect, Robillon removed all political and spiritual values from the staircase but exhibited his strong technical capability, particularly in the forking of the ramps.

105 top The fountains in the garden create intimate corners ideal for quiet interludes.

105 center The park at Queluz offers a wide variety of scenery: there is the geometric regularity of the French garden and the wide tree-lined avenues bordered by azulejos. These Iberian tiles were used to line the walls of the Dutch Canal (now dry) that crosses the lower part of the garden and once fed the ponds.

105 bottom The strict French design of this garden is well-suited to the light-hearted but rational harmony which is seen everywhere at Queluz.

106-107 *The splendid
Entertainment Room (later the
Throne Room) is characterized by
soberness of color and limited,
though always very elegant,
decoration. The ceiling design,
with its multi-lobed form, bears
some resemblance to the Italian
airiness of Juvarra. The huge
Venetian chandelier quite
evident: chandeliers played a
fundamental role in 18th-century
houses.*

Portugal to consider difficult oligarchic modernization without losing the essence of their cultures. This was a complex process not without damaging conflicts; in Spain it led to the anti-Napoleonic War of Independence and in Portugal to the return of the royal family from exile in Brazil. Queluz had been the permanent residence of the Prince Regent João VI and his wife Carlota Joaquina since the fire in their Lisbon palace of Ajuda (1794) but it was abandoned in 1807 by the fleeing royal family. The court only returned to Portugal in 1821 when the palace was lived in by Carlota Joaquina and, on and off, by Dom Miguel and Dom Pedro, the two sons of João VI, who were jockeying for the throne. Dom Pedro actually died at Queluz in the Don Quixote room. Now the palace is used to host foreign heads of state visiting Portugal.

decorative majolica tiles generally in a blue (*azul*) pattern on a white background. The tiles were used to create large scenes from the 17th century onward; the Spanish version remained more faithful to the geometricality of the original Arab tiles, while the Portuguese version abandoned geometrics.

The evidence of a foreign influence is most evident in Robillion's Oriental pavilion. The balustrades and Doric columns remind one of the French 18th-century Classicism in which the architect was trained, but the beautifully decorated stairway created to obviate the difference in level between the the palace and the underlying ground is certainly among the most creative features of the building.

Architectural structure only becomes fully meaningful, at Queluz as at other European palaces, if other elements in other styles and

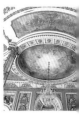

106 bottom The loveliest ceramic tiles in the palace are to be seen in the Azulejos Corridor. The blue and white tiles of the lower section show hunting and fishing scenes in Rococo style. The larger polychrome tiles higher up are almost Neoclassical and depict allegories and singeries *(cheerful scenes). The tiles have replaced the original trompe l'oeil frescoes that imitated azulejos. The carriage on the left is notable: Portugal has one of the world's best collections at the Museu Nacional dos Coches in Lisbon.*

Oliveira (who was responsible for the central section of the building and the two wings) decided that the palace should not be huge in size and that it should be pleasantly livable (although comparisons abroad do not always match Oliveira's opinion). The strikingly local choice of several important decorative aspects also contributes to this goal: the large panels of white and blue *azulejos* on both the interior and exterior of the palace are one of the most original examples of decorative Portuguese art. Azulejos are

from other ages are considered. It is necessary to bear in mind the gardens designed around the palace; although partly modified in outlay and choice of species, and later embellished with various decorative elements, they still give a good idea of the original plan created by Robillion and the Dutch gardener Joseph Van der Kolk in 1760 on the occasion of Prince Pedro's wedding. The Neptune Garden (or Hanging Garden, as it rests on huge stone counterforts that level the soil), onto which the internal facade of the palace opens, is

107 The Ambassadors' Room (originally the Entertainment Room) receives abundant light from the north and south. The canopy over the spot where the thrones used to stand does not match the style of the room and was in fact an artificial addition. Foreign ministers were only received here from the 19th century on.

108 top Lighthearted and lively, the Tea Room is remarkable for its wall paintings of still lifes and country life. The profusion of silverware contributes to an atmosphere of friendly, cheerful luxury.

108 bottom The Don Quixote Room takes its name from pictures showing scenes from Cervantes' magnificent novel. Note the continuation in the wooden flooring of the circular themes of the ceiling.

particularly impressive: ponds, waterfalls, statues, azulejos and the French design of the flower beds made (and to a certain extent still make) the overall design incomparable. The loss of the original furniture, mostly dispersed, is keenly felt. It is very difficult to repair such losses, as members of the 18th-century European aristocracy took great care, sometimes over several generations, in the choice of their furniture, in order to create varying degrees of intimacy according to individual taste. As Mario Praz wrote in his fascinating book, *The Philosophy of Furnishing*, a piece of furniture took on significance and worth insofar as it was chosen (or, as usually occurred, designed and made) for a particular

setting (i.e., for its upholstery chosen to suit other furniture in the room, for the light it gives off or for the people who normally lived there). A room stripped of its proper furniture can no longer be itself, however generous purchases in the antiques market may be.

It is through the decoration of Queluz, much of it original, that we can bring the palace's era and atmosphere to life once more. The rooms were arranged in rows (a style that was to continue at least until the end of the 19th century) and had particular functions, but both the public and private rooms were decorated with an overabundance of materials, techniques, colors and lights. Wood or plaster (often gilded), on the one hand, and mirrors, on the other, help to create the dominating image. At Queluz as at analogous European houses, the tendency to create a unique atmosphere in a single room rather than to create coherence throughout the whole building is apparent. The objects also contribute to this effect: there are Oriental and European porcelain, carpets from Arraiolos (where the most famous embroidered carpets in the country were made) and goldsmith's pieces from the royal collections. The choice of pictures and their themes plays a similar role; examples are the panels by Manuel da Costa and José Antonio Narciso in the Don Quixote room, the cherubs in the queen's changing room or the rustic banquet scenes in the tea-

room. Consequently, the eye derives pleasure not so much from architectural and decorative continuity as from the continually changing emotions that are aroused.

Yet all this gives Queluz an enjoyable intimacy: for instance, the facade of the central section (two stories high, while the wings are single stories) faces inward toward the garden, and the colors are always tenuous, as was *de rigueur* for Rococo style.

The Royal Palace of Queluz

Baroque Taste for the Crown of Portugal

The "Portugueseness" of Queluz emerges when it is compared to the two other best examples of Iberian architecture from the same era: the Royal Palace in Madrid (an urban residence, unlike Queluz) and the Granja di San Ildefonso in Segovia, a splendid country house famous for its fountains. The two Spanish palaces display a grandiosity and a triumph of Italian and French taste in structure and details, but Queluz stands out as a vital example of Portuguese art. In the first place, it is natural to contrast it to the nearby palace of Sintra beloved by European Romantics, including Byron, for the beauty of the nature surrounding it and for its late-Medieval atmosphere. In this sense, Queluz becomes the symbol of a new aesthetic vision that could only be 18th-century. But Queluz is also the most illuminating example of the Rococo style in southern Portugal which, strongly influenced by the presence of the court, contrasts resolutely with that of northern Portugal (e.g., Braga and Porto). The first, elegant and cultured, is an expression of French taste featuring large, undecorated areas on its exterior but a concentration of decoration within. The second is an example of sacred architecture with a strong use of granite on the facade sculptures and friezes that integrates decoration into the architecture with a degree of expressiveness that reaches its maximum eloquence in Brazil in the Aleijadinho.

108-109 The Queen's Toucador (toilette room) contains a series of beautiful paintings showing cupids at play. Note the tenuous colors of the ceiling and the abundance of mirrors. The lovely cabinetmaker's effect on the floor was created by alternating different types of wood. Many of the palace's examples of boiseries used high-quality Brazilian wood.

109 bottom This bedchamber has many Neoclassical features; examples are the use of brass on the bed and bedside table and the widespread use of yellow gold (especially on the ceiling).

Buckingham Palace

REFLECTION OF THE MONARCHY

Buckingham Palace is one of the best known buildings of London. The principal official state residence of the British monarchy, it is the home of the Queen when she is not staying at Windsor, Sandringham or Balmoral. It is particularly fascinating because it is not a museum—although containing many treasures it remains a working royal palace. An imposing classical structure, it stands imperiously on its own, a central focus in the city's West End. (London claims to be two cities: the City of London where business is focused, and the City of Westminster, which first began as a residential suburb to the west.)

Buckingham Palace is not old as royal palaces go, its first appearance being in 1633 as a private residence. It is very much a mixture of periods and styles, with the best work dating from 1820 to the 1830's, although much of this is concealed by the East facade, added in the middle of the last century.

To truly appreciate the palace you need to know its setting. With elegant houses to one side of the wide approach, the green depths and lakes of a park to the other, the palace is indeed handsomely framed. As you pass under Admiralty Arch from Trafalgar Square and approach Buckingham Palace, there follows to your right a parade of handsome buildings. Note the early 19th-century cream-colored classical fronts of Carlton House Terrace and Clarence House, the home of the Queen Mother.

Marlborough House, home to the Queen's grandmother, Queen Mary, when a widow, is early 18th-century red brick. (George V's queen interested herself greatly in the restoration of palace interiors and furniture. She instituted a historically accurate approach still followed today.) Next comes the Palace of St. James's with Tudor buildings, tiled roofs and a chapel, where the late Princess of Wales lay the night before her burial, and last is Lancaster House, the Government hospitality house, beside Green Park.

Buckingham Palace is everyone's ideal royal palace. It appears as you approach along the half mile length of a grand, tree-lined avenue. This is the Mall, a triumphal way, often used for royal processions from state events to weddings, from formal visits by foreign heads of state to somber funerals. Although the Mall gave its name to American shopping centers, it has nothing to do with buying and selling goods, and apart from souvenir vendors there are no shops. The name comes from a 17th-century bowling game played by aristocrats in the gardens of the stately mansions facing the route—the game of pell-mell.

The palace stands behind high gilded railings and gates in its own extensive private gardens, with a lake, surrounded by brick walls. The public park to your left is St. James's Park and is also famous. It has been an open space for more than 350 years and is often mentioned in classics of English literature. If you don't want to walk along the Mall, take a stroll through the park to pause and view the palace from the bridge over the ornamental lake—it looks as if it stands deep in the country, for it rises massively above the clustered trees. With many colorful ducks and geese on the water this viewpoint is a marvelous one for photographers.

The grand facade of the palace stands out as you approach it, flanked with open spaces and formal flower beds, wide roads leading right to Hyde Park Corner and the Duke of Wellington's house beyond Green Park, left to the Guards' barracks. The road edging the far southern side of the park is the charmingly named Birdcage Walk which eventually

110 top A painter who achieved considerable fame under Victoria was Franz Winterhalter. His skill at presenting figures dressed or draped with exotic fabrics is seen here in the portrait of the queen.

110 center right Originally the heraldic beasts bearing the royal coat of arms were leopards—now they are the famous lion and unicorn. Framed with a French style gilded wreath, this essential symbol of the monarch is mounted on an entry gate.

110 bottom left On the Dining Room's walls, among the rich collection of paintings, hangs this portrait of King George IV. The monarch is here wearing the uniform of the Order of the Garter.

110-111 Set in gardens with a pool, here you see the original 18th-century house, behind the later east wing, surrounding buildings, its parade ground and gilded grilles facing the Mall.

111 top St. James's Park and Green Park form an extensive garden setting encompassing the palace. From the former's lake you look up to the facade. It would have been more spectacular if Nash's design still existed: you would be looking into a court inside two tall wings fronted with statuary.

112-113 The Grand Hall is a rather low-ceilinged apartment, stressing the fact that it is below the piano nobile. To create the effect of space Nash lowered the floor, made of Carrara marble, as are the pillars. The great chimney piece is very fine, carved by Joseph Theakston. Originally the walls were of colored scagliola; the present white and gold decor dates from 1902.

conducts you to the well-known Big Ben clock tower and the Palace of Westminster with its Victoria Tower on Parliament Square. Beside the Mall Horseguards' Parade has a second, and more intimate, Changing of the Guard which takes place with the Queen's Lifeguards on horseback each afternoon.

Such extraordinary neighbors! Yet the palace in its very commanding position is a real centerpiece. If a brilliant red, blue and gold flag, the royal standard, is fluttering high on its mast from the central flagstaff it means the Queen is in residence. The banner flies only then, whenever or wherever the monarch is present as Britain's sovereign, and head of state.

And what a home Buckingham Palace is! The vast building with a graveled parade ground before it is actually a hollow square, its original front concealed. Behind is a central courtyard hiding the principal part of the palace from view by the spectators who crowd the noble grillework of railings. Inside sentries march, often in familiar red uniforms and black bearskins, on the parade ground in front of the stone facade. Here every day at noon traffic is stopped and the famous Changing of the Guard is played out with various uniformed regiments marching to music and drums. It's a huge tourist attraction, and in summer the "rond point" before the palace can become very crowded. This traffic circle is dominated by a statue of the present queen's great-great-grandmother, the long-lived Queen Victoria. The monument is a very grandiose one with steps and balustrades—and makes a good viewpoint for seeing the palace.

Although first built in the reign of Charles I in what were then open fields to the west of the City of London, the house has been much altered since. Early prints show that three

Reflection of the Monarchy

centuries ago this was a large mansion in a
country setting west of London, belonging to
Lord Goring, and later to the Earl of
Arlington, who rebuilt it. When acquired by
the Duke of Buckingham, whose name it
retains, it was rebuilt again 25 years later;
even so it was nowhere near as imposing
and large as it is now. It was remodeled once
more under George III from 1762. Its
greatest period dates from 1820, however,
for it is to this rather dull king's cultured son,
the Prince Regent, later George IV, that we
owe so many of the present aspects.

George IV employed a star designer,
John Nash. This inventive architect worked
well with the king, for both liked marked
theatrical effects. (The Nash Terraces in
Regent's Park and the wondrous Brighton
Pavilion, an Eastern exotic dream, were their
concepts.) Within the Quadrangle, hidden
from public view, many of Nash's designs
exist—but his construction could be weak
and methods were not well thought out, so
his elegant work often suffers from this fault.
Yet it reflects the often Francophile good
taste of the king, and his immense flair when
it came to the arts. Poor Nash was dismissed
on the king's death in 1830 and replaced by
the competent yet insensitive Edward Blore,
who effectively spoiled Nash's concept.
There was new building to be done and the
king's young niece, Queen Victoria, was
freshly married to Prince Albert of Saxe-
Coburg. The couple had ideas of their own
to make it a home, for after 1840 there were
children on the way.

Blore equipped the palace with a new
east wing. Bedrooms and nurseries were

114 top The Green Room is one of the handsomest. From its high coved "Mogul" ceiling to its parquet floors it is sumptuously Nash in style, the whole expressed in ultimate Georgian taste. Here guests gather for receptions in the Throne Room. The marble fireplaces were supplied by Joseph Browne.

114 bottom Over 40 meters long, the Picture Gallery occupies, like a tall corridor, the first floor rooms of the old Buckingham House and was designed to contain George III's Dutch and Flemish pictures, part of the rich collection of paintings owned by the queen. Wood carvings are in the style of the great English 17th-century limewood sculptor, Grinling Gibbons.

added, and the kitchens modernized. The pillared gray Portland (originally Caen) stone facade you see is essentially the one added by Victoria in the mid-19th century. In addition to accommodation for her growing family she also aimed to provide bigger state rooms, including a ballroom. Now it is also used for up to 170 guests at state banquets.

The new wing closed off the open courtyard front of the late-Georgian palace, which had been flanked with two grand side wings, turning it into a hollow square. (The original concept of George IV was for a triumphal entry called the Trafalgar and Waterloo Arch. It stood in front, but Nash's design was too narrow for Queen Victoria's state coach to pass through, so it was moved and the Marble Arch, as it is popularly known, now stands at the northeast corner of nearby Hyde Park.)

front hides the golden brown Bath stone of the older part of Buckingham Palace.

Until quite recently, except by going in to view the exhibitions at the Queen's Gallery, to the south of the main building on Buckingham Palace Road, there was no way people without the official entry could see the grand interiors. Now, every summer when the royal family is on holiday in Scotland at Balmoral, Buckingham Palace is open to a flow of visitors. They traverse a set route along two floors through grand corridors to view the decors, the antique furnishings and the many works of art in gilded saloons and reception rooms. These overlook the parks, private gardens, lakes, and the Mall from tall windows.

The palace is open for the months of August and September each year. You pass through the Entree with portraits of the

Due to the erosion of the soft Caen stone this new front had to be replaced, and it was redesigned and refaced from 1913 in the reign of King George V, the architect being Aston Webb. Now the East facade is the best known part of the palace, instantly recognizable. Here in the center at first floor level is the famous balcony upon which the royal family make appearances on state occasions. Within the palace in the Quadrangle you can see and compare the different stone of the walls of the original. The recent pale Portland stone of the

Hanoverian kings from the South entrance, on to the Prince of Wales Door and the Ambassadors' Court to arrive beside the inner Grand Entrance. The rooms in the East range are not seen by the public, but the only interesting one is the heavily gilded Center Room, leading to the first floor balcony.

The facade before you is the original one by Nash with a handsome double portico of Doric and Corinthian columns, the Grand Entrance. It was influenced by Charles Perrault's design for the Louvre entrance in

114-115 The Throne Room is a most theatrical saloon with twin winged genii descending from the coving to hold garlands over the chairs of state. They are sculpted by Bernasconi, the leading plasterer at the palace. The plaster frieze attempts a rare medieval theme. The crimson silk hangings were recently restored, and the four gilded trophies may have come from Carlton House.

115 bottom One of a pair of Japanese lacquer bowls, mounted in gilt bronze in the French style of the mid-18th century, among the treasures of the Picture Gallery.

Paris. The contrast with Blore's East range, its rear walls in stucco across the Quadrangle, underlines the craftsmanship and elegance of the old palace. Its style is undeniable.

To your right is the Grand Hall with floor and pillars of Carrara marble. On the other side of the entrance, you ascend the ceremonial Grand Stair to the first floor. The stairway is double one and has a fine bronze balustrade. It conducts the visitor to the grand suite of rooms that are a shortened form of a stately sequence that can be appreciated more fully in Wren's enfilade of royal reception rooms at Hampton Court.

The State Rooms still bear the style and artistic stamp of John Nash and are among the most opulent in the world, reflecting the grand style and glorification of British arts under King George IV. They are the Guard Room, then the Green Drawing Room, followed by the Throne Room. The first is a narrow apartment, lavishly decorated with sculptures. The Green Drawing Room, once Queen Charlotte's Saloon, acts as an assembly room for functions in the Throne and Music Rooms. It seems at first more gold than green—the predominant color, except for the silk wall panels and pelmets. The red of the ensuing Throne Room is far more dominant. This spectacular long room has a proscenium surrounding the chairs of state and is dominated by the crimson of the

hangings, gilt trophies, a deep plaster frieze, and a huge chandelier. All three of these rooms have a strong indebtedness to Nash.

The Picture Gallery, the spine of the first floor rooms, is sandwiched between two sets of state rooms and has several entrances. A very long apartment, it is lit from above with a glass ceiling. It contains some fabulous pictures including many of George IV's collection of Flemish and Dutch works. Unfortunately they are not clearly numbered to coincide with the catalogue.

From this gallery you progress through the Lobby, Silk Tapestry Room and into the East Gallery, then cross to the West Gallery. These contain treasures, but are essentially grand corridors to connect the suite of Nash state rooms to later additions by his pupil James Pennethorne from 1853. However on the way there is much to see in the form of furniture, pictures and porcelain in these otherwise rather plain "corridor rooms" leading eventually to the dramatic State Dining Room. It is in red with the principal

116 The present decor of the White (originally North) Drawing Room dates from a century ago. It retains the glorious Nash ceiling, however, with its Italian plasterwork. The palace contains one of the most interesting furniture collections of the U.K.

117 top left The most prominent aspect of the garden front of the palace is the bow window of the Music Room. Inside, lapiz lazuli scagliola columns support an extraordinarily detailed gilded ceiling. Its parquet floor, seen here framing the carpet, is of exotic woods. It has been used for royal christenings: three of the queen's children were baptized here.

117 top right The East Gallery is really a connecting anteroom, but like the other links to Queen Victoria's grand ballroom of 1853-55 it is interesting for its furniture and paintings—here hangs a vast canvas of Queen Victoria, Prince Albert, and their children.

117 center The Marble Hall beneath the Picture Gallery seems low-ceilinged but is harmonious, its marble floor and columns from Carrara. Wooden swags over the fireplaces, from Carlton House, remind one of English woodcarving skills of the seventeenth century.

117 bottom Canova's sculptures have always been much appreciated in England. This one, Nymph with Putto, dates from 1817.

features being the vast mahogany dining table and the set of full-length royal portraits under a ponderously coved, gilded ceiling. Here the presiding portrait is appropriately that of George IV in his coronation robes by Thomas Lawrence. After viewing the State Dining Room with its garden views, shared by all the state rooms on the west side of the palace, one enters an enfilade of three of the finest rooms in the palace, beginning with the Blue Drawing Room.

This is a most opulent apartment, used for state and diplomatic gatherings. The overarching ceiling is Nash at his most sublime, and the effect of the decorations from pillars to molded plaster reliefs is of a breathtakingly splendid room.

Next is the Music Room with a huge semi-circular bow window that is its most telling

118 top right This opulent circular table top was probably never intended to be used. It is a typical work of the early 19th century, tending toward heavy opulence. The cameo heads of generals throughout history gave it the name Table of the Grand Commanders. It was a present of Louis XVIII to the then Prince Regent.

118 center Mostly the work of the architect Blore for William IV, the State Dining Room with its ponderously supported ceiling is impressive with its rank of portraits of kings and queens. The two fireplaces are of white marble and female figures playing instruments show the intended original function was as a Music Room.

118 bottom One of the Prince Regent's great pleasures was collecting and commissioning extraordinary pieces to decorate his houses. Many of the clocks here, often in surprising forms, such as this gilt-bronze and marble Apollo, were ordered by him. This one, purchased in 1810, depicts the passage of the sun. It is French, by Pierre-Philippe Thomire.

120-121 The Blue Room is the epitome of fashionable Georgian design. Originally a red room with porphyry scagliola columns, crimson curtains and wall hangings, it changed under Queen Mary in the early 1900s to become blue with flocked paper, the tall Corinthian columns painted to resemble onyx. Nash's bold coved and bracketed ceiling is stupendous.

feature, although the vaulted and domed ceiling and the costly rare wood parquet floor, a triumph of English art, are magnificent. Here guests are presented to the monarch before a banquet or dinner.

The final state room is next, the White Drawing Room. The French-inspired room is warmly gold and white, the wall decorations late 19th century under another Nash ceiling with its superb plasterwork by the Italian master Bernasconi. Here the royal family can enter by a secret mirrored door to assemble before meeting guests in the Music Room.

From here one descends the Ministers' Staircase to the Marble Hall, with notable Canova sculptures. Like so many of the priceless objects in Buckingham Palace they were commissioned for Carlton House, home of the Prince Regent, and brought here when that fabulous mansion was torn down.

The Bow Room was intended to be a Library, part of the apartments of George IV. Although so much of the building is due to this king, he did not live here, and on his death completion of the work was handed on to his brother, William III, who also did

not live long enough to see completion. Its marble fireplaces of 1810 were added by Queen Mary and are French.

Visitors exit from the Bow Room beneath the West Wing's curved window (another of Nash's bold designs; he also landscaped the gardens). The Bow Room opens onto the park, where there is a walk to Grosvenor Gate. The Royal Mews are nearby and still in daily use. The famous gray horses are stabled there, and the royal coaches, including the Gold State Coach which has been used for coronations since 1760.

Hampton Court

A TUDOR PALACE ON THE THAMES

Great Britain

LONDON

120 top As a young man Henry VIII started well. He and his brother king, François I of France, were a pair of handsome young monarchs. Growing older, heavier and

diseased, Henry became venal and hard—the greatest painter of the age, Holbein, hints at a later grossness in this 1536 portrait of the king.

homas Wolsey built for his pleasure the most splendid palace in Britain to have come down to us from the 16th century: Hampton Court Palace, which still stands in a fine position by the River Thames. It gives a vivid impression of the life of a wealthy man of almost 500 years ago—a huge house set in a wide hunting park with gardens down to the water. It stands on the edge of a pretty riverside town west of London containing handsome old houses.

Many of the great houses of Britain were built by aristocratic families, some old and established, some rich merchants. Occasionally a member of an ordinary working family could make a mark, however, and so it was with the son of a Suffolk butcher who rose to ecclesiastical glory as a prince of the church, and in one of the greatest offices in the land. It was possible for a young entrepreneur to go far in those days

almost five centuries ago, for the country had new strengths as it consolidated under the leadership of Henry VII, first of the Tudor dynasty.

An astute and supremely ambitious politician, Thomas Wolsey from Ipswich worked his way up the levels of power established by the new Tudor kings of England to become England's Lord Chancellor, a most powerful man. Henry Tudor had put out the light of the previous line of kings when he stormed in from his native Wales to battle with King Richard III, killed at the Battle of Bosworth Field in 1485. (Shakespeare's great history play chronicles the history and death of this hunchback king, heralding the arrival of the new royal family.)

Henry's first son, a brilliant boy, died as Prince of Wales and his place was taken by the second son, also named Henry, later to become well known as a husband to six

120 center The king's coat of arms outside the Chapel Royal shows two angels holding the crown over his quartered shield. Many of the major events in the king's life occurred here: this sculpted shield loomed over the baptism of the king's son, Edward VI, and saw his fifth queen attempting to reach the king in the chapel to plead her innocence of adultery. The marriage to his sixth queen took place in the nearby Queen's Closet.

120 bottom The two main apartments of the Wolsey Rooms contain historic art and a range of Renaissance pictures. This one shows the palace after Wren's alterations.

121 top The Family of Henry VIII was painted in 1545 and set in Whitehall Palace. In this picture the king is seen with his third wife who bore Edward VI. Henry's only son died young, and his sisters, seen here, were queens in their own right.

120-121 The Privy Garden was indeed the royal "private" garden first laid out for Henry VIII from 1530. It has seen many changes and was recently restored to its 17th-century state to complement the beautiful balanced South Front as it was when created for William III. At the river end are wrought iron screens by the French master Jean Tijou.

121 bottom Although the palace seems to occupy much space, it is surrounded by extensive deer parks and the reason it was preferred by many monarchs was the hunting. Before Wolsey it was a property of the Knights Hospitalers. This general aerial view shows the west entrance with the two Tudor courts and the roof of the Great Hall.

122 top The atmosphere in the enclosed Base Court is totally Tudor. It is easy to imagine Wolsey arriving here in state. Through the Anne Boleyn Gatehouse with a bell once belonging to the Knights Hospitalers is a much altered Clock Court, the inner courtyard of Wolsey's house, seen here. It is bordered by the Great Hall and the walls of the Cumberland Suite.

122 bottom The circular fountain is the focal point inside the Privy Garden which develops symmetrically from the south side of the palace toward the river.

wives. As a young and promising man, the eager young King Henry VIII turned to new people and one of the men he chose was the fast-ascending Wolsey. He served the king so well that he became fabulously rich, overshadowing his master in the magnificence of his life. It is dangerous to arouse envy in royal masters, for like the later Fouquet under Louis XIV in France, power went to his head and he indulged in a love of luxury and display. Wolsey acquired the land and a country house for his new palace from a religious order when as Archbishop of York, chief minister to Henry VIII, he signed a lease to the Manor of Hampton in 1508.

Made a cardinal in 1515, he proceeded to turn a simple country house into what was to become Hampton Court Palace. Then Wolsey

the Pope and turned England and Wales into a Protestant kingdom. It caused national havoc and poor Tom Wolsey's disgrace, downfall and death, even though Wolsey—the last powerful English cardinal for many decades—tried to ameliorate his position by giving the king his great monument, Hampton Court Palace, as a gift.

Henry spent an enormous amount on rebuilding the palace until it was finally completed in 1540. It contained private apartments and reception rooms, several courtyards, a Great Hall, a fabulous chapel, huge kitchens, bowling alleys, tennis courts, pleasure gardens and the park. Much of the Hampton Court built by the prelate can still be seen however, notably the spacious Base Court.

122-123 On each side of the main entrance of the western facade of the palace rises a series of columns topped with war trophies. This entrance, called the Trophy Gate, was built by William III. On top of the gate, flanked by two turrets, is Henry VIII's coat of arms.

123 top The Astronomical Clock, a complex machine with a huge face, was made for Henry VIII by Nicholas Oursian.

fell foul of Henry's imperious desires to be a great king and a progenitor of kings. In his frustration at producing only a princess from Katherine of Aragon, his first wife, he wished to remarry, and he chose Anne Boleyn. As a Catholic he needed the approval of the Pope to get a divorce, and this was difficult, as the first queen was related to the Holy Roman Emperor. Charged with effecting the divorce so Henry might remarry, Wolsey was in a hard position as intermediary. In love with Anne, the king waited impatiently, but when at last patience gave way so did the whole social structure of the country, for in order to remarry he defied

One hundred fifty years later William and Mary, joint monarchs, began leaving London for the country for a few days after each week in the city. The king commissioned a star architect, Sir Christopher Wren, to renew Hampton Court; work was sped up after the 1698 burning of Whitehall Palace, the prime royal residence in central London.

A successor, George II, redecorated the royal apartments, but 1737 was the last year that Hampton Court was used by the court. The palace dwindled in importance, and although the great house and gardens were well kept up (a famous designer, Capability

123 bottom View from the Pond Garden. The Pond Garden's three sunken gardens were once ponds for keeping freshwater fish until they were needed for the kitchen. Under Henry VIII it was decorated with statues of heraldic beasts on poles and sundials. Nearby is the Knot Garden, planted in 1924 to show how the gardens might have looked in the Tudor period.

Brown, was on the staff as Royal Gardener for 20 years) the royal family left the Tudor palace and court life no longer continued here.

Queen Victoria took an interest in restoring the building when it was open to the public after 1838. In typically Victorian style a concerted attempt was made to give it back its first 16th-century aspect. Much of what you see is actually skilled 19th-century work. The most dramatic recent event in Hampton Court's history was a fire that badly damaged much of the King's Apartments in 1986. Repairs took six years during which the largest restoration for a century took place, and after 1995 the palace reemerged looking as splendid as it ever has. The most recent renovation was that of William III's spectacular terraced Privy (Private) Garden running down to the Thames, in 1996.

As the river was a highway for so much of London's history, you should try to arrive from Kingston on Thames by boat and dock beside the palace. You will be doing just what Henry and his courtiers would have done when they arrived, rowed by strong young men up the wide river from Whitehall Palace, more than 12 miles to the east. The new palace must have been a fine sight for the envious young king, and it is even more impressive today, a series of handsome red brick facades set against the green spaces of its park and framed with the elegant wrought iron gates and screens of Jean Tijou.

You can also get a fine view of the palace, however, after arriving at the local station by train from London. You cross the river and the palace is set to your right. A walk through the

Hampton Court *A Tudor Palace on the Thames*

124 top At 34 yards long and 20 yards high, the Great Hall is the largest room of Hampton Court. The hammerbeam roof is splendid, achieving a 44-yard width with the aid of cantilevered beams. A fire once burned here (marked with a brass plate in the floor), the smoke exiting through a vent in the middle of the painted ceiling. Stained glass commemorates the king, Wolsey and Henry's six wives. You see the hall as restored in 1840.

124 bottom The Tapestries of Abraham may have been specially made for the Great Hall. They were woven in 1540 by Brussels weaver Wilhem Pannemaker using gold and silver thread and were only displayed on special occasions. Six can be seen here, others are in the King's Apartments. Henry VIII owned over 2,500 tapestries.

125 The Chapel Royal is one of the few rooms to remain from the Tudor period. It is still a place of worship. With an exotic gilded and heavily bossed ceiling in a peculiarly English vaulted style, and a richly decorated altar wall, it and the Great Hall are the only survivors of Henry's magnificence.

A Tudor Palace on the Thames

Trophy Gate along a range of Tudor buildings takes you to the entrance. The first court you enter, past sculpted King's Beasts and through the main gate, is the Base Court, still much as it was built by Wolsey. Stand in the center of its yard and look around to the west end of the Chapel, completed by Henry VIII—his arms are on the gate with the arms and the initials of his daughter, the great Elizabeth I, to each side. Her mother, Anne Boleyn, is commemorated in the gate opposite, which leads to the Clock Court. Named for the great Astronomical Clock here (1540) this would have been Wolsey's inner courtyard, but it is much altered. The supremely elegant Fountain Court, designed for William and Mary by Christopher Wren, contains the State Apartments. A doorway leads to Wren's spectacular baroque East and South fronts.

Visitors now have a choice of six routes through the palace. They conduct you to the contrasted aspects and periods of the house. First are the State Apartments of Henry VIII with the magnificent Great Hall and the Chapel Royal remaining. Here is the Great Watching Chamber, the Pages' Chamber and (touchingly) the Haunted Gallery. Here the fifth of Henry's wives, Catherine Howard, convicted of adultery, tried to reach the king in the chapel before being beheaded, and was seized by guards to be dragged away, screaming. The Wolsey Rooms are thought to have been the cardinal's private lodgings. These small Tudor chambers are evocative of the period with original fireplaces, fine paneling and early Renaissance features. The rooms, together with the Renaissance Picture Gallery, contain a great collection of 16th-century paintings.

The third route takes you to the King's Apartments, a set of rooms in grand Baroque style furnished as they were when made, in 1700, with tapestries and furniture. The suite has been restored since the fire of 1986. The Queen's State Apartments contain some fine rooms and look over the park. And the Georgian Rooms represent the private life of the last courts to be held here.

126 Truly splendid are the King's Stairs, mounting up with shallow stone risers and built for William III by Wren on the site of the old state apartments. Antonio Verrio painted the walls and ceiling in a style not approved by Horace Walpole.

127 top left Intended not as a practical bedroom but as a ceremonial room where the monarch dressed, access to the King's Great Bedchamber was controlled by a favorite courtier. The air is opulent with gilded chairs, a ceiling painted by Verrio, and carving by Grinling Gibbons. The mirrors by Gerrit Jenson are notable.

127 bottom left and top right Started in 1694, the Queen's State Apartments were designed for Mary II. Her sister Queen Anne, who succeeded her, commissioned the decorations of the Queen's drawing room. She is the central figure in both paintings.

127 bottom right Galleries in English houses were used for exercise as much as for display. The Queen's Gallery was built for Queen Mary. Originally hung with Mantegna's Triumphs of Caesar, it now has early 18th-century tapestries. The stools were made for this grand room in 1737 and there is a spectacular marble fireplace.

128-129 The Great Watching Chamber retains its original scale, its gilded ceiling and its tapestries. Four, known as armorials, displayed over the doors, depict coats of arms—this one was of Cardinal Wolsey.

128 bottom This portrait of Cardinal Wolsey depicts the prince of the church at the height of his power. The existing Wolsey Rooms are believed to have been his. Although his fall came about because he was unable to effect the royal divorce, the great brick palace he created made him appear loftier than the king. It became both his triumph and his nemesis.

129 top The Queen's Bedchamber is one of the Georgian Rooms and was used by Queen Caroline. Mortlake tapestries depict English naval victories. The rooms mark the last time a king lived here; after the queen's death in 1745 George II never returned with the full court.

We are fortunate that Hampton Court fell out of royal favor, for it has been preserved and not damaged by the fashion changes of more than 200 years.

129 bottom George II's large family required space at the palace, and when his second son,

the Duke of Cumberland, was entitled to his own household and establishment, the Cumberland Suite was created on the east side of the Clock Court. Along with the other rooms, this elegant bedchamber was designed by the painter William Kent.

Home Park, said to be 1,000 years old.

The oldest of the plants is the Great Vine, claimed to be the oldest and largest in the world, thickly draping its greenhouse. Planted in 1768, it measures more than eight feet in girth and produces up to 700 bunches of sweet black grapes each September. Home Park, where the Royal Horticultural Society has a flower show each year, has a herd of 300 fallow deer, descended from the original collection of Henry VIII.

As befits a palace of such surprises, perhaps one of the best can be reserved for last. Like George IV, Charles I was one of the greatest of royal collectors. Much of his collection was dispersed under Cromwell, yet surviving here in the beautiful redesigned Lower Orangerie are the fabled nine panels of the *Triumphs of Caesar* by Andrea Mantegna, in a new presentation recreating the way the tapestries were once seen in the palace of San Sebastiano in Italy.

The Kitchens offer a sixth visit. They occupied the north side of the palace and originally provided two meals a day for the 800 members of the king's court. The Great Kitchen has six fireplaces, with one still having cooking equipment. Spices and fruits, wood, coal stores for charcoal and a chandlery for wax tapers as well as meat and fish were stored in the more than 50 rooms. There is a Confectionery for desserts, a pastry house with four large ovens for pies, and three cellars for the storage of wine casks and ale. Part of the kitchen has been set up to give an impression of the time when thousands of sheep, deer, oxen, and pigs, were cooked here with the Flesh Larder hung with pheasant, rabbit and wild boar, and pewter dishes carrying pies and stuffed fish.

The gardens of Hampton Court are the most visited in the country. Staffed by 41 gardeners, they include three acres of the Privy Garden with its terraces, the South Gardens with the Knot and Pond gardens and a Banqueting House, and the extensive Wilderness where many spring bulbs flower. Here can be found the Maze, first planted in 1690 of hornbeam hedges 6.5 meters high, now yew. Of the 7,500 trees the most venerable is an English oak in the 620 acre

The Castle of Brussels

THE HALLMARK OF THE "BUILDER KING"

Whoever wishes to study the history of the city of Brussels will quickly recognize how complex it is: a whirling succession of dynastic events and revolutions and the passage of powerful and famous people contributed to the formation of what is today the capital of united Europe. The original structure of the small market town on the river Seine underwent gradual expansion and transformation as a result of the policy adopted by the local dukes of Brabant and, later, the dukes of Burgundy. This was the historical and

and cultural development of the city were born at or stayed in the austere palace. Two of these rulers were the Duchess Maria of Burgundy, future wife of Maximilian of Austria, and the Hapsburg king Charles V. During his reign, Brussels and the whole of Flanders experienced extraordinary progress in the fields of art and philosophy. In 1522, Charles V ordered the construction of a magnificent chapel in late Gothic style which, from an architectural point of view, was an extension of the Great Hall. In 1596 the Infanta Isabella,

cultural background against which the foundations of the Royal Palace were laid. The oldest part of the building dates from the end of the 11th century.

The importance of Brussels quickly grew during the first decades of the 15th century when the dukedom of Burgundy was annexed to the kingdom of the Netherlands. After designating the old fortress in Brussels as his new principal residence, in 1431 Duke Philip the Good began to turn the original modest structure into a ducal palace that would be worthy of the dynasty and the city.

The building stood on Coudenberg hill near the church of St. Gudula which was later to become the cathedral. Recent archeological excavations have uncovered the superb remains of the Great Hall attached to Coudenberg Palace. It was a jewel of Gothic architecture built by Philip the Good in 1452 to host festivities and meetings.

During the 15th and 16th centuries, many potentates who contributed to the economic

niece of Charles V, and her husband, Archduke Albert of Hapsburg, Governor-General of the Netherlands, came to live in the palace. The two were greatly admired by the people of Brussels and its neighboring territories: not only did they promote great artistic and industrial activity, they were also the first governors to suggest that Belgium become independent of the hegemony of the Netherlands.

The glory of the ducal palace of Coudenberg was not destined to last for long. The building was devastated by a fire on the night of 3 February 1731.

The square where the palace had stood— the Place des Bailles, today the Place Royale— remained covered with rubble for 40 years as no governor bothered to have it cleared up. In 1744 Charles of Lorraine, brother-in-law of Maria Theresa of Austria, was appointed Governor-General of the Netherlands; as the ducal palace no longer stood, he bought and rebuilt the palace of the Prince of Orange near

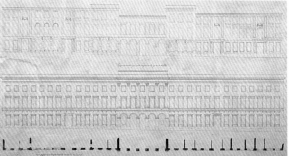

130-131 The allegorical paintings on the ceilings of the Long Gallery were produced at the end of the 19th century by Georges Van den Bos and Leon Cardon. The armchairs in the style of Louis XIV, adapted to the tastes of the 19th century and covered in red damask, are particularly valuable.

131 bottom This drawing held in the palace archives shows Tilleman-François Suys' modernization plan for the facade. Suys restarted the work that had been interrupted on the death of Vander Straeten, thus allowing William I of Orange to move into the palace in 1829.

132-133 The imposing Throne Room is divided into three sections by solid square-based columns. Famous sculptors such as Rodin and Vinçotte worked here. Vinçotte created the bas-reliefs over the two entrances that depict the rivers Meuse and Schelde, symbols of the two districts of Flanders and Wallonia. Rodin produced the four bas-reliefs in the center of the room, each of which represents two Belgian provinces.

132 bottom The Venice Staircase provides the main access to the upper floors. In 1867, the painter Jean Baptiste Van Moer painted several pictures of Venice and its Grand Canal, and the name was forever linked with the staircase.

133 top left This miniature by Henry Delacroix is held in the palace archives. The Belgian coat of arms is at the top, flanked by allegorical figures and the motto "Union gives strength." In the lower section there are symbols of the country's provincial capitals and framed portraits of Leopold I, king of Belgium from 1831 until 1865, and his wife Louise d'Orléans. Finally, the emblems of the three children of the royal couple appear in the lower band.

133 bottom left The Marshals' Room was originally an audience room but was turned into a dining room and salon in the 19th century. There are distinguished portraits of King Leopold I and Queen Louise-Marie.

133 top right The elegant bas-relief that runs around the walls of the Large Antechamber was the work of the French sculptor François Rude and the Fleming Jean-Louis Van Geel in the first half of the 19th century. The first represented allegories of Trade, Navigation (in the picture), Abundance and Prudence; the second, Industry, Agriculture, Peace and Power, plus the union of the north and south of the Low Countries.

133 bottom right A marble statue of Minerva, an allegory of Peace, dominates the Grand Staircase designed by architect Alphonse Balat. The stairs were designed to facilitate access to the reception rooms and also to invest the route with great splendor.

corner of Rue Héraldique and Rue Bellevue) were turned into residences for, respectively, the diplomats Luigi di Barbiano Belgioioso and Baron Bender.

The political situation during the following decades became darker and more complex. The low popularity of Joseph II and the echoes of the French Revolution contributed to the explosion of the Brabant Revolution which in turn led to a provisory independence of the Netherlands from Austria. On the death of Joseph II, however, Austria once more reigned over the territory and, under the Holy Roman Emperor Leopold II, dominated it with iron discipline.

The French occupied Brussels in 1794 but they had no interest in embellishing its architecture, so even the palace was not modified at all. After the fall of Napoleon in 1815, William of Orange proclaimed himself king of the Netherlands, and Brussels assumed the role of capital.

The state representatives immediately wanted to resolve the problem posed by the absence of a royal residence in Brussels. All the pieces of land around the Bender and Belgioioso residences were bought back and various architects successively attempted to design a structure that could connect the two buildings. The first of them, Gislain Joseph

Henry, began construction of a majestic, five-column arch that crossed the Rue Héraldique to link the two buildings, but the plan was interrupted on his death. Charles Vander Straeten, his successor, did not manage to complete Henry's plan, as the works proceeded too slowly, mainly due to lack of

money. The last of the architects appointed to the task, Charles Tillman François Suys, had the large arch demolished. He finally unified the facade with a five-arch portico topped by six Corinthian columns and the Rue Héraldique was turned into an internal courtyard. Suys completed the work in 1829 but the palace still did not have the air of a proper royal residence—it was more like a sumptuous reception building for the successful bourgeoisie. The end of the works during the following year can be considered a milestone in the history of Brussels and its territory: the revolutionary and independent ferment that opposed the power of William of Orange exploded.

the Place des Bailles. It was thanks to his successor, Joseph II of Hapsburg Lorraine, who came to power in 1780, that the future Royal Palace came into being. Joseph built four buildings to the south of the park (known by the Flemish word *Warande*, which roughly translated means "hunting reserve") where the Palace of Coudenberg had stood. These were used to accommodate the plenipotentiary of the king of the Netherlands, diplomats and the army chiefs, and were also the first stage in the reconstruction of the original palace of the governors of Brussels. This reconstruction was not an event in itself but was part of a new plan for the entire area, now called the "Royal Quarter." Several architects, in particular Guimard and Zinner, were commissioned with redesigning the park which, at the time, was surrounded by four roads lined with beautiful buildings. On the basis of a plan by the architect Barrè, the Place Royale was created (where once the Place des Bailles had stood) surmounted by the impressive church of St. Joseph of Coudenberg, completed in 1785. During the Austrian domination, two of the four original buildings (the pavilions on the

In 1830 Brussels arose, bringing the independent state of Belgium into existence. The Belgian people nominated Leopold I of the Saxe-Coburg family as king. He went to live in the palace but without making any large alterations to it. For official receptions he used the other building, Charles of Lorraine's magnificent palace, which he embellished and decorated in the style of Versailles. In contrast, his son Leopold II, the duke of Brabant and future heir to the throne, showed great interest in the architecture of the Royal Palace. In 1858, he began a close professional relationship with the architect Alphonse Balat, which was to last nearly 50 years. Leopold II was responsible for rebuilding the left wing of the palace which he had chosen to be his personal residence. By degrees he improved it with fountains and glasshouses. The plans for enlarging and renewing the building previously proposed to Leopold I were approved without obstacles of any kind and a series of favorable circumstances permitted the financial support of the state. This meant that Alphonse Balat could undertake a rebuilding project that over the years was to turn the palace into a distinctive and prestigious royal residence.

One of the most important stages of the project was the transformation of the facade into Louis XVI style to harmonize with the surrounding buildings in the Royal Quarter. Unfortunately, the modification was interrupted in 1861 due to slow progress and the fact that the money had run out. Only the ascension to the throne of Leopold II, Belgium's great royal builder, brought new energy to the redecorating of the interiors. Attention was first turned to the main staircase; then the rooms to be used for guests visiting the court of Brussels were renovated and furnished, followed by the reception rooms.

Balat also designed the Large Gallery, the Throne Room and what is known as the Thinker's Room, which is still used today as a funeral chamber for the members of the royal family. Above the elegant pilasters in the Throne Room, the visitor can admire bas-reliefs by the famous French sculptor, Auguste Rodin. The Marble Room is also worthy of note: paintings by Louis Gallait of Emperor Charles V and Goffredo of Buglione hang over the fireplaces. The huge doors that give access to the two palace wings were decorated with bas-reliefs by Thomas Vinçotte showing the two large rivers that cross the country, the Meuse and Scheldt. Balat's project was due to end in 1860 but it was only terminated 20 years later.

In 1903, the state agreed to spend the necessary funds to complete the renewal of the facade. This was carried out by the architect Maquet following Balat's original design. Leopold II however was not entirely satisfied and wished to make a further modification to render the whole more harmonious. He bought the old building of the Hotel Bellevue and incorporated it into the palace via a sort of semi-circular pavilion. He then made a similar integration to the opposite wing by connecting it with the Hotel Walkiers. A garden was created in front of the main facade and the pediment embellished with bas-reliefs by Vinçotte with allegories of the two regions of Belgium, Flanders and Wallonia.

Other interiors aimed at conferring distinction on the palace were created and furnished, such as the Room of Mirrors

and the Fontainebleau Apartments. The king's ambitious projects went much further but were interrupted by his death in 1909. Since then, no more important alterations have been carried out in the Royal Quarter except for the modernization of the Rue du Bellevue, which was also renamed the Place des Palais. The palace apartments were occupied by the royal family until 1935 but after the early death of Queen Astrid her husband Leopold III decided to live in Laeken Castle as his successors have done ever since. Today, the building built over the ruins of the ancient ducal residence of Coudenberg is a fine example of a blend of 18th and 19th century architecture; it serves as an administrative center and is also is used for royal receptions.

134 top left The Large White Room of Paintings was part of the apartments reserved for important Austrian officials. It was rebuilt by Maquet on Leopold II's orders and appointed with elegant Empire style furniture.

134 bottom left The salon in the photograph is called the Vase Room after the large Berlin porcelain vase made in the 19th century. Note the chandelier in the style of Louis XIV and the bust of Leopold II on a pedestal.

135 top The Goya Room was used to host important Austrian officials. Its name came from the large wallhangings made from cartoons designed by Francisco Goya and realized by the royal manufactory of Santa Barbara in Madrid.

The Hallmark of the "Builder King"

134 right The picture shows another detail of the allegorical miniature painted by Delacroix in the 19th century and held in the royal archives.

134-135 The Empire Room, situated in the oldest wing, is one of the palace's most splendid rooms. It was used to host the Austrian plenipotentiary when Belgium was under Hapsburg power. The original design of the room was by Louis Montoyer but it was later remodeled by other famous architects. The pomp of the furnishings is emphasized by the fluted semi-circular columns, the vaulted ceilings decorated with bas-reliefs and the chandeliers in the style of Louis XVI which replaced the original Empire-style ones. This room is still used to hold important ceremonies today: it was here that the civil wedding between the current sovereigns of Belgium, Albert and Paula, took place.

135

136 top The rear facade of the corps de logis or middle section is here seen from the Lower Garden full of blooming flowers. The Fountain of Venus rises just in front of the stairs leading to the royal building.

136-137 This bird's eye view clearly shows the importance of symmetry ruling the location of fountains and small canals and the shape of hedges. The Fountain of Venus can be recognized in the middle of the Lower Garden, while the King's Fountain and the colonnades are seen in the Upper Garden.

136 bottom left The private garden of Queen Mary, called the Queen's Garden or the Princess's Garden, was designed by Marot. Its intimate character is exemplified by a network of berceaux, or arbored pathways.

136 bottom right The Fountain of Venus, which is almost entirely reconstructed, stands out against the background of the colonnades. Its central position along the Middenallee testify to its preeminence in the Lower Garden.

Het Loo Palace

A SHELTER IN THE WOOD

When Prince William III of Orange (1650–1702) was named Stadtholder of Gelderland in 1672, he received the hunting rights to the provincial region called the Veluwe. As this was a sparsely populated area extremely rich in wildlife and as Prince William III was a passionate devotee of this sport, it is little wonder that he felt the need for a hunting lodge there. In 1676 a house in Hoog Soeren was adapted to this purpose. But William III's sights were set considerably higher and in November 1684 he purchased the castle of Het Loo, with the intention of building a new and more palatial hunting lodge somewhere on the castle property. In September 1685 the stonework of the middle section or *corps de logis* of what came to be known as Het Loo was completed.

In 1686, the year given on the facade of the building, the wings, originally linked by colonnades to the corps de logis, were added, the walls were built and the gardens were laid out.

Construction was carried out under the supervision of the Dutch architect Jacob Roman (1640–1716) probably after designs by the Académie d'Architecture of Paris. It seems that the French designer Daniel Marot (1661–1752) became involved in the project of Het Loo after the majority of the construction had been completed. Daniel Marot was a French Protestant designer who, subsequent to the revocation of the Edict of Nantes in 1685, had fled to the Netherlands where he became chief architect to William III. His influence can be seen primarily in matters of detail and various decorative finishing touches.

Thus Het Loo became the favorite hunting seat and country palace of William III and his wife Princess Mary II (1662–1695) and until the Prince's death in 1702 furnishings and decorations both inside and outside underwent repeated alterations and embellishments. The construction of a regal and elaborate country residence like Het Loo required that attention be given as much to the surroundings as to the building itself, and the palace and gardens were regarded as integral parts of a single unified whole. At that time symmetry was considered ideal and the design for the building and grounds featured a central axis with mirror-image components on either side. Inside the palace the axis consisted of the Entrance Hall, the staircase and the Great Hall on the first floor. West and east of the Great Hall respectively were the apartments of William III and Mary II. The apartments of the courtiers and the Dining Room were on the ground floor.

The main garden was enclosed on three sides by terraces and divided into the Upper Garden and the Lower Garden. The unity of house and garden was manifested in various efforts to blur the distinction between indoors and outdoors. Inside, the walls of the staircase area and the main hall were painted with scenic perspectives to give the impression of being in the open. The entrance to the garden from the palace, situated in the exact center of the rear of the building, was not an ordinary closed door but was instead a pair of openwork gilded iron gates.

Daniel Marot made designs for various features of the buildings and garden, employing a single formal language and thereby achieving a high degree of unity throughout. When William III became King of England this elevation of his position and power brought an enlargement of Het Loo. Between 1691 and 1694 the colonnades were

137 top left Gold, blue and red characterize the coat of arms of William III, the monarch who championed the royal residence of Het Loo.

137 top right This decorative element by Daniel Marot can be seen on the golden iron gate of the corps de logis. It features an orange tree in a vase, long the symbol of the royal dynasty of Orange-Nassau.

137 bottom Plenty of documents and drawings available, such as this painted engraving dating from the 19th century, helped in the reconstruction of the complex and its garden.

replaced by four pavilions in which new rooms and apartments were set. In the garden a new section bounded by curving walls was added to the northern end so that the avenue leading to the palace now came within its confines, crossing it neatly from side to side. Water, the essential element for garden maintenance, was supplied by means of artificial streams.

Next to the walled area a park was created containing various means of diversion such as a small wood with paths, a labyrinth, an aviary and an arragement of narrow canals from which hidden fountains could spout unexpectedly. In addition there were also vegetable gardens, fish ponds, dog kennels

and a falcon house; while the stable, orangerie and coach houses were located in a wing of the palace itself.

In 1702, years after William (or Willem) III's death, Het Loo descended to Willem IV (1711–1751). Both Willem IV and his son Willem V (1748–1806) used the house as a hunting seat and summer residence. Willem V had the layout of the upper garden remodeled in more natural landscape style, after the fashion of the day, by the architect Philip W. Schonck (1735–c. 1823).

From bills and other documents of the period it appears that maintenance of the complex remained a problem throughout the 18th century. Moreover, after Prince Willem V's flight in 1795, the entire garden was plundered and fell into ruin.

According to subsequent historical events the palace changed its aspect drastically in 1807–09 when it was appointed as a summer residence by Louis Napoleon (1778–1846), brother of Napoleon I and king of Holland from 1806 to 1810. The exterior was coated with a layer of gray stucco and provided with sham joints, to suggests blocks of natural stone. The new Empire windows were fitted with shutters. Louis Napoleon had the architect Alexandre Dufour (1750–1835) draw up a design for landscaped surroundings which would include a park and garden. To create a single-level surface the terraces were removed and the lower areas were filled in.

Later the son of Willem V, returned to the Netherlands and became King Willem I (1772–1843) in 1815. Het Loo was assigned to the head of state as a summer residence and although Willem I lamented the loss of the old garden, he did nothing to alter the profound changes that had been made. The only

substantial change he brought about was in the park where he had the six rectangular fish ponds redug to form the two-level artificial lake. An island was built in the middle and a natural look was created by rounding the edges of the lake and covering them with a thick growth of vegetation, for the most part rhododendrons.

King Willem II (1793–1849) was not very interested in Het Loo, but his son King Willem III (1817–1890) lived frequently there. The latter added an art gallery also used as a foyer to the theater in the east

138-139 *The Old Dining Room was used as such between 1686 and 1690. On t he walls hung a series of tapestries representing Meleager and Atalanta, and Cephalus and Procris, derived from Ovid's Metamorphoses.*

wing in 1875. He was fond of trees, unusual plants and seeds. The arboretum which he had created east of the walled garden remains as a testimony to this royal hobby. The wooden tea pavilion and bathhouse next to the artificial lake were brought there by King Willem III, who loved swimming.

During the 19th century the color of the stucco became whiter and the mock joints disappeared. Willem III's daughter, Queen Wilhelmina (1880–1962), restored some apartments in the style of William and Mary, but these activities were stopped in 1911 when

it was decided to enlarge the palace. It was partly heightened, and enlarged on the east side to the detriment of the original shape and symmetry.

After her abdication in 1948 Queen Wilhelmina retired to stay at Het Loo until her death in 1962; Princess Margriet and her husband Mr. Pieter van Vollenhoven lived at the palace from 1967 to 1975, when they moved with their four sons to a new house in the park.

The most recent chapter in the history of Het Loo began in 1970 when the decision was

139 top left Prince William III of Orange, Stadtholder of Gelderland then King of England, is here portrayed by Jean Henry Brandon. The monarch was responsible for the creation of the wonderful palace of Het Loo and further enlargements and changes to it.

139 top right This 18th-century portrait by Jean Henry Brandon shows Mary Suart, the queen who played a fundamental role in the construction of Het Loo, a place she was very fond of.

made to turn the palace into a national museum. In 1974 it was determined that the 19th- and 20th-century additions should be removed, to return the exterior to its original state. Given the unity of the total design, this necessarily involved the reconstruction of the garden. The comprehensive restoration took place between 1977 and 1984.

Today, the furnishing of the central part of the house and the pavilions tries to give an impression of how the palace was lived in by different rulers. The furnishing is based on contemporary documents. In the 17th and 18th century these documents consisted of inventories, accounts, descriptions and the prints by Daniel Marot. Only a few objects dating from before 1795 are left and to fill this gap furniture has been selected in accordance with the inventories. However, most of the original furniture from the 19th and 20th century still exists, and watercolors and photographs of some of the royal apartments show us how the rooms looked.

Old Dining Room, with its painted boards and original tapestries, the New Dining Room with its gold-striped pillars typical of Marot, and the White Hall or the Stone Room where portraits of the Frisian Nassaus hang.

Another "public" place is the Chapel with its ceiling ornaments designed by Marot and an altar for the Anglican services of the English Queen Mary. Marriages were never held in the chapel, but it was used for the confirmation of members of the royal family.

The East Wing of the palace contains paintings, prints, medals, objets d'art, costumes, banners and documents that put the House of Orange into its historical perspective. The lower floor of the West Wing originally served as the stables for the king's horses; on the upper floor of the same wing is the Museum of the Chancery of the Netherlands Orders of Knighthood, housing the biggest collection of decorations in Europe (apart from that of the Musée de la Légion d'Honneur in Paris).

140 The room of King Willem II is characterized by a suite of rosewood furniture in Neo-Gothic style made by Matthieu and Willem Horrix. Willem II had a predilection for the Gothic style.

Because the princes lived in the same apartments successively, the restorers had to choose how to allot a room to each prince—William III and Mary II were given their original apartments because they were the builders of the house. In their day, only people of the highest rank or the most intimate friends of William III and Queen Mary II were admitted into their private rooms.

In the palace there are no corridors: the apartments lead one into another. Among the "public" rooms which can be visited are the

From reports of the Académie d'Architecture in Paris we know that the Dutch ambassador asked for designs for a palace or hunting seat in 1684. These were destined for an unnamed person of high rank who later turned out to be "Monsieur le prince d'Orange." Since the drawings are lost it is impossible to check whether Het Loo was built in accordance with them. Stylistically the plan and the austere classical building are related to the Dutch tradition rather than to the French architecture of the end of the 17th century.

However, the interiors show the influence of the French style of Louis XIV. As for the gardens, the wealth of available information about them made their reconstruction possible. In fact they were quite famous during the 17th and 18th centuries: they are pictured in numerous prints and frequently described by visitors in letters and journals. The restored gardens of Het Loo recreate of one of the peaks of Dutch Baroque garden art, and gives us a faithful impression of the wealth of this aspect of Dutch 17th-century culture.

A Shelter in the Wood

140-141 The original decoration of the Great Hall or Audience Chamber, designed by Marot in 1692, has been preserved. The landscapes were painted by Johannes Glauber. This room is also called the Abdication Room because it was here that Willem I abdicated in 1840.

141 bottom left In the Room of Willem I is a set of Empire chairs, part of which dates from Louis Napoleon's epoch. The portraits of Willem I and his daughter Marianne, Princess of the Netherlands, hang opposite in a corner.

141 bottom right The walls of the Long Gallery are covered with green damask alternating with portraits of members of the House of Orange-Nassau and its Frisian branch, Nassau-Dietz.

The Castle of Neuschwanstein

Germany

THE FANTASTIC PALACE OF LUDWIG II

NEUSCHWANSTEIN

142 top left The colors of Bavaria, white and blue, stand out in a coat of arms that decorates the pane of one of the bow-windows of the castle.

142 bottom left This portrait of Ludwig II by Franz X. Thallmaier highlights the handsome features that the king is so famous for. Tall and slim, his gait and manners were marked by great elegance and distinction.

142 right The whiteness of the castle, shining out from a distance, gives the impression that it is miraculously supported by tree tops. With is profusion of towers, pinnacles and columns, the building recalls a sandcastle.

143 Resembling the castle of Sleeping Beauty in the woods, Neuschwanstein was built amongst the snow-covered pines of the Alps in southern Bavaria.

Every great king has built at least one residence for himself as an architectural symbol of his power and a display of his wealth, using state resources to glorify his image in a material manner that will last through the centuries. But the Bavarian castles of Ludwig II—the Linderhof, the Herrenchiemsee and the Neuschwanstein—were not built to represent royal authority to either the people or the powerful. The king's Cabinet Secretary Friedrich von Ziegler declared, "The castles are treated by His Majesty as sacred places." Ludwig II spent very little time in the three residences which, despite being very different to one another, have in common the fact that they are all fantastical settings where the king was able to project himself in roles denied to him in reality. The Herrenchiemsee was his own Versailles in which he could play the Sun King; in the Arabian Linderhof palace, Ludwig became a Pasha from the *Thousand and One Nights* surrounded by his retinue in Oriental costume, while at the Neuschwanstein he was crowned king by the grace of the Holy Grail surrounded by mythical heroes from German legends. Few but trusted people witnessed or took part in these role-playing sessions. The castles were never used for state ceremonies and it was Ludwig's wish that they would be destroyed on his death. Not only did this not happen, but Neuschwanstein was actually opened to the public as a museum just three weeks after the king's premature end. Ludwig was also a source of debate and dispute in life. His mysterious death on Lake Starnberg, where he was confined to house arrest after being deposed and disqualified from office due to his mental problems, was no more than the expected end of an enigmatic and strange man who was despised by his government but adored by the people won over by his peculiarities. In the mid-1800s, the imaginative and individualistic Bavarian people found themselves governed by a young and good-looking king who combined the greatness of the Sun King with the ways of

King Arthur. How could they resist him? In fact, Ludwig's governing power was almost nonexistent and, after the first examples of his odd behavior, was limited even further. He was born at a historical moment completely out of phase with his monarchic ideal of the absolutism of the Sun King, for constitutionalism and democracy made no sense to him even after the proclamation of the Reich that signaled the end of Bavarian sovereignty. Profound problems and delusions marked his personality, which was perhaps susceptible due to hereditary defects. (There were signs of madness on the side of his mother, Princess Maria of Prussia, and his brother Otto was locked up as a result of mental illness). Little Ludwig grew up almost without human affection; his mother was strict and distant and his father, Maximilian II, who ascended the throne when Ludwig was three, ignored his children. Ludwig kept to himself even as a child, avoided all contact, and hated being touched. He became king at the age of 18 without ever having studied anything, let alone politics, and found himself completely unprepared both culturally and emotionally to take the reins of government. His only opposition to the government was over the war between Bavaria and Prussia which ended with Bavaria's defeat and brought about Ludwig's definitive withdrawal from the affairs of state. The government even opposed his great friendship with Richard Wagner, and chased the composer out of Munich against the king's

wishes. The affection between Ludwig and Wagner was almost certainly platonic as was his love for his cousin Sissi, Empress of Austria. With Sissi (Elizabeth) it was a union of two narcissistic personalities in which each recognized the opposite sexual component in the other. Elizabeth was independent, athletic and "masculine," while Ludwig was effeminate, romantic and contemplative. Both were beautiful, and were great aesthetes; each mirrored the other. But Ludwig's great problem was his homosexuality: this was unthinkable at the time and particularly for a figure of state. For the king, a fervent Christian, his "mortal sin" was an agonizing torture from which he was unable to free himself.

This description of Ludwig II perhaps helps to explain the torment that oppressed him, and

who that musical genius was able to revive in powerful melodies that touched Ludwig's soul deeply. During his travels, the nostalgic king visited several old mansions that corresponded to his dreams of the ideal medieval castle. At the fort of Wartburg near Eisenbach, the king was less interested in Martin Luther's room than the Room of the Bards, the site of singing contests between minstrels during the late Middle Ages, known to Ludwig through literature and the works of Wagner.

He was especially struck by the castle of Pierrefonds in the forest of Compiègne in France. It was built in the late Middle Ages and restored during the Second Empire in Neo-Gothic lavishness in the exaggerated style of the *parvenus*. Ludwig II shared his ideas with the restoration architect and art critic Eugène

his extreme desire to escape reality. He had to create walls that both protected his dreams and hid his madness; barriers that defended him from the attacks of his enemies and made an enclosure of peace and beauty around him. As king, he had the means to find the material solutions to these needs, and he built real walls, towers, gardens and sumptuous rooms in which "imagination is the model from which reality is created." This acute observation was made not by Ludwig but by Walt Disney who took the castle of Neuschwanstein as the model for the emblem of Disneyland, the most extraordinary creation of the "king of fairy tales."

The idea of a medieval castle came to the adolescent Ludwig while he lived in the castle of Hohenschwangau, an ancient fort restored by his father Maximilian II. Its Neo-Gothic style and late Romantic paintings of medieval knights impressed the fervid imagination of the young prince who fantasized about the ruins of a medieval castle built on the steep slopes opposite Hohenschwangau. In 1868, as king, he wrote to his friend Richard Wagner that he had decided to restore an old ruin, the Schwanstein (the stone swan), which was the ancestral home of the Knights of Schwangau. "It is one of the most beautiful places, holy and unapproachable, a worthy temple for the divine friend; thanks only to him, salvation and true happiness has bloomed." Ludwig had a sort of theatre in mind, very different from the future Festspielhaus at Bayreuth, where the heroes of his dreams could be brought to life in a meticulous historical reconstruction. It may be better to define it as a setting for the characters given voice by Wagner (whom the king already knew from German mythology)

Viollet-le-Duc. What he wanted was a medieval castle with modern services built for modern purposes. The king was not content to create an "archaeological re-creation" because, despite his nostalgia for the past, he was also attracted by the achievements of his own age.

Neuschwanstein is still a unique monument of its type; a demonstration of the extraordinary artistic and technical possibilities of the era. The early signs of Art Nouveau can be seen in the designs of its interiors, while the large, single pane windows and sliding glass door to the winter garden were amazing technical innovations for the time. Another example of late-19th-century technology in this medieval castle is the electric bell system which allowed servants to be called from any room in the castle. The modern kitchen was equipped with two gigantic automatic grills and a large cast-iron stove also used to heat the water sent to the upper floors via metal pipes. Ludwig's idea was to build a new castle in Romanesque style but without leaving his ancient world completely; it was necessary to take into account the progress made in the worlds of the arts and sciences "which certainly would have been used at that time if they had existed."

The first design presented by Eduard Riedel in 1867 was too Neo-Gothic, but the second, proposed in 1868, was closer to Ludwig's ideas: it had a palace for the king, rooms for women, the house of the knights, a connecting building and an entrance building. In 1874, Georg Dollman, a traditional classicist, replaced Riedel. He simplified the facade and eliminated many of the romantic and Gothic decorations to concur with the wishes of Ludwig, who wanted a Romanesque and holy

144 The Throne Room combines the oriental atmosphere of an Arab mosque with the majesty of a Catholic cathedral. The throne was never placed in the room that, with its mixture of the sacred and the profane, represented the ideal of Ludwig II: subject of God but monarch of men by divine will.

145 top right A marble staircase leads from the Throne Room to the gold-plated apse featuring, as models of power granted by God, six canonized kings and the twelve apostles, in a picture portraying Christ in His Glory.

145 center right The elegant mosaic that covers the floor of the Throne Room like a large carpet features decorative forms with portrayals of plants and animals that are reminiscent of the painted motifs in Pompeian houses.

146 top This wall painting in the Waiting Room of the royal apartments on the third floor portrays a scene from the legend of King Sigurd. The young monarch is seen here as he kills the dragon that guards the treasure stolen from the Nibelungen.

Castle of the Holy Grail (the chalice used to collect Christ's blood). The king made an important contribution not only to the architectural but also to the figurative design in all his projects. He placed great importance on historical truthfulness in the furnishings, wall decorations and paintings. He was a severe critic if he thought that the work carried out was either not historically realistic or poorly-finished. There were many painters who were offended by the criticisms of the king and refused to produce further works; others, some

famous artists, did not even accept the commissions, as word had spread of how difficult it was to work for a client who was not only very attentive to historical content but also considered himself qualified to make cutting artistic judgements. For Neuschwanstein, the king wanted only painters of historical subjects who had studied medieval poetry and who took pains to remain faithful to historical reality, or what Ludwig considered to be such, based on his own knowledge and reading. His passion for history overthrew even his original idea of making Neuschwanstein a temple dedicated to Wagnerian creativity. "The paintings in the new castle must be based on the legends and not on Wagner's instructions," Ludwig ordered.

The monarch was not present at the laying of the first stone on 5 September 1869 but his mind was always busy on his great scheme. He often followed the works from Hohenschwangau with his binoculars, overseeing not just the overall project but also the details. The furnishing of the interiors was by Julius Hofmann, who became director of all the king's works from 1884. The predominant style in the rooms is Neo-Romanesque and only the bedchamber and oratory retained the Neo-Gothic style designed by Peter Herwegen.

The castle is located in one of the most panoramic positions in the Bavarian Alps and seems to stand on the tops of the trees. The Romanesque style is apparent in the construction overall and in its decorations: the rounded arch entrance, the windows and towers, the position of the columns and the bow-windows and spires. The entrance building is to the east, the Kemenate to the south, the connecting building containing the house of the Knights and the Square Tower to the north, and the Palas is to the west. The entire construction is covered with rectangular sandstone slabs taken from a nearby quarry.

In order to oversee the works personally, until the Palas was finished in 1884 the king lived on the second floor (not accessible to the public, as it was never finished and is now completely bare). Ludwig was held prisoner for a short while in the rooms on the first floor on 10 June 1886 when the regency was proclaimed and he was placed under technical arrest.

Inside the Palas, the king's rooms and the reception rooms on the third and fourth floors were more or less complete in 1886. The servants' quarters were on the first floor and an Arab Room, a large bath area and other

146 center The Room of the Bards ends with arches supported by marble columns that act as a frame to the painting of the forest of the Wizard Klingsor. Portrayals of other characters from the legend of Parsifal (to whom the room is dedicated) decorate the area above the arches.

146 bottom *The divan and the table of the living room are covered by a rich damascened cloth bearing a favorite symbol of Ludwig II's: the swan. This room is dedicated to the Knight of the Swan, Lohengrin, whose exploits fascinated the young Ludwig and inspired the building of the castle. On the wall is painted the miracle of the Holy Grail.*

146-147 *The Room of the Bards is shown here in all its grandeur, highlighting the beauty of the lacunar ceiling enriched with decorative motifs and the signs of the zodiac. The series of branched candlesticks and the huge brass chandeliers support over six hundred candles.*

147 top *This painting in the Waiting Room to the Room of the Bards portrays King Attila courting Gudrun, the widow of Sigurd. Here too, as in other halls of the castle, an evident effort was made to bring to life the legends of Germanic mythology, of which the king was very fond.*

servants' rooms were planned for the never-completed second floor. A spiral staircase in the North Tower connects the four floors and its central column is decorated with friezes showing hunting scenes. On the third floor, the walls of the waiting room outside the royal rooms is decorated with painted scenes from the Saga of Sigurd. This corresponds to the medieval saga of Siegfried and is the version recounted in the *Edda*, the oldest collection of German legends in existence. An antechamber fitted with an electric bell to call the servants leads to the Dining Room

lined with oak panels and painted with scenes from the time of the landgrave Hermann of Thuringia, and portraits of minstrels. Next there is the Bedchamber which Ludwig wanted, as in all his castles, to be particularly sumptuous in contrast to all the other rooms in Romanesque style. The Bedchamber is decorated in late-Gothic style with engraved oak panels and with a ceiling made of carved beams.

The furniture is also made from richly engraved oak, including the four-poster bed hung with brocade in blue, Ludwig's favorite

color. The whole room is dedicated to the poem *Tristan und Isolde* by Gottfried von Strassburg. A small prayer chapel has been built in one corner of the room; this too is lined in oak and decorated with Neo-Gothic motifs. The wall pictures, the paintings on the windows and the center of the triptych are all devoted to St. Louis or Louis IX of France, Ludwig's patron saint (Ludwig is the German version of the French name Louis). The dressing room was inspired by the work of two famous German medieval poets, Walther von der Vogelweide and Hans

148 top The Dining Room, on the third floor, is adjacent to the Bedchamber and the Study. The decorations date back to the time of the landgrave Hermann of Thuringia, and the portraits are by Minnesänger. The paintings above the arches of the windows depict allegories of chivalrous virtues: wisdom, temperance, justice and strength.

148-149 The inlaid oak ceiling of the study is lightened by geometric motifs. The room on the third floor, which houses the royal apartments, is covered with oak paneling and decorated with furniture in the same wood. The paintings on the walls depict scenes from the saga of Tannhäuser.

149 top A conversation corner set up in a bow-window in the king's apartment. Bow-windows are typical features of Nordic architecture, designed to let in as much natural light as possible while using the same space in the facade as would a flat window.

Sachs, who are portrayed over the bow-window. To emphasize the bucolic atmosphere of the poems of the two poets, the ceiling was painted as a blue sky with clouds and birds in a manner that lightens the heavy and opulent decorations of the castle.

One passes from the dressing room to the living room, which is dedicated to the myth of Lohengrin, a theme closely linked to the castle for the king: Neuschwanstein means "new stone swan" and Lohengrin is also known as the Knight of the Swan. The theme of the swan

dominates the room in which episodes of the saga cover the walls, are molded in the decorations of a large vase that stands on the majolica stove, and are also woven into the silk curtains.

The room that follows is a complete surprise: it is an artificial grotto with stalactites and stalagmites; it is lit by colored lights and originally featured a small waterfall. Having passed through this original corridor, the visitor enters the more severe atmosphere of the Royal Study. Like the other rooms, it is

lined with oak panels and decorated with oak furniture supplied by the famous Pössenbacher and Ehrengut workshops of Munich. The tapestries on the walls depict the saga of Tannhäuser. Passing back through the antechamber, one reaches the the room that most recalls a fairy tale: the Throne Room. This occupies two floors and was designed by Eduard Ille and based on the design of the church of St. Sophia in Constantinople and on the Allerheiligen-Kirche in Munich. It was supposed to be the throne room not of the king

of Bavaria but of the king of the Holy Grail. According to the legend, discovery of the Holy Grail would redeem man's soul and save the king's power. In Neuschwanstein's Throne Room, Ludwig wanted to exalt the ideal of the monarch in the traditional sense, not to display it before his people or the state, but to have it for himself. The central painting of the apse shows Christ in His Glory. Six canonized kings pay homage to the heavenly king for having followed and preserved the divine laws; the six kings are Casimir of Poland, Stephen I of Hungary, the Holy Roman Emperor Henry II of Germany, Louis IX of France, Ferdinand III of Spain and Edward the Confessor of England. To Ludwig, the six kings were not only saints and patrons, they were models of a power conceded by God and limited by His commandments but absolute over their subjects. That power was almost obsolete by the 19th century, and was something that Ludwig could not have attained except in his personal fantasy kingdom. The grandiose gold and ivory throne with four lifesize angels that held up the symbols of Wittelsbach, Bavaria and Schwangau was never placed in the center of the apse of the Throne Room, with the result that the hall was even more like a sanctuary. The balcony has splendid views over the lakes of Alpsee and Schwansee, the countryside around Füssen, Mount Sauleing and the Schwarzenberg chain. Legend has it that the chain is the dragon from the story of the Nibelung turned into stone. The hill with Hohenschwangau can be seen as the dragon's head, and the castle is his crown; the chain of hills forms the humps of the dragon's back; and his tail encircles the lake Alpsee.

The king's ideal of royal authority derived through the grace of the Holy Grail inspired the creation of the Throne Room. Furthermore, this ideal was also responsible for the modification of the original idea of the magnificent Room of the Bards which, together with the Throne Room, fills the fourth floor. Inspired by the Room of the Bards at Wartburg Castle, this space was intended to be used for a permanent poetry contest.

To bring the mystery of the Holy Grail into the Room of the Bards, the minstrels were placed in the background (only their names appear in the scrolls in the passage that leads to the room) and the walls were covered instead by paintings by August Spiess. These

narrate the story of Parsifal (Perceval) created by Wolfram von Eschenbach in the Middle Ages. Ludwig's faith in Christ sometimes wavered and, tortured by knowledge of his sin and resulting guilt, he believed that a new savior might be found in Parsifal, in whose story the king recognized his own suffering. In his attempt to pursue justice and attain salvation, Parsifal, the Christian knight, fell into sin and suffering and doubted God. In the end, Parsifal submitted to God's will and through

149 center Access to the magnificent Room of the Bards is through the Waiting Room with its splendid Gothic vault and ornaments of Byzantine taste.
The paintings on the walls depict the Saga of Gudrun, Sigurd's widow, who marries and later kills Attila.

149 bottom The richly inlaid table in the Dining Room, which is dominated by the color scarlet, holds an imposing centerpiece in gold-plated bronze depicting the struggle between Siegfried and the Dragon.

150 top left The paintings on canvas that cover the upper part of the Dressing Room are inspired by the poetic works and the lives of two famous medieval German poets: Walther von der Vogelweide and Hans Sachs.

150 bottom left Unlike the other rooms, designed in the Romanesque style, the King's

Bedchamber was designed and decorated in the late-Gothic style; as in all his castles, Ludwig II wanted it to be particularly sumptuous. While the king enjoyed medieval sagas, his spirit, tormented by his impossible desire, drew him toward the great love stories, such as the one of Tristan and Isolde, depicted in the room.

divine grace he found the holy chalice and was elected king of the Grail. The pictorial cycle culminates in two scenes: first, Parsifal is led to the castle of the Grail, where he relieves the ailing Fisher King of his suffering and becomes king of the Grail. Then Lohengrin, Parsifal's son, leaves the castle of the Grail to save Elsa of Brabant. Of the original idea, the minstrel's stage remains, below a small gallery decorated with scenery of the "holy wood" where Parsifal learned of the secret of the Holy Grail.

Though imagination can inspire reality, it is

The Fantastic Palace of Ludwig II

psychiatrists (who never examined Ludwig) to declare the king mentally ill. On 9 July 1886, the government decided to interdict him and proclaimed Luitpold, Ludwig's uncle who was over 60 years old, as Regent. The next day, a commission of psychiatrists, nurses and government representatives tried to take Ludwig "into custody." The king was staying at Neuschwanstein at the time, and the commission ran into opposition from his retinue and from the local people, who loved Ludwig and considered him eccentric but not mad. After a day's emotional agony worse than his worst nightmares, the king gave in to the request for him to abdicate and surrendered himself to the doctors. He knew he could not survive as a man or king after such an outrage

also true that reality can strongly delude the imagination. The Grail saved neither the man nor the monarch. Ludwig did not even have the power to ensure the castle construction timetable was respected; the praise and small gifts he generously handed out to the painters, architects and workers were to no avail, and the money from his own resources began to run out. In 1880, an estimate was made that an annual expenditure of 900,000 marks was required for construction of Neuschwanstein, originally begun in 1869, to be completed by 1893. Ludwig was unable to scrape together such a sum, particularly as he had begun construction of another castle, the Herrenchiemsee, after the Linderhof was completed in 1878. The Herrenchiemsee was to be a copy of Versailles and to be a setting for Ludwig to play the role of the Sun King. This squandering of the royal finances and his ever more bizarre and hallucinatory behavior were the reasons given by a commission of

and thought he would never set foot in Neuschwanstein again. His last words to the orderly as he left the castle were, "My little Stichel...look after these rooms like a sanctuary; do not leave them be profaned by the curious." Three days after his abdication, on 13 June 1886, Ludwig was found drowned together with his doctor in Lake Starnberg, where he had been locked up in his castle, now an asylum. The few people close to Ludwig knew that the idea of suicide was not alien to him; he had always tried to inhabit a different reality, epitomized by the dream castles he could no longer build as settings for his personal fantastic world. The most suitable epitaph for Ludwig II is probably these lines from the poem "Le seul vrai roi de ce siècle" dedicated to him by Paul Verlaine, the bard of mystical symbolism: "A poet, a soldier, the only king of a century in which kings are such ashen figures, a martyr to Reason according to Faith."

150 top right The windows of the King's Dressing Room open on to the upper courtyard. The peacock, one of the king's favorite birds and a recurring symbol, together with the swan, in the castles of Ludwig II, is woven into the damascened cloth of the drapes and upholstery.

151 The Bedchamber leads to a small prayer chapel, the King's Oratory, decorated in the Neo-Gothic style. The paintings, windows and wooden triptych portray St. Louis, Ludwig II's patron saint.

The Castle of Charlottenburg

FOR LOVE OF SOPHIE

More than 300 years were needed to build Charlottenburg, one of the most sumptuous palaces in Germany and the largest castle in Berlin; but in just a few months it was reduced almost completely to rubble. Despite bomb damage, Charlottenburg has been carefully rebuilt, although not all the furnishings and objets d'art dispersed across East Germany during World War II have been returned. The castle was used for longer than two centuries as a summer residence by the Prussian royal family. New sections were added and architectural alterations made to the original small palace, generation after generation, in accordance with personal taste and the fashion of the age.

In 1695, the Electoral Prince Frederick III ordered the construction of a "maison de plaisance" for his second wife, Sophie Charlotte, on a hill in the marshy area of the Spree river a mile from the residential city of Lützow. The first design was drawn up by the court architect Johann Arnold Nehring in a late Baroque style, but Nehring died during the first year of construction. The palace was very small, with an oval pavilion at its center that faced toward the park in French style. With two floors and a mezzanine, the castle had from the start been considered a strange construction for the age, as Sophie Charlotte had decreed that she wanted her apartment on the ground floor and not on the main floor. She also wanted each room that faced the park to have direct access to it. The princess was the daughter of Duke Ernst August von Braunschweig-Lüneburg and was married to the electoral prince for dynastic reasons after the death of his first wife, who had not given him an heir. The princess had been given a full education and had a lively interest in sciences, literature and Italian chamber music (there are cymbals and portraits of Italian composers in her rooms at Charlottenburg) but at the age of 16 Sophie Charlotte was obliged to exchange the animated court of her family for the austere court in Berlin, where military affairs were

dominant and the only music to be heard was fanfares. Her intolerance of the boring atmosphere of the Berlin court was demonstrated by her running away as soon as possible to her paternal house in Hanover. Her royal husband, certainly more in love with his vivacious wife than she was with him, gave her this castle to keep her longer in Berlin. The princess's apartment was small as it was designed only to be used for a few hours during the summer. On the ground floor there were two wings each with two rooms, a bedroom, an audience room and an antechamber. To create the illusion of space in these rooms chock-full of furniture and ornaments, long walls of mirrors alternated with strips covered with brocade. Most noticeable are the many pieces of Oriental and particularly Japanese porcelain. These were so valuable and sought after at the time that Sophie's son, Frederick William I (called the "king of soldiers"), received 600 grenadiers from the king of Poland in exchange for two large vases, like those that can be seen in the Porcelain Room of the palace, and about 100 other small objects. Since then this type of large Oriental vase has been called a "Grenadiervase." As a result of his diplomatic skill, and without having had to declare war, the Electoral Prince

154-155 *The central section of the building was the core of what was to become a royal palace. It was originally built as a country house for Princess Sophie Charlotte but,* *after her death in 1705, King Frederick I followed the model of Versailles and had a domed tower, 156 feet high, built by his architect Johann Friedrich Eosander* *(1669-1728), known as Göthe. The guard boxes at the entrance to the main court are overlooked by statues that were part of the decoration of the park.*

154 left *The statue of the Great Electoral Prince of Brandenburg was commissioned by his son Frederick I from the court sculptor and architect Andreas Schlüter. It was due to be erected by the bridge that leads to the castle of Berlin. The artist, influenced by monuments to the Farnese family in Piacenza, created a pedestal with chained slaves as a symbol of the Prince's defeated enemies. The Great Prince is dressed partly in Roman and partly in contemporary fashion.*

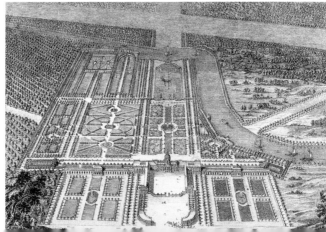

Frederick III managed to elevate himself to the position of king of Prussia in 1701 with the name of Frederick I. From that moment, he decided to enlarge the small Charlottenburg palace and turn it into an official summer residence. The Swedish architect Nicodemus Tessin the Younger enlarged the building by adding two further wings to create a courtyard in which a bronze statue of the Great Electoral Prince Frederick William (father of the builder) has stood since 1952. It is one of the most important equestrian sculptures created during the Baroque era and was made from a single cast in 1700. It originally stood near the royal residence in the city center but, to save it from damage during World War II, it was sunk in the Tegeler See, from which it was recovered after the conflict.

Poor Sophie Charlotte was unable to enjoy her renovated palace, for she died as soon as the works were complete. But the king still chose the palace to be his permanent summer residence from April to October and, in memory of his young wife, he called it

replaced since 1993 and the room has regained its lost splendor.

On the death of the king in 1715, the 155-yard-long west orangerie had only just been completed and the east one not even started. All works were suspended during the reign of Frederick William I who, unlike his mother, had completely absorbed the Prussian love of the army and chose the military city of Potsdam as his residence. His successor, Frederick II (known as Frederick the Great) was obliged to place advertisements in newspapers to recall to Prussia artists and craftsmen who had been left without work during the reign of the "king of soldiers" and had emigrated to other countries. The king had the second orangerie at Charlottenburg designed by the court architect Georg Wenceslaus von Knobelsdorff, but not with the aim of producing fruit; instead he wished to create splendid apartments for himself and make the castle his principal residence. A great admirer of the French painter Antoine Watteau and his pupils Nicolas Lancret and Jean-Baptiste Pater, whose works he

154 bottom This copper engraving was produced by Martin Engelbrecht at the beginning of the 18th century and shows the project by architect Eosander Göthe, which was never completely executed. The layout of the park is unusual: Sophie Charlotte chose a site for the palace near the river Havel on which she arrived from Berlin by boat, and this position did not permit the customary symmetrical park.

155 The French garden with its parterre approximately 270 yards long by 110 yards wide can be admired from the top of the central pavilion of the palace. Before designing the park, Sophie Charlotte had visited the gardens of Fontainebleau, St. Cloud and Versailles, and was in correspondence with the famous French landscape gardener, Le Nôtre, who later sent his pupil Simeon Godeau to Berlin to collaborate on the design of the gardens.

Charlottenburg. Great investment was made to decorate the residence: a lovely stairwaywas built, as was a large dome fitted with a turret and carillon. The Palatine chapel was decorated as was the famous Porcelain Room, where more than three thousand different types of Japanese objects in all different sizes are an integral part of the mirrored and gilded walls. Unfortunately, the majority of the porcelain was so solidly affixed to the walls that it was impossible to detach it and save it from the destruction of the war. With the help of money from the Berlin State Lottery, however, the lost pieces have been gradually

owned, Frederick dreamed of creating an existence full of *fêtes galantes* as idealized in the pictures. Fate, though, pulled him in the opposite direction. Hardly had the works begun than the war for the reconquest of Slesia started; but numerous missives still exist with reports to the king on the state of the construction. Ironically, the first rooms to be finished were those on the ground floor for the queen, but she never went there to live. The 13 rooms making up the king's apartments on the main floor were much more simply decorated. Only three now remain in their original condition: the silver anteroom, the library and the study, all elegantly decorated in Rococo style. Displayed in the library are eight superb gold snuffboxes decorated with precious stones or enamel and diamonds. They came from Frederick II's large collection, which was dispersed over the years. The two large rooms in the center of the building are unique in the world of royal castles. They are exquisitely decorated with examples of Frederick's personal taste in Rococo style. The White Room was covered with a pink powdered marble paste and then blanched; it was used as the dining room or throne room. The Golden Gallery, with its elegant green and gold decoration, recreates a

happy garden party and was used as a ballroom and for musical evenings. A year after the construction of the Golden Gallery, the king decorated a second, four-room apartment, to house his famous collection of French paintings rather than to live in. Though the collection was plundered by the Austrians after the war of Silesia, many outstanding works can be admired by painters such as Watteaue du Lanret. The office and the bedchamber were furnished after World War II with period furniture. Expansion and decoration of Charlottenburg did not stop with the palace: Frederick II planted more than 7,000 lime trees in the park. Frederick the Great died without an heir, and his successor, Frederick William II, was the son of his younger brother. In his short reign (1786–97), the new

ruler furnished two apartments, one for summer and the other for winter, and added two new buildings: the Belvedere and the Theater. The Belvedere was constructed on a small island in the park that the king began to change into an English park. The architect was Karl Gotthard Langhans, who had designed the Brandenburger Tor. The two upper floors of the small three-floor palace with Baroque and Neoclassical elements were decorated with wood inlays that covered the floors, walls and ceilings. Today it is used as a museum for the porcelain products of the the royal porcelain manufacturer, the famous KPM company, which still operates near the castle.

Frederick William II loved music and had personal contacts with some of the great

composers such as Mozart, Boccherini and Beethoven; he was also passionate about the theater. Unlike his uncle, who preferred French authors, the nephew favored contemporary German authors like Lessing and Schiller. The architect Langhans added the theater onto the orangerie so that it could be reached from the castle. Its Neoclassical interior was fully changed in the early 20th century and the building is now used as a museum. For his summer apartment, the king chose the ground floor of the new wing, once the apartment (never used) of Frederick the Great's queen. As the apartment was only used for short visits, the decoration was simple compared to his apartments in other castles. The five rooms, which were seriously

156-157 The Golden Gallery, 137 feet long, is situated on the first floor of the New Wing next to the White Room. It was used for balls and musical evenings arranged by Frederick the Great. The gallery is the most richly ornamented room in the palace. Its light green coloring and large windows give the impression of a space in the heart of a park. The joyous atmosphere is created by shallow reliefs in Rococo style that cover the ceiling and walls. As inspiration for the decoration, Georg Wenceslaus von Knobelsdorff used engravings with grotesque ornaments by French painter Antoine Watteau, which he succeeded in adapting perfectly to the architecture of the gallery.

156 left The White Room in the center of the New Wing was used as a throne room and for large dinners. It is built in a simple manner with double pilasters between the tall windows. Only the doors are decorated in a magnificent manner, with gilded reliefs depicting the four seasons. The ceiling fresco by Antoine Pesne was destroyed during World War II.

157 bottom left The library in the New Wing is structured like a gallery. It is one of the seven libraries that the king maintained in his various residences. The walls are lined with wood and painted light green with silver decorations. The cedarwood bookshelves are original, while the books are those from the king's library in the castle of Potsdam.

157 bottom right The Royal Chapel and the royal box on the north wall were also designed by Frederick I's favorite architect, Eosander Göthe.

158-159 *The Red Chamber in the king's suite derives its name from the red damask wallcovering with rich gold ornamental braiding. It was designed by Eosander Göthe between 1701 and 1713.*

158 bottom *Sophie Charlotte's apartments are elegant and originally furnished. On the left is an English black lacquer wardrobe with gilded paintings and base from the late 17th century.*

damaged in a 1943 bombing raid, were decorated in Japanese and Etruscan styles. Seven rooms of Frederick II's first apartment on the main floor of the new wing were renovated to become the winter apartment. The floors, inlaid with native and exotic woods, are of exquisite manufacture; but the apartment was never lived in by the king, who died before it was completed.

His son Frederick William III reigned for 43 years, through a very difficult period. After the French Revolution came the Napoleonic Wars and the trading blockade with England, which brought the country to its knees. But after the Congress of Vienna, Prussia got its strength back again. Art and science flourished once more, and Berlin became a cultural center with universities, museums and theaters. The king had married the beautiful and widely-admired Princess Luise von Mecklenburg-Strelitz and used Charlottenburg as a summer residence for his numerous family. Until 1809 he occupied the west part of the new wing without altering the furnishings. A fashionable young architect, Karl Friedrich Schinkel, who had created the new image of Berlin with the construction of several important buildings, altered the bedchambers of the couple in the new Imperial style; only a little of this is left, in the queen's apartment. This castle, named after a queen, seems to have a strange curse: its queens are unable to enjoy its sumptuous appointments for long. Princess Luise died in July 1810 at the age of 34. To stay close to his dead wife, the romantic king gave detailed instructions to Schinkel for the rapid construction of a Greek mausoleum in the castle's park. At Christmas of the same year,

159 top left The Porcelain Room contains over 3,000 pieces from Japan and China. It was finished in 1706 and was considered a marvel of its time. It made such an impression on the kings of Denmark and Saxony, who admired it during their meeting with the king in 1709, that they imitated it in their own palaces in Copenhagen and Dresden.

159 bottom left Most palace rooms have been rebuilt more than once and furnished with items of different origin. In this Chinese Room in the Summer Apartments of Frederick William II, the china and lacquered furniture help to create an exotic atmosphere emphasized by the Chinese style wall paintings.

159 right The Audience Chamber is located on the ground floor of the central section of the palace and was part of Sophie Charlotte's apartments. The drum table from Java is part of the original furniture. The Berlin wallhangings by Charles Vigne show scenes from the commedia dell'arte and were added in 1740.

For Love of Sophie

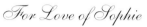

Luise's body was transferred here, but it was another five years before the monument above her gravesite was ready. Among designs from famous sculptors like Canova, Thorwaldsen and Schadow, the king chose that of the young Christian Daniel Rauch, who created a model at Charlottenburg under the king's strict supervision. Actual production in Carrara marble took place in Rome, and transportation of the monument turned into an odyssey that lasted eight months. Over subsequent years, the mausoleum was enlarged to include the monument dedicated to the king and, fifty years later, that of his son William I, the first emperor of the second German Empire, and his wife Augusta von Sachsen-Weimar. During his long reign, Frederick William III had the entire park transformed into English style by the famous landscape gardener Peter Joseph Lenné, who was later to create the famous park at Sans Souci. Fourteen years after the death of Luise, Frederick William III made a morganatic marriage with the Countess Auguste von Harrach and built for her what is known as the "Schinkel Pavilion" in the park. Schinkel designed not only this building but also the decoration and interior furnishings in Neoclassical style. Little is left intact of the apartments on the first floor of the central body of the castle, which were decorated for Frederick William IV and his wife Elisabeth, Princess of Bavaria. Only the king's library has

been reconstructed since recovery of the furnishings from Potsdam, where they were transferred during the war. As a young man, the king was a collector of books and at the end of his life he possessed more than 20,000.

Charlottenburg became the imperial residence for three months in 1888, when Frederick III, already seriously ill, moved there with his wife Victoria. The rooms were restored and furnished so elegantly that guests like Queen Victoria of England, the mother of the empress, could be respectably accommodated. During the reign of Emperor William II, the castle was only used as a royal residence for a few days, but the apartments were often used for the Emperor's guests and today they still welcome guests of honor to the city of Berlin. Worthy of note are the Silver Rooms and the Crown Treasure which was

displayed in the castle after World War II. Just the "skeletons" of the royal crowns are exhibited, for their precious stones were only mounted for coronations, and used in other contexts for the rest of the time; also on view is the sword, consecrated by Pius II, which the Electoral Prince, Albrecht Achilles, received from the hands of the pope in Mantua in 1460. The goldsmith was the Florentine Simone de Martino. The Silver Rooms have been the vaults for the castle's silverware since the 16th century. Among the 2,694 pieces of silver collected over three centuries, the most recent is a silver plate given by the cities of Prussia on the wedding of the imperial heir, William, to Cecilie von Mecklenburg-Schwerin in 1904. Another room contains porcelain that Frederick II ordered from KPM and pieces from Meissen.

The Castle of Sans Souci

THE "VERSAILLES" NEAR BERLIN

Lying amid gentle, rolling hills and surrounded by small lakes created by the river Havel, the city of Potsdam is considered the Versailles of northern Europe. The thousand-year-old city situated a little more than 20 miles from Berlin clearly shows the marks of history. It has been the luxurious residence of the Hohenzollern dynasty, a fulcrum of absolutist power, the homeland of religious tolerance, a school of German-Prussian public bureaucracy and a city of art.

Set in an idyllic location and surrounded by the tranquil rural setting of a vineyard northwest of the residential city of Potsdam.

After Frederick's initial design for a private refuge, a complex of ten buildings developed over the course of a century. The complex spread across the 717 acres, making one of Europe's loveliest and most important parks.

The work was first begun in 1744 with the preparation of the ground. One of the hills to the north of the Havel plain was transformed into six deep, curved terraces connected by a central stairway which led to the palace at the

160 top This form is typical of Rococo decoration. It has no real function: its only purpose is to embellish the wrought iron grating.

160 center Thirty-five caryatids border the glass doors of the south front. The figures, by Friedrich Christian Glume, appear in a variety of positions and shapes atop the pilasters decorated with grapes, flower garlands, musical instruments and masks.

copses of larch trees and pavilions scattered around its gardens, the palace of Sans Souci was an island of peace where Frederick II of Prussia went to forget his problems. "Sans souci" is French for "without troubles," an ideal of life that frankly is impossible for a monarch to achieve; but Frederick went ahead and created this splendid refuge where he could hide away for short periods. The preferred interests of this "philosopher on a royal throne" were art, literature and French music; he chose an almost private palace for his project, far from the court and immersed in

top of the hill. Separated by indigenous trees and vines, glass-doored niches were built on each terrace to house exotic fruit trees, which could provide the much-favored delicacies for the dining tables of the aristocracy.

The architect Georg Wenceslaus von Knobelsdorff, who had already built the New Wing at Charlottenburg for Frederick, drew up the design of the palace on the basis of a sketch made by the king. Extending across the hilltop, the golden-hued, single-story building consists of a domed, oval pavilion with two wings that end in semicircular pavilions.

160 bottom Sans Souci palace stands on a hill cut to form six deep terraces with a flight of 132 steps. The architect Georg Wenceslaus von Knobelsdorff built the 315-foot-long palace in just two years, on the basis of a sketch made by the king.

160-161 The center of the palace is emphasized by a pavilion of the same height and decoration as the wings, but with a green dome that was erected later. The richly decorated oval windows are false; the real skylight in the Marble Room is hidden behind the small balustrade over the dome.

161 top The portrait of Frederick the Great by Franz Dudde, painted a century after the death of the king, shows the old monarch (nicknamed "Old Fritz") as he usually presented himself, not in official dress but in the uniform of the supreme commander of Prussia, and decorated with the medal of the black eagle, the emblem of the Hohenzollern family.

161 bottom left The painted copper engraving entitled View of the Royal Country Palace Sans Souci near Potsdam was created by Johann David Schleuen only a year after the palace was completed.

161 bottom right Karl Friedrich Schinkel (1781-1841), here painted by Carl-Friedrich Schmid, was the architect who built the Neoclassical palace of Charlottenhof for the heir to the throne, Prince Frederick William.

The king requested that the building be raised three steps above the ground to allow him immediate access from the palace to the terrace for his walks. The tall windows were crowned with caryatids of Bacchantes, the roof balustrade was decorated with vases and the windows of the dome with groups of putti. Porches to the east and west were added to the building, as was a trellis pavilion that looks like an enormous golden cage. The back of the palace is simpler and more traditional, surrounded by two quarter-rondo colonnades that form a courtyard. The unobstructed view of the hill beyond takes in a group of fake ruins inspired by the king's classical taste for ancient monuments.

The summer palace's official inauguration took place on 1 May 1747 after only two years of construction. There was a lunch party for 200 guests and a musical evening, although the

The "Versailles" near Berlin

162 top left A detail of the colored plaster wall decorations in Voltaire's Room; it shows a wading bird resting on a basket of fruit.

162 center left Voltaire's Room is a brilliant example of "capricious" Rococo style. Its elegant decorations were the work of J. A. Hoppenhaupt the Younger.

162 bottom left Frederick II's library held more than 2,100 volumes. The cedarwood furnishing with gilded decoration, the proportions, the colors and the harmony of the round room with four niches (one of which was for the fireplace) still create a sense of peace and relaxation.

162 top right The magnificent Marble Room is topped by a domed ceiling decorated with gilded stuccoes and supported by eight pairs of Carrara marble columns. The room was reserved for learned conversation. Note the floor decorated with floral motifs made from semiprecious stone.

163 The Concert Room is a marvelous example of the "Frederick" style of Rococo. It is decorated with paintings, sculptures, furniture and handcrafts; it was the setting for musical evenings in which the king was often a performer.

building was not completely finished. Beyond the vestibule and the Marble Room, Sans Souci had only five rooms on each side; those at the east end had a small gallery to the north and were for use by the king, while those to the west were reserved for friends. The parties Frederick held at Sans Souci became famous throughout Europe.

One hundred years later, Adolf Menzel, a famous 19th-century illustrator and painter, immortalized the atmosphere of the festivities at Sans Souci in two famous pictures: *Frederick II's Lunch Party at Sans Souci* and *Flute Concert at Sans Souci*. The first event is being held in the Marble Room, a room in Italian style with eight pairs of Carrara marble columns rising from a richly decorated floor made of semiprecious stones and supporting a gilded stucco dome. Among the Corinthian columns, the guests at their meal philosophize and argue. In the middle of a group of witty lovers of philosophy, Frederick often had beside him his favorite philosopher, the famous Voltaire, with whom Frederick had been corresponding since he was heir to the throne. Voltaire lived at Potsdam as Frederick's guest from 1750 to 1753 though the reserved Frenchman did not like the life of the court and preferred to retire to the quiet of his apartment in the royal palace, rather than occupy what is known as "Voltaire's Room" at Sans Souci.

The small Audience Room is next to the Marble Room and was used as a dining room when the king dined alone or with just a few friends. The principal decorations are pictures by famous French painters, such as *The Concert* by Antoine Watteau. The gilded reliefs over the doors are decorated with putti who read books with sentences in French chosen by the king; they encourage the viewer to live a life *sans souci*, without worries. Next there is the lovely Concert Hall, a jewel of Frederick's preferred style of Rococo design. Opposite the two windows that overlook the terrace are two

164-165 *The frivolity of Rococo alternates with the grandeur of the Neoclassical style at Sans Souci. One of the entrance halls,* lined with marble columns with gilded capitals and classical statues, demonstrates the height of Neoclassicism.

niches with mirrors that reflect fragments of the room into infinity. Paintings, sculptures, furniture, decorations and objets d'art combine to create a global work of art. This room was the setting for famous musical evenings during which the king would entertain his guests by playing his own flute compositions.

The study with an alcove for a bed was redesigned in Neoclassical style in 1786 soon after the king's death, but toward the middle of the 19th century, when interest in Frederick's Rococo style was being revived, some of the original furnishings were put back, including the armchair in which the king died.

After the Seven Years' War (1756–1763), few of Frederick's many friends were left. Frederick II became the "hermit of Sans Souci" and lived alone, surrounded by his dogs and

that encourages concentration. The little gallery that extends to the north of the apartment was used to hang some of his pictures by French artists including Antoine Watteau, Nicolas Lancret and Jean-Baptiste Pater and sculptures from the collection of Cardinal Polignac.

Each of the five guest rooms to the west of the Marble Room has an alcove for a bed opposite the windows, and two side doors, one of which goes to a servant's room and the other of which opens into a wardrobe. Each room is decorated differently: the first and fifth are in Chinese style, one in light pink, the other in green; the second is decorated in blue and white, and the third in red and white; and the fourth, Voltaire's Room, has intaglios of multicolored wood on a yellow background.

165 top right A gilded section of a door in the fifth guest room, dedicated to Chinese decoration. Each of the six guest rooms is decorated in a different color: there are both pink and green Chinese rooms, a white and blue room, and a red room; Voltaire's Room is yellow.

164 bottom left The painting Dance near the Pegasus Fountain by Nicolas Lauret shows a playful moment in the large park of Frederick the Great's summer palace.

164 bottom right Like Voltaire's Room, this is another one of the six rooms reserved for guests; all were situated in the central body of the palace and all had the same dimensions and layout. Note the inlaid wooden floor and landscape paintings on the walls.

books. His library here contained more than 2,100 volumes (but he had six other large libraries in other palaces) which contained only works of history and Roman and Greek poetry, all translated into French, as well as works of French literature, including Voltaire's complete works. All the books have red or light brown leather bindings, colors that best harmonize with the cedarwood and gilded decorations. The proportions and colors of the round room with four niches (one for the fireplace, one for the armchair and two for glass doors), create an atmosphere of peace

Monkeys, cranes, storks, squirrels, different types of birds, garlands of flowers, fruit and bushes create a relaxed atmosphere like a garden in summer.

Even before building began, Frederick had chosen the highest terrace toward the east to be the site of his grave. He had it decorated with busts of Roman leaders and the group of Spring and Zephyr. "I have lived as a philosopher and as such I wish to be buried," he wrote in his will, but it was only 205 years after his death, on 17 August 1991, that the sarcophagus of the king was buried on the

165 bottom This guest reception room is rendered particularly elegant by the white Empire-style chimney-piece, the great mirror that seems to enlarge the room, the lovely wall and floor surfaces, and above all the many classical paintings. Especially worthy of note are the furniture and the gilded plasterwork that frames the room.

166 left The extraordinary variety of monuments, fountains and statues in various styles gives great charm to the Sans Souci park. This "classical" fountain uses ancient elements, but the final effect is of a "modern" design.

166 below top The Art Gallery to the east of the palace was built by architect Johann Gottfried Büring between 1755 and 1764, on the spot where the glasshouse had been. The gallery, like the palace, has a central pavilion and two wings.

166 below center The New Rooms were built as the first Orangerie by von Knobelsdorff in 1747, but the king had the building reconstructed as a guest residence in 1771. Behind it rises the mill whose presence so annoyed the king.

The "Versailles" near Berlin

terrace beneath a simple stone slab near the tombs of his dogs, the only faithful companions of his old age.

To the right and left of the palace, but further down the hill, the king built two other single-story buildings, the Art Gallery and the Orangerie. The Picture Gallery was constructed between 1755 and 1763 on the design of Johannes Gottfried Büring with the original intention of hanging the king's private collection of paintings and Italian, Dutch and French sculptures bought explicitly for this gallery. The works displayed are by Raphael, Guido Reni, Annibale Carracci, Tintoretto, Rembrandt, Rubens, Van Dyck; there are also classical Roman sculptures and works by Gian Lorenzo Bernini.

Knobelsdorff's design for the Orangerie to the west was begun soon after completion of the palace in the spring of 1747. It had seven rooms with stoves to heat more than 1,000 orange trees in winter. Oranges were considered to be the golden apple of mythology and regarded as a symbol of power and strength. During the summer, the empty rooms were used for balls, large dinners, concerts and French and Italian theatrical shows. Two other small Orangeries were built 25 years later, and the original one was used for a different purpose: twice a year, in autumn and spring, military parades and maneuvers were organized in Potsdam, attracting from abroad generals and guests of the nobility who required suitable accommodation. The king therefore decided to create what are called the New Rooms in the west part of the Orangerie. These are three apartments, two with two rooms and one with a single room, all with rooms for servants. They were also used during the 19th century by different members of the royal household and their guests, but there was a catch: the court provided food but drinks had to be paid for separately.

The central and eastern parts of the building were transformed into a row of four party rooms. The entrance to the east was linked to the royal palace by a stairway and led to the Blue Gallery, the reception room. Then

166 left, bottom Behind the palace can be seen the "ruins" inspired by ancient monuments, a fashionable decoration. The function of such constructions was not just evocative; these also served to hide the water reservoir necessary to supply the fountains in the park.

167 top left The extensive park at Sans Souci is an ensemble of small parks in different styles. There are parks in French and English style, and gardens based on Dutch, Sicilian, and other layouts.

167 top right The Neptune Grotto, designed by Georg Wenceslaus von Knobelsdorff shortly before his death in 1753, exemplifies the artificial grotto of Rococo gardens. It was decorated with all kinds of sea shells and protected by an elegant grating.

166-167 The most recent and largest building on the site stands between Sans Souci and the New Palace. The Orangerie was designed by architect Ludwig Persius in Italian Renaissance style and built between 1851 and 1860.

167 bottom Two wrought iron pavilions decorated with images of a golden sun flank Sans Souci palace. The kitchens and the outbuildings with rooms for secretaries and domestic staff are hidden behind the pavilions. Frederick the Great's tomb can be seen on the right.

168-169 The magnificently decorated Art Gallery was built by architect Johann Gottfried Büring with copious gilded plasterwork. The two-tone marble floor tiling accentuates the sense of perspective. The gallery holds the king's personal collection of Dutch, French and Italian paintings and sculptures, which were bought specifically to be housed here.

169 top left The gilded reliefs were the last work by the sculptor brothers Johann David and Johann Lorenz Wilhelm Räntz. The two moved to Berlin after the death of the Marquess Wilhelmina von Bayreuth, Frederick's favorite sister and a great art patroness. From 1764 on, they influenced the development of art at Frederick's court.

169 top right Ovid's stories of love between gods and human beings were part of the education of nobles and artists of the time, so they were often used as themes for interior decoration. Scenes from the love lives of Apollo and Zeus were the predominant decorations chosen for the Ovid Gallery.

168 bottom left The central section of the Orangerie was never used as a greenhouse. It was designed to be an apartment for King Frederick William IV. He was a great admirer of Raphael and for these rooms he had copies made of 47 of the master's paintings.

168 bottom right The Jasper Room in the New Rooms is decorated in typical style for a banqueting hall, with walls paneled with precious stones and a painted ceiling. Ancient white marble busts stand out against the warm color of the jasper.

there was the buffet room, which was probably used for small groups but also to place the food that arrived from the palace kitchen (the New Rooms had no kitchen). Ovid's Gallery derives its name from the gilded reliefs showing amorous scenes from the works of the Roman poet, and was used for musical evenings. The room used for festivities was decorated in a traditional manner with walls in stone: gray marble alternated with compartments lined in jasper which were used as bases for the busts.

Standing between the New Rooms and the palace is an ancient mill, seemingly out of place, which has an interesting story. Fed up with the sound of the grinding at the mill,

Frederick wanted to confiscate it from the miller but the latter, sure of his rights and trusting in the just administration of the Prussian federation, refused to leave and went to the court of appeals in Berlin. The king acknowledged the importance of his justice system; he changed his mind and allowed the miller to stay.

To the south of the main avenue in the park, the king had a Chinese Tea House designed by Büring—the architect of the Picture Gallery. China was almost unknown at this time, as the spices and valuable porcelain arriving in Europe were only imported by Dutch traders. The image of the exotic Chinese

169 bottom The Ovid Gallery, which was used as a music room, is situated between the Jasper Room and the Buffet Room in the New Rooms. The walls are decorated with 14 scenes from Ovid's Metamorphoses *set among the five windows, the mirrors and the side doors. The white and light green ceiling is decorated with the elegant Rococo shapes typical of Frederick's residences.*

world was supplied by the scenes painted on the porcelain. In 1720, a vogue started for pavilions and small houses built in a blend of Chinese and Rococo styles and Frederick's is certainly one of the best examples of this fashion. It is impressive artistically, but the gilded, lifesize statues are also amusing. They are dressed in clothes created from pure imagination, and have European facial features.

The largest building in Sans Souci park is the New Palace. This was designed before the Seven Years' War but only built after Frederick was saved from certain defeat, in the third battle for the conquest of Slesia, by the sudden death of the Russian Czarina Elizabeth. The construction was the king's enthusiastic means of expressing the enormous triumph he felt for this war he had not lost. He later called it "a fanfaronnade" (bragging) which was the term given to local rural buildings that had marvelous facades in order to look like small, independent castles. The New Palace—230 yards long, with 322 windows, 230 pilasters and 428 statues—looks like a majestic and luxurious

170 top The Chinese House was built between 1754 and 1764 by architect Johann Gottfried Büring with a roof in the shape of a large tent that terminates in a drum. This was topped by a gilded statue of a mandarin sitting on a cushion with a parasol and stick; the statue was produced by Friedrich Jury from a model by Benjamin Giese.

170 center The bucolic atmosphere outside is reflected in the colors of the central room in the Chinese House, and the light green walls correspond to the Carrara marble floor.

royal residence with a major court and annexes, but it was not really designed as a royal house. Apart from the rooms dedicated to festivities, the many bedrooms were used only by guests. The whole was designed by the architect Büring, but construction was finished by Carl von Gontard, who was mainly responsible for the interiors.

Although Rococo had by now been replaced by Neoclassicism, Frederick II remained faithful to his preferred style, and so some of the rooms resemble those in Sans Souci. The Grotto Room, however, was completely new. Grottoes and grotto rooms reflect the typical attempt of Rococo to merge nature and architecture. Furthermore, their nooks and crannies were also the most suitable places for "games of society," i.e., amorous trysts. During Frederick's lifetime, the decoration of the walls was not as attractive as it is today. There were only imitation stalactites,

170 bottom left Eighteen figures grouped in threes around columns in the shape of palm tree decorate the atrium of the Chinese House. The figures were made from sandstone and entirely gilded.

170-171 The themes of the groups only partly reflect Chinese life—one group, for example, is eating pineapples, and another is drinking coffee. The group shown is the Melon Eaters by Johann Peter Benckert, created in 1755.

171 top left Chinese tea was imported to Prussia by Dutch traders toward the middle of the 17th century. It remained an aristocratic drink until the start of the 19th century, partly due to its high price. Two of the six groups in the pavilion atrium are dedicated to the drink: one is preparing it and the other, here, is drinking it.

171 top right The ceiling of the Chinese House was painted with a trompe l'oeil effect so typical of the Baroque period. Groups of people in Chinese dress (but with European faces) move behind a balustrade to create the impression of another room above the real one.

171 bottom right The illustration of a Buddha appears several t imes in these scenes. The Buddha in this picture seems to be oblivious to the monkeys next to him, so engrossed is he in observation of the company in the room below, celebrating with the king. The three-dimensional effect is strengthened by monuments and pale backdrops, which create the illusion of a deeper space behind.

172 top left Most of the 200 rooms in the New Palace were used for lodgings, but in the center of the building exist some richly decorated rooms for court celebrations. Originally planned as rooms for guests only, the New Palace was used by succeeding kings as their own residence.

172 bottom left The Grotto Room was divided into three sections by four pilasters. It was decorated, even in the wall niches, with horizontal stripes of white marble alternating with a mixture of natural materials like crystals, metals, minerals, glass and shells. It was designed by Carl von Gontard and was built by a team of local artists and craftsmen.

172 top right The Marble Room was the palace's main room. It was furnished by Gontard in the style of the Marble Room at Potsdam castle. The floor was decorated with lovely inlays and the walls were lined with Slesian marble.

172-173 In constructing the New Palace, Frederick the Great wanted to show the world that after three wars against Slesia, the Prussian kingdom still had the wealth for such a project, which he himself called "a fanfaronnade"—bragging.

173 top The theater occupies two floors in the south wing of the New Palace. It has been renovated several times; its current version dates from 1865, and the original design is unknown. This small court theater, still used today, can only be visited when musical or theatrical performances take place.

white marble and compositions of shells, crystals, minerals, glass and metal. In the second half of the 19th century, gold, fossils, ammonites, precious stones and silicified wood from all over the world were added, so that now the room is decorated with over 20,000 different pieces.

The exquisite furnishing of the New Palace was chosen with the particular aim of astonishing the guests. The wood- or brocade-lined walls, the ceiling frescoes, the valuable pieces of furniture with rich inlays, the more than 250 pictures and objets d'art remained intact for the most part after Frederick's death, and even as late as the second half of the 19th century when the palace was delegated as a house for the royal princes. The New Palace is now a museum, but the theater in the south wing, last renovated in 1865, still hosts concerts and plays. The facade of the palace is the backdrop for a musical festival that ends every year with a performance of Beethoven's Ninth Symphony.

Later generations added a few other buildings. Charlottenhof Palace was built in 1826–29 by Karl Friedrich Schinkel in Neoclassical style for the heir to the throne, Frederick William, but it seems more like an Italian villa than a palace. Twenty years later, when the prince became King Frederick William IV, the longest building on the site, the Italianate, 357-yard-long Serra, was built. The Serra was constructed by the pupils of Schinkel in the style of the Uffizi in Florence or the Villa Medici in Rome. The central section, in Imperial style, housed the apartments for the king and his guests, and a special room for the collection of 47 copies of paintings by Raphael.

The nearby Roman Baths of the same era were used not as baths but as apartments for the court gardener; they are another element of a fictitious, idealized world, indicative of the romantic and nostalgic nature of the age.

173 bottom left Architect Karl Friedrich Schinkel designed Charlottenhof, the Italian-style villa in the heart of Sans Souci park, for Frederick William IV between 1826 and 1829.

173 bottom right The Roman Baths was the name given to a group of buildings built by Ludwig Persius following ancient and Renaissance designs that had nothing to do with bathing.

The Castle of Schönbrunn

LAST GLOW OF A GREAT EMPIRE

Schönbrunn was supposed to have been the Versailles of the Austrian Empire, but the Hapsburgs were very different from the kings of France and would never have wanted to present themselves to to their subjects as living gods. Therefore Schönbrunn was built as both a palace and a summer residence for the numerous families of the rulers.

In the two centuries of its official existence, the palace and its immense park shared the destiny of the Hapsburg dynasty, which—from the matriarch Maria Theresa of Austria to the scrupulous bureaucrat Franz Joseph I—based its life on prudence and thrift. Consequently, the splendors of Schönbrunn are related more to the power and position of the Hapsburg dynasty than to the daily life of its royal inhabitants. Its attraction even today is that it was the setting for the arc of history that led from the enlightened rule of Great Empress Maria Theresa and her son, Joseph II, to unstoppable decline under Franz Joseph I and his consort Sissi.

Custodian of a famous and happy past, Schönbrunn seemed an ideal place even as early as the time of the Austrian Secession, and so, when architect Otto Wagner built the imperial family's private railway station not far from the palace, it was designed as a Baroque temple to celebrate glories of the recent past. Yet the architecture of the rest of the palace does not proclaim the building as a triumphant symbol of a superb and divine monarchy: the central section was indeed used for receptions, but it was squeezed by two private wings, for Maria Theresa and her sons on one side, and Franz Joseph and Sissi on the other.

Construction was started at the end of the 17th century, but the history of Schönbrunn had begun much earlier than that. It is said that Emperor Matthias II, returning from the hunt one day near the country residence of Katterburg, found a spring of crystal clear water that he called "schöner Brunnen" (lovely spring). It had also been chance that led Maximilian II to the spot in 1569. He fell in love with the estate and bought it. Twice the old residence was destroyed, the first time by the Hungarians in 1605, and the second by the Turks in 1683. Once the latter had been chased out of Vienna, Leopold I decided that he would build the Hapsburg summer residence on the site of the pile of rubble. The most renowned Austrian architect of his era, Johann B. Fischer von Erlach, was commissioned to design the palace. (Von Erlach had also designed the church of St. Karl in Vienna.) Von Erlach had spent fifteen years working in Rome and Naples and wished to blend classical architecture with the Baroque style of Bernini, but when the design was placed before the emperor in 1690, the plan for a Hapsburg Versailles was rejected.

Construction based on a second, revised design by von Erlach began in 1696 and was carried forward by Joseph I (1678–1711). While Jean Trehet was designing the park in the French style, the central section and the court were completed. After the death of Joseph I, the work came to a halt, although Empress Amalie Wilhelmine managed to furnish the interiors. The golden age of

174 top right On the side of the roof that faces the park sits the symbol of the power and glory of the Austro-Hungarian monarchy, the two-headed eagle. The two eagles on the pair of obelisks at the entrance to the palace are from a very different source; these were put there by Napoleon during his stay at Schönbrunn.

174 bottom The Neptune fountain, built in 1775 by Anton von Zauner, stands in the center of the park on the main axis in front of the palace. The impressive sculptural group is composed of tritons, mermaids and the dominating statue of Neptune.

174-175 The Ehrenhof, the main courtyard, has two fountains built during the reign of Maria Theresa by Franz Zauner and Johann Hagenauer. The fountain on the right symbolizes the empire's most important rivers—the Danube, the Inn and the Enns—while the fountain on the left represents the reunification of the Transylvanian dominions under the Hapsburg crown.

175 top Emperor Franz Joseph and Empress Elizabeth (Sissi) were married in 1854. In the castle there are still many objects recalling the couple.

175 bottom left In this painting by Fritz L'Allemand (1812-1866) is the scene of a reception in the park of the castle. Schönbrunn was for the sovereigns the ideal stage set for the magnificent receptions and court celebrations like those that took place during the Congress of Vienna.

175 bottom right This painting, in Franz Karl's Study, is a masterpiece by Martin van Meytens depicting Emperor Franz I and Maria Theresa of Austria and their family sometime in 1745-55. As a backdrop the painter chose a nonexistent terrace which opens onto the main courtyard to create a strong scenographic effect.

176 top Contrasting with the geometrical structure of the park are the numerous mythological statues and the fountains. The palace and gardens together cover nearly one square mile.

176-177 Ornamental flowerbeds mark the central axis of the large park at Schönbrunn. Designed in 1705 by Parisian Jean Treher in the French style, the park had to harmonize with the rigid geometry of the palace.

Schönbrunn began with Maria Theresa of Austria (1717–1780) and was only to end with the definitive decline of the Hapsburg empire. The Empress commissioned court architect Nikolaus von Pacassi with the remaining works, which were completed between 1746 and 1749. He concentrated on the interiors, lightening the original Baroque style with many touches of Rococo. The Great and Small Galleries were completed to be used for state receptions and, at Maria Theresa's personal request, a court theater was built as an addition to the original plans. The park too was finally completed and took on the appearance it still has today.

A lot of history has taken place in these rooms but not all perhaps of the sort that one might imagine. Affairs of state, diplomacy and government of the empire as a whole continued at the Hofburg, the imperial palace in the heart of Vienna. What the rooms of Schönbrunn saw was the family life of the rulers, as well as huge festivities and sumptuous banquets.

Maria Theresa raised her 16 children here, spending much of her time directly looking after the smaller ones and in feminine pursuits such as crocheting. Maria Theresa's fifteenth child, Marie Antoinette, future wife of Louis XVI of France, spent her childhood

*176 bottom The sharp
geometry of the palace is clear
in winter. At the height of its
splendor, Schönbrunn hosted*

*1,000 people in its 1,441
rooms (of which 390 were
used for accommodation or
receptions).*

Last Glow of a Great Empire

here. Later, Schönbrunn was used by
Napoleon as his general headquarters
between the battles of Austerlitz (1805) and
Wagram (1809). The Frenchman also became
a member of the family when he married
Marie Louise of Austria in 1809. Once
defeated and exiled to St. Helena, Bonaparte
also lost his only heir, the king of Rome, who
died from tuberculosis after being abandoned
by his mother.

The two defeats of the French forces at
Leipzig (1813) and Waterloo (1815) brought
Vienna to the center of the European stage.
The Hapsburg capital became the seat of the
Congress that had to restore the balance of
power among the large European nations
overrun by Napoleon. Schönbrunn was the
ideal setting for the balls and banquets that

the revolution of 1848 and remain in power
until the eve of the end of the thousand-year
dynasty.

The age of absolute monarchy was
already coming to an end and even the
Schönbrunn of Franz Joseph seemed
increasingly to be a gilded cage. This was
particularly true for Empress Elizabeth,
whose restless personality could not tolerate
being shut up in elegant rooms and hemmed
in by court ceremonial. The only part of this
palace that Sissi (as she was known) really
liked was the park, in which she went for
long walks. The violent deaths that the
Hapsburgs suffered during Franz Joseph's
reign—the execution of Maximilian in Mexico
in 1867, the suicide of the heir Rudolf in 1889,
the assassination of Sissi in 1898, and the

*177 top A massive stone suit of
armor stands out on the terrace
at the top of the Gloriette. The
Gloriette is a symbol of victory but
also a monument to the dead in
the Seven Years' War.*

accompanied the complex diplomatic games.
Supreme political strategist and incomparable
master of ceremonies Chancellor Klemens W.
Lothar Metternich (1773–1859) impressed the
city on the Danube and gave the emperor's
country residence one of its most dazzling
moments. This was the start of the period of
the waltz and the associated image of
gracefulness of life indissolubly linked with
Vienna.

This period was followed by the
Biedermeier era, when Vienna turned *petit
bourgeois* and Schönbrunn too lost some of
its splendor. Then, in 1830, Franz Joseph I
was born in the palace. He was to put down

attack in Sarajevo in 1914—spread a dark
cloud over the palace that had once been a
delight. Franz Joseph I died in 1916 and only
two years later, in the Blue Room at
Schönbrunn, Karl I signed his renunciation of
all affairs of state. The history of the
Hapsburgs had ended, but the legend was
just beginning. It was kept alive by the entire
city of Vienna, which preserved their legacy,
particularly Schönbrunn, with pride and a veil
of nostalgia.

Of the palace's 1,441 rooms, today the
public can visit about 40 on the main floor.
Perhaps the attraction that the rooms retain is
due less to the history which occurred here

*177 bottom One of the most
beautiful views of Vienna is seen
from the elegant Neoclassical
porch of the Gloriette, erected in
1775 by Ferdinand von
Hohenberg. It was on this hill that
architect Johann Fischer von
Erlach had initially planned to
build a palace, but he met
with the outright opposition
of Leopold I.*

178 top The Old Lacquer Room, designed by Isidoro Carnevale in 1770, is a fine example of chinoiserie *and a real masterpiece, lined with long lacquer panels decorated with Japanese scenes, exotic birds and plants engraved in gold.*

178-179 The Walnut Room is named for the wood used to line the walls and to make the furniture. It was used as an audience chamber by Joseph II and later by Franz Joseph. The finely gilded chandelier is of great value.

178 bottom left All the rooms of the palace are still redolent of the atmosphere of the Vienna of Maria Theresa and are furnished in a style that combines the elegance of Rococo with the moderation of Neoclassicism.

178 bottom right Fine portraits by court painter van Meytens are hung on the walls in the large corner room next to the drawing room of Archduke Franz Karl.

179 center The Horse Room was once a playroom for the princes and princesses. It takes its name from the many copper engravings of horses made between 1719 and 1722 by Johann G. Hamilton, and from a large painting showing Joseph I at the hunt, painted in 1752 by Philipp F. Hamilton.

179 bottom The Court Chapel stands beside the Bergl Rooms. It was built at the beginning of the 18th century by Joseph I and slightly altered by Maria Theresa. Paul Trogger's 1744 depiction of the Virgin Mary can be seen on the altar and Daniel Gran's ceiling fresco of the same year shows the apotheosis of Mary Magdalen.

than the memories and private anecdotes that the richly frescoed, lacquered or gilded walls jealously retain. The figure who left the deepest imprint and speaks loudest to the modern visitor is Maria Theresa of Austria. She was without doubt the sovereign who loved Schönbrunn most and who most deeply impressed her taste on the palace, leaving marks visible even before one enters: she was responsible for the ochre color, nicknamed Schönbrunn yellow or Maria Theresa yellow, of the once-pink facade with gray pilasters.

The farsighted empress was also a devoted mother who remained unperturbed when she saw her children and grandchildren running around the Great and Small Galleries, with their white and gilded stucco walls and frescoed ceilings, reserved for official banquets. Nor did she hide her enjoyment of simple feminine pursuits such as crocheting. The 24 medallions that adorn the Breakfast Room are evidence of her favorite pastime. Maria Theresa was an enlightened ruler, and not only in affairs of state. She loved music and theater and the Mirror Room, where newly appointed ministers swore loyalty to the Empress, was regularly transformed to host concerts. It was here that Mozart performed for her at the age of six in 1762, and then, they say, jumped into her arms and kissed her passionately. It was she who ordered the building of the theater that was inaugurated in 1747 with a magnificent banquet; when she was young, she had liked to sing and recite on the stage herself. Gluck, Haydn and Mozart all performed in the Schönbrunn theater and, on occasion, the empress would prompt her fold of children to put on complete homemade performances. She was also happy in her married life, finding that her husband, Francis of Lorraine, also shared her enthusiasm for the palace. Reluctant and reserved in public life, Francis was happy to dedicate himself to Schönbrunn's enormous park and it was he who created the basis for a menagerie. Often the imperial couple would have breakfast in the octagonal pavilion, built in 1752 by Nicolas de Jadot, as they quietly watched the animals. Francis's interest in the natural sciences induced him to finance expeditions to bring back rare species of plants to his botanical garden. These and the other sights in the park were made available to all when the couple's son, Joseph II, opened the park to the public in 1779. In 1882, Franz Joseph built the Palmenhaus, a conservatory, taking Kew Gardens in London as his model.

The building and surrounding park formed a harmonious whole. The park is an intriguing mix of Baroque and early Romantic styles based on the contemporary French rules of garden design: on the one hand, there was the search for an ideal design and formal perfection to make the garden the explicit manifestation of man's control over nature; on the other hand, there were also elements such as false grottoes, artificial ruins and mazes that turn the garden into a place of illusion and artifice.

179 top Unpretentious like all his rooms, Emperor Franz Joseph's study had white walls covered with brown fabrics. The portrait by Franz Russ of his 23-year-old consort, Princess Elizabeth, hangs on the wall. Franz Joseph spent 18 hours a day in this room dealing with the administration of the empire.

Last Glow of a Great Empire

180 top, 181 top left The Million Room takes its name from the huge sums spent on the rosewood panels with miniatures showing scenes from the life of the Mogul rulers in India, and from the finely made and gilded Rococo frames.

180 center In the magnificent Gobelin Salon, in the east wing, 18th-century tapestries depict busy harbors and markets. On the chairs are scenes from each of the 12 months of the year.

Whereas the focal point of the palace is the group of reception rooms, that of the garden is the geometrically perfect set of ornamental flowerbeds. Their very geometry seems to attract the gaze toward the highest point where the Neoclassical portico, the Gloriette, is outlined against the sky. The Gloriette was built in 1775 and gives a superb view over Vienna.

Continuing the similarities between the designs of the interiors and the park, just as the eye is distracted from the rigid geometry of the Baroque, tree-lined avenues in favor of the dozens of mythological statues and the edges of the distant wood, so inside the palace the eye is attracted by details and the mind tends to dwell on the names of rooms

rather than observing the official portraits of the Hapsburgs or the sumptuous furnishings. It happens, for instance, in the Million Room: the name is a joke, perhaps one of the few by Maria Theresa. The room took its name from its cost, high in 1765, of one million gulden, which was mainly represented by the valuable rosewood floor, for which materials had been imported from the Antilles, and the 60 decorative medallions that frame beautiful miniatures which Maria Theresa had ordered directly from Constantinople. Then there is the Napoleon Room, which had in reality been the bedroom of the empress before the death of her beloved consort. It must certainly have pleased Napoleon with its magnificent 18th-century Belgian tapestries that depict scenes from military life. The French ruler left another mark on Schönbrunn: the two eagles that dominate the obelisks of the entrance. In addition he left reminders of his son, who died in the palace and to whom a room was dedicated. The funerary mask of the son, known as l'Aiglon (the eaglet), lies next to his portrait and the stuffed skylark that the unhappy King of Rome considered his only friend.

Although Maria Theresa spent much of her time at Schönbrunn, she did not neglect affairs of state and often retired to one of the two circular Chinese studies which served as her private office. Her favorite study is decorated with lacquered panels and delicate porcelain and has a secret stairway connecting with the overhead apartments of her Chancellor and advisor, Wenzel A. Kaunitz (1711–1794). She certainly did not spend as many as the 18 hours a day that Franz Joseph spent working in his study, in the right wing of the palace where his and Sissi's apartments were located. But that was not the only difference in character or lifestyles between the two rulers: compared to her satins, her tapestries in the Gobelin Room, her Chinese lacquers in the Old Lacqeur Room, and her pieces of porcelain and crystal in the reception rooms and other apartments, the soberness of the rooms lived in by the penultimate Hapsburg leader almost seems like self-inflicted punishment. And while the study of Empress Maria Theresa, the famous Porcelain Room, was decorated with 213 pieces of china made by her husband together with their children, Franz Joseph's study was bare, functional and modest. There were few pieces of furniture

180 bottom Napoleon's famous room in the left wing of the palace faces onto the park and gives a splendid view of the Gloriette. It was originally Maria Theresa's bedroom. Note the 18th-century wallhangings from Brussels showing scenes from military life.

180

181 top right The Blue Room is also known as the Chinese Room, as the walls are covered with rice paper and the room furnished with small lacquered Oriental sideboards. In this room Karl I signed his renunciation of all affairs of state.

180-181 The Great Gallery, on the main floor of the central wing, is 140 feet long. Official receptions are still held here and, just as at the time of the Congress of Vienna, guests are still dazzled by the crystal chandeliers that reflect light on the walls and the ceiling frescoes painted by Gregorio Guglielmi.

181 bottom The Mirror Room is at the end of the right wing of the palace. Here Maria Theresa received newly appointed ministers for their swearing-in ceremony. It was in this room, with its superb mirrors, that the young Mozart performed in 1762. It is said that at the end of his performance he jumped onto Maria Theresa's lap and kissed her.

and the dominant color was brown, as it was in the bedroom, where the emperor's famous camp bed can still be seen. As protocol demanded, both Franz Joseph and Sissi were given five rooms each, but after rearrangements made by Archduchess Sophia, the mother of the Emperor, on the occasion of his wedding, almost nothing was changed again. What redecorations the couple did make were always discreet; for example, the bedroom of Empress Elizabeth is lined in pale gray against which the red brocade of the furniture stands out. But this was not simply a question of taste. The choices and rigor that dominated the life of Franz Joseph were dictated by a punctilious sense of duty deriving from his position, and the almost obsessive desire to promote the image of a good father who did not live better than his subjects/children. Sissi's motives however were very different: she fled Schönbrunn and everything that the palace represented for her—a hated mother-in-law and a ceremonial court life. She preferred to stay in the Laxenburg Palace or

182 top and 182 center The name of the Porcelain Room comes from the white and blue ornaments of flowers and birds made of wood in imitation of porcelain. There are also 213 ink drawings by Francis of Lorraine and his daughters based on paintings by Boucher and Pillemont. Four bas-relief medallions with portraits of Franz Joseph I, the Archduchesses Elizabeth and Christina and Duke Albert of Sachsen-Teschen decorate the walls. The porcelain clock was manufactured in Meissen.

Hermesvilla that the emperor built for her in 1884 in the former hunting lodge of Lainz. Even more she loved to travel and to spend time in the Villa Achilleion on the island of Corfu to which she transferred the beautiful Louis XIV secrétaire that had belonged to Marie Antoinette and which until then had remained in the Children's Room. That room in particular, decorated with tapestry portraits of Maria Theresa's children, strikes the visitor with its the absence of the portraits of Sissi, Sophia, Gisella, Rudolf and Maria Valeria. This is another proof of how much the unhappy empress hated Schönbrunn.

The era of the Hapsburgs was, however, coming to an end, and the shine that Schönbrunn had once given off was now reduced to a weak glow while Franz Joseph left his mark in the center of Vienna with the Ring. As the city of Vienna experienced its "merry apocalypse" the great imperial carriage, completely lined with gold and decorated by the school of Rubens, which had been used for the coronation of Karl VI in 1711 and three other sovereigns since, now

prepared for its last journey: the coronation of Karl I in 1916. His reign, though, lasted no more than the blink of an eye before the lights went out for ever on this dynasty. Today the imperial carriage can be seen in the Wagenburg at Schönbrunn, one of the witnesses to an era that many call *Austria Felix*.

182 bottom Two Chinese Studies open onto the Small Gallery: one is oval, the other round; the round one was Maria Theresa's secret study. The studies are named for the precious lacquer panels that line the walls and for the Oriental porcelain ornaments.

182-183 and 183 right The Bergl Rooms on the ground floor of the palace were decorated by Johann Bergl between 1769 and 1777 for Maria Theresa of Austria. The gold-covered ceramic stove depicting a tree and

birds is a masterpiece. The paintings on the walls of the Bergl Rooms show the Hapsburgs' love of nature. They were executed to be a continuation of the park but with much more tropical vegetation.

The Castle of Esterháza

A THEATER FOR A PALACE

184 top This image shows a detail of the decoration on the façade of the castle of Esterháza.

184 center The right wing of the Esterháza palace slopes down into a low, covered colonnade that reaches as far as the main entrance. Similarly, the left wing reaches the same entrance in another covered colonnade, creating the U shape that embraces the court. Pilasters intersect the fan-shaped steps and support putti and gaslights. The wrought-iron fence is in the same style as the entrance gate.

The small village of Fertőd lies near the lake of the same name in the province of Győr-Sopron in the most western part of the Transdanube. The tiny village, with fewer than 3,000 inhabitants, is the site of an architectural jewel known to art scholars around the world and visited by numerous tourists: it is the castle of the Esterházy family. The village was long called Esterháza after the family, but its name was changed to Fertőd in 1950, shortly after the Communist regime came to power, as the regime wished to prevent further homage to a family considered to be "an enemy of the people."

The castle was built in three years (1763–66) by Prince Miklós (Nicola) Esterházy, nicknamed the Magnificent or the Grand. The man had unlimited aspirations, as was revealed by his motto, "What the Emperor can do, so can I." When Empress Maria Theresa of Austria visited his residence in 1773 and expressed her particular admiration for the recently built Chinese Pavilion, Prince Miklós replied that it was nothing but a "bagatelle," and the building retained the name.

The Magyar aristocrats were numerous, equal to the Polish and Spanish nobility, but at their head several families stood out, families whose ascendancy was largely due to services rendered to the Hapsburgs. Thanks to political marriages, the Hapsburgs had become masters of the northern part of the kingdom of Hungary from the first half of the 16th century, following the death of King Louis II at the Battle of Mohács (1526), just when a large slice of the land belonging to the monarchy had fallen into the hands of the Ottoman Turks.

After pushing back the vigorous Ottoman advance which culminated in the siege of Vienna (1683), toward the end of the 17th century the Hapsburgs took possession of vast regions belonging to the Crown of St. Stephen. The Magyar nobles who had followed them and served during the struggle against the Turks also benefited from the imperial victories, partly fought against rebel Magyar nobles (particularly in Transylvania) led by Ferenc Rakóczi II. After that, the aristocracy began to be absorbed into the Viennese court (the founder of Esterháza had had a German upbringing) and much of the wealth of the nobles was spent on conforming to the level of that court rather than on the creation of a national army worthy of respect (as emphasized by the Frenchman, Riesbeck). At the same time, the French cultural model spread to all the territories under the control of the Hapsburgs, influencing the construction of imperial and princely residences.

In 16th and 17th centuries the Esterházy family, in particular the earlier Miklós and his son Pál, rapidly ascended to the leading rank of the aristocracy thanks to their conversion to Catholicism during the full force of the Counter-Reformation, and due also to a prudent marriage policy that allowed them to acquire the properties of such important people as the Dersfy, Nyáry and Thökoly families. Pál

184 bottom left The south façade toward the park is similar to the main one, though designed by Melchior Hefele. The central, protruding section features pilasters that frame 11 windows and are topped by a balustrade and lookout.

184 bottom right On the second floor of the palace's south face, a wrought-iron balcony in Rococo style rests on four Tuscan columns.

184-185 In the middle of the palace front (by the Austrian architect Johann Ferdinand Modlhammer), a double fan-shaped stairway leads to the balcony supported on paired columns. The pediment is decorated with statues and trophies, as is the balustrade.

185 top left On the death of Miklós III in 1833, Prince Pál (shown here with his family) inherited the enormous estate and residences of the Esterházy family. A diplomat and for a short period the Minister of Foreign Affairs in 1818, he was the last of the family to maintain the properties intact. His son Miklós IV sold 643 paintings (including works by Raphael and Rembrandt), 3,500 engravings and 51,000 prints to the Hungarian National Gallery.

managed to acquire 25 castles and palaces and 1.5 million acres. In 1662, possession of Munkács was ceded on the order of the Emperor to the *voivode* of Transylvania, Gábor Bethlen, and in exchange the Esterházy received the safer Kismarton (Eisenstadt) and Franknò properties near the Austrian border.

Three years later, Miklós was made *nador* or palatine of Hungary, a sort of imperial viceroy. Pál received the same title and was also invested as a Prince of the Empire, a title that became hereditary after 1712. The castle of Kismarton was built on Pál's command by the Italian architect Carlone; Pál was also a poet, composer and actor who loved the theatrical events at Sopron and Nagyszombat. In his residence at

Kismarton, he built a stage (in the room now called the Haydin Saal) where plays were put on at Christmas and Easter. These were the first of the theatrical events for which the Esterházy family later became famous; also memorable were the festivities that took place in the artistic castle and the distinguished guests who enriched it with their work. The most famous example was the great composer Joseph Haydn, who lived there from 1768 until 1790, during which time he composed around 700 pieces. After being invited in 1761 by Pál Antál Esterházy, Haydn spent some years at Kismarton, then moved to the other family residence, Esterháza, to live with the palatine and Prince Miklós the Great in what is today

185 top right Miklós Esterházy appears in this painting by József Dorfmeister. The work dates to the end of the 18th century and is kept today at the Museum of Fine Arts in Budapest.

185 bottom The Hungarian Rococo gate, made of wrought iron by K. J. Franke, is the main entrance from the north to the Esterházy house. This is the meeting point of the two colonnades that curve around to the wings of the palace. The gate leads into the main court which boasts several fountains.

186-187 A large painting, Apollo on the Chariot of the Sun, covers the ceiling of the Banquet Room or Salon d'Honneur. Although the room is on the main floor, it is high enough to include the second floor. Like many other frescoes in the palace, this one was painted by the artist Josef Ignatz Milldorfer.

186 bottom Statues representing the seasons stand in the four corners of the Banquet Room, among them Summer (left) and Autumn (right).

forward than the central section and ending against the railing in front of the residence. The railing was made from wrought iron by K. J. Franke and is considered a masterpiece of Hungarian Rococo style.

Fountains play in the main courtyard in front of the central section of the building decorated with a pediment, statues and trophies. As at Schönbrunn, a fan-shaped double stairway leads to the upper floor. Inside is a great variety of styles produced by different Italian craftsmen such as Cantini, Pietro Travaglia and Alessio and Girolamo Bon, who did not skimp on stuccoes and frescoes. The Sala Terrena is the most celebrated room: pillars divide it into three parts and it is decorated with green and gold stuccoes and frescoes probably by Josef Ignaz Milldorfer. Milldorfer also painted the outstanding oval chapel. The ceramic stoves that once heated the various rooms are now collected in one room.

The loveliest room is, however, the two-story Salon d'Honneur on the upper floor. Here are frescoes by Johann Basilius Grundemann,

17th-century Flemish tapestries; and statues of the four seasons in the four corners. Next to the prince's apartments is still a music room; and the castle now has a permanent display of objects related to Haydn and the works he composed there.

As in the Hapsburg palace of Schönbrunn, there is no shortage of rooms decorated and furnished in Oriental style and called Chinese rooms. Outside the railings is the Muzsikaház and the house of the Grenadiers, the Granátosház. Time and war have done away with not only the Chinese Pavilion and the temples but also the Hermitage, the staff quarters, the stalls and the opera theater.

The history of the Esterházy residences is linked with the theatrical events that took place there. No less than the productions of schools or city theaters, these activities signaled the beginning of the Hungarian theater—although not in the national language. The Esterházy court theater came into being in the second half of the 18th century but did not survive into the next

A Theater for a Palace

the Music House (Muzsikaház) just outside the perimeter of the residence. Popular Hungarian dances influenced Haydn's compositions, giving them rhythm and liveliness. After the death of Prince Miklós in 1790 the residence lost some of its attraction and members of the Esterházy family preferred other houses, but time did not bring an end to that partial decadence. Only World War II inflicted heavy blows upon the castle: the rooms were stripped of their rich furnishings and temples dedicated to Diana, Venus, Fortune and the Sun were destroyed, as well as the Chinese Pavilion in the surrounding park. Restoration work begun in 1959 has only partly been able to restore the castle to its previous condition. The 741-acre park behind the palace is once again crossed by wide avenues laid out in geometrical shapes like a French garden. The park contained "the limitless green woods" that Ernst Hoffman could distinguish in Haydn's symphonies, in which "a gay multicolored swarm of happy men" moves.

To return to the origins: in 1720 Anton Erhard Martinelli built a small hunting lodge; the Hungarian Miklós Jacoby used this as the nucleus of the Esterházy residence that he began building in 1763. The building was carried out by the Austrian architects Johann Ferdinand Modhammer and Melchior Hefele. Creation of a large artificial waterfall in 1784 signaled the end of construction of the entire complex, which cost 13 million florins. The style of the palace and its 126 rooms is Baroque, tending to Rococo. The ground plan forms a rounded U with wings placed slightly further

187 top left The parlor decorated with Rococo paneling was formerly the bedroom of Prince Miklós the Magnificent.

187 bottom left Several salons among the 126 rooms in the palace are decorated with Chinese or Japanese wall paintings, furnishings and knick-knacks.

187 top right The great Austrian musician Joseph Haydn (Rohrau 1732-Vienna 1809) became closely tied to the Esterházy family in 1761 at the request first of Prince Pál and, a year later, Prince Miklós. When Prince Miklós died, Haydn moved to Vienna with a pension and became the friend of Mozart. He produced his best operatic works, based on the librettos of Goldoni,

while with the Esterházy family. His musical genius shines brightest in quartets, symphonies and sonatas.

187 bottom right The Music Room, like the Banquet Room, is on the main floor. It too reaches the second floor and was painted by Grundemann. The two rooms occupy the central section of the building.

century. The first theatrical events that took place at Kismarton date back to 1749 and were linked to the Italian Gian Maria Quaglio. The first opera was performed in 1755 and the first production at Esterháza was *Lo speziale* by Haydn (1768).

The following year, all the musicians, actors and workers were transferred from Kismarton to Esterháza castle. The first company engaged was that of Joseph Hellmann and Friedrich Koberwein in 1769, followed a year later by the company of Franz Passer. In both the prima donna was Katharina Rösslin. The passage from comic to serious works is linked to Passer. The "summer" season lasted from the end of Lent to October with performances as often as every day. A year-round season began in 1778, with three alternating companies. The investment required was enormous, which justified the fame of Prince Miklós and his residence. The

orchestra and actors sometimes performed elsewhere, for example at Schönbrunn for Empress Maria Theresa. The main productions offered—as everywhere at the time—were Italian, by writers such as Cimarosa, Piccini, Paisiello, Salieri and many others. Fundamental contributions over the years were made by stage designer Pietro Travaglia and choreographer Luigi Rossi. The first arrived to illuminate the palace and the gardens with more than 4,000 lamps on special occasions or for receptions. The Prince's Grenadiers were probably included in performances, either on the stage or elsewhere, for combat scenes requiring lots of shooting and marches.

Special guests would be shown folk dances performed by farmers jumping out from behind trees as the guests were driven around the park in a carriage. The *dolce vita* of the

Esterházy family was celebrated by the poet Geörgy Bessenyei. During the period of Esterházy castle's greatest splendor, 1769–1790, one of the most dramatic events was without doubt the fire of 18 November 1779 that spread from the Chinese dance hall to the theater, destroying the latter completely. The prince wanted performances to restart a few days later in the more modest puppet theater (which was according to some inspired by the Cave of Thetis at Versailles) and in just a short time, a new theater was built and inaugurated in October 1780 with the tragedy *Julius von Tarent*. The new building was designed by architects Stöger and Haunold and constructed in ten months by Paul Guba. The company in residence at Esterháza at the time was that of Franz Josef Diwald, which constituted an important link between the Esterházy family and the Hungarian theater in the German language, as it later performed throughout

various cities in Hungary and Transylvania. A couple of amusing stories are connected to this company; one was the flight of Johann Schilling who, taking his romantic role as "the lover" too seriously, attempted to run away with the prima donna, Diwald's wife, and ended up spending several weeks in prison. In the same period, the Italian actor Benedetto Bianchi played a joke on prima donna Katharina Poschwa: while laid out on the stage during a performance, on a couple of occasions he lifted the actress's dress with his stick. Following the protests of the lady and her husband, the prince decided that the offender should receive a good beating, be shut up for a few days and make his public apology from the stage at the next performance.

Two other important companies played at Esterháza after 1785, that of Johann Mayer (which boasted a corps de ballet of eight people) and that of Johann Lasser. In 1780 even a company of children was engaged.

Prince Miklós died on 18 September 1790 and his successor, Antál, a man with little feeling for the arts and a major interest in military campaigns, brought to a close the theatrical season, which had lasted since 1768. During that period, many operas had been performed—over a hundred during the last decade alone—many of them world premieres.

Actors and musicians were dismissed by Antál, except for Haydn and the military band. A few years later, Prince Miklós II abandoned the enormous complex of Esterháza and returned to live at Kismarton, to which he transferred much of the theatrical furnishings and paraphernalia to start up artistic events again. At the start of the 19th century, many rooms at Esterháza were in ruin. All artistic and theatrical events came to a stop in 1813, even at Kismarton where Cherubini had replaced Haydn and where Mozart's *Magic Flute* had been triumphantly received.

The amazing contribution of the Esterházy family to Magyar and European culture became a part of history. In 1860, Hungary purchased the family's collection of paintings to create the Museum of Beaux-Arts; but not until the late 20th century was the Versailles of Hungary restored as a cultural attraction.

188-189 The largest room at Esterháza is the Sala Terrena, on the ground floor. It lies below the Music and Banquet Rooms and is divided into three sections by pilasters. Green and gold plasterwork embellishes every wall and the marble floor is still the original one. Frescoes by Josef Ignaz Milldorfer decorate the ceilings.

188 bottom left This fresco by Milldorfer in the Sala Terrena shows a monogram E (for Esterházy).

189 left The so called Tobacco-colored Salon on the first floor takes its name from the dominant color of the wall covering that matches the soft shade of the wood floor. On the table that appears at left can be to seen one of the precious clocks belonging to Esterháza collection; this one, in gilded bronze, dates to the 18th century.

189 top right This figure is a detail of a fire-enamel decoration on a piece of furniture in the Tobacco-colored Salon.

189 center right Prince Miklós was very proud of his library, which contained over 22,000 volumes.

189 bottom right The Chinese Rooms of Esterháza have wall decoration and furniture echoing the exotic taste that was so common in Europe at that time.

A Theater for a Palace

190 top The cathedral of St. Vitus, St. Wenceslas and St. Adalbert is seen here from the garden on the terrace of the riding track in the castle gardens. The garden was created during the 1950s on the roof of the garage of the Czech President's office. The garden contains elements found in other historical gardens of the castle.

190-191 The castle area is dominated by the Gothic cathedral and crowned by a Baroque dome from the end of the 18th century. The oldest Gothic bridge in Prague, the Charles Bridge, can be seen in the foreground decorated with Baroque sculptures.

190 bottom left The Royal Gazebo is situated in the royal garden. The building is one of the loveliest examples of Italian Renaissance architecture north of the Alps.

The Castle of Prague

THE PANTHEON OF CZECH HISTORY

The imposing and dominant symbol of the city of Prague is its castle. It was the palace of Bohemian princes, kings and emperors for centuries, and more recently served as the residence of the President of Czechoslovakia first and then that of the Czech Republic.

The castle has played a prominent role in the history of the city and the entire country. Decisions affecting European events have often been taken within its walls. In the rooms where visitors today admire the furnishings and architecture, great figures of history have lived: from the Holy Roman Emperor Charles IV and Rudolf II to their contemporary democratic successors.

The origin of Prague castle dates from the second half of the 9th century when the Premyslid family—first princes, then the founders of the royal dynasty—moved to a rocky hill above the river Moldava. As the importance and power of the Czech state grew, so did that of Prague castle. It was already a massive fort with a perfect defensive system in the 11th century. It also contained churches, a bishop's palace and two monasteries. Under Emperor Charles IV in the 14th century the castle enjoyed its period of maximum development. The French architect Mathieu d'Arras and the German builder Peter Parlér launched a large reconstruction project in a mature Gothic style for the demanding emperor. The golden reflection of some of the castle roofs dates from that period, built as they were to symbolize the wealth, power and fame of the Czech kingdom.

A Renaissance renovation took place after a disastrous fire in 1541. Emperor Rudolf II, in power at the turn of the 16th century, turned the castle into a center for science and art as well as a gallery for his famous collections. Some of the most famous contributors to the richness of the castle were the artists Paolo della Stella, Hans Tirol, Bonifacio Wolmur, Oldrich Avolstalis and Giovanni Maria Filippi; the painters Hans von Aachen and Bartolomeo Spranger; the sculptor Adrian de Vries; the astronomer Tycho de Brahe; and the mathematician/astronomer Johannes Kepler. During Rudolf's reign, the garden became an important laboratory for nursery gardening and botany. It was instrumental in acclimatizing various tropical plants to European weather conditions.

Things changed after Rudolf's death. The putting down of the insurrection of the States in 1620 and the Thirty Years' War that followed were responsible for the Hapsburgs (who were at the time rulers of Bohemia) moving their capital to Vienna, with the result that the castle was downgraded to a family residence. It only regained its former luster in the second half of the 18th century when the buildings of the castle were rebuilt by Nicolò Piccasi, the court architect of Empress Maria Theresa, and took on their current appearance.

The most recent rebuilding works were undertaken after 1918 when the complex once again became the symbol of an independent state and the official seat of the President of the Republic. Much of this 20th-century work was linked with the name of Slovenian architect Josip Plecnik.

Currently the Office of the President of the Republic, which is situated in a part of the castle, coordinates a broad program of restoration work which has more than the simple aim of conserving the castle's artistic and historical heritage: its goal is to transform the whole into a busy complex that is always open to visitors. The restored palaces are used today as display spaces for continuously changing exhibitions and the magnificent ecclesiastical buildings are the settings for

191 center The sunny south side of the cathedral of St. Vitus, St. Wenceslas and St. Adalbert. The castle's main tower was partially built by the cathedral's second architect, Peter Parlér, in the 14th century and was completed at the end of the 15th century.

191 top left This detail of the ceiling fresco in the Bohemian Registry Office in the Old Royal Palace shows the emblem of the Czech monarchy, a rampant lion.

190 bottom right A military band plays in the first courtyard of Prague Castle. The castle's garrison band plays whenever heads of state visit.

191 bottom right The Great Ballgame Room game faces onto the royal garden and is one of the loveliest Renaissance buildings in the castle. Allegorical figures of the forces of nature and human characters can be seen next to Oriental motifs on the richly decorated facade in the north section of the building.

PRAGUE

Czech Republic

192 top left The royal mausoleum occupies part of the cathedral's main nave. The upper slab contains effigies of Bohemian kings.

192 center left A Baroque bas-relief in oak showing Prague and the castle. It is in the choir passage in the cathedral. A bronze statue of Cardinal Schwarzenburg from the 19th century can be seen in the background.

192 bottom left The lower part of the walls of St. Wenceslas chapel is covered with more than 1,300 precious stones; the frescoes showing moments from the saint's life are from the early 16th century.

192 top right The insignia of the Bohemian crown are part of the country's most important cultural treasures. The crown was made for the coronation of

Charles IV in 1346. The Crown Jewels are kept in the treasure rooms inside the cathedral.

193 The cathedral's main nave is over 100 feet high. The cap vault over the unusually high choir was designed by Peter Parlér. The colored windows at the end of the choir were added shortly after World War II and tell the story of the construction of the cathedral.

The Pantheon of Czech History

The Castle of Prague

ancient and contemporary music concerts.

For more than 600 years, the roofs of the castle have been overlooked by the towers of the Gothic Cathedral of St. Vitus, St. Wenceslas and St. Adalbert. The cathedral, seat of the Prague archbishopric, was where the coronations of the kings of Bohemia took place until the year 1836. Beneath its high cross-vaults, saints, kings, princes and emperors of Bohemia have been buried. The spiritual center of the cathedral is the St. Wenceslas Chapel built by Peter Parlér directly above the saint's tomb. Its decorations glitter with gold, precious stones and paintings that are an interesting expression of the medieval devotion this saint and national patron received. Charles IV also left the insignia of the crown of Bohemia under the symbolic protection of St. Wenceslas. The most valuable part of the treasure, the crown of St. Wenceslas, was commissioned by Charles IV as a symbol of the hereditariness and holiness of the state's highest office; it is only exhibited on very special occasions. The original versions of the royal insignia have only been put on show nine times since 1900.

The cathedral's ingenious supporting system of columns, the bizarre faces of the gargoyles, the majestic portraits of the royal family, important prelates and constructors sculpted from stone, and the solemn sarcophagus lids bearing effigies of the princes and kings of the Premyslid dynasty are evidence of the high artistic level achieved in Parlér's workshops. From the Middle Ages until the beginning of the 20th century generations of architects, artists and craftsmen, whose names have now been forgotten, passed though the cathedral workshops. From an architectural point of view, the Cathedral of St. Vitus, St. Wenceslas and St. Adalbert is one of the true peaks of Czech art.

The nucleus of the castle has always been the famous royal palace. This is where the princes and kings of Bohemia ruled until the end of the 16th century and where, later, the

highest levels of Czech and imperial government and judiciary were based. It is no surprise that major episodes of Czech history have taken place within its walls. The rooms of the Bohemian Chancellery, for example, saw the Second Defenestration of Prague by the Czech Protestants, the first signal of the anti-Hapsburg uprising and Thirty Years' War. The attention of visitors to the Old Palace is especially directed toward the Vladislav Room which is an example of the highest quality late-Gothic architectural style in all of medieval Prague. For the first time in Bohemia, the features of mature Gothic are infused with the seeds of Renaissance forms. The aesthetic effect and the technical precision of the vaulting ribs are an example of the virtuosity of its builder, Benedict Rejta. The late-Gothic monumental beauty of the interior of the Vladislav Room is still the setting for state ceremonies like the investiture of the President of the Republic which has been celebrated here since 1934.

Government celebrations at Prague Castle mostly take place in the south wing. The furnishing of the individual rooms, where the head of state receives his guests and where official dinners are held in their honor, meets the requirements dictated by the protocol of the Office of the President of the Republic (reproduction furniture, beautiful carpets, paintings and magnificent wallhangings). This is why areas not normally open to the public can only be entered two or three times a year on what are known as Open Door Days.

The oldest heart of the castle is the Third Square, beneath which important archaeological finds have been unearthed. During rebuilding of the square in the 1920s, the walls of many old buildings were found, which prompted a systematic investigation. The excavation was unique in its size and difficulty; it uncovered so many important finds concerning the history of Prague Castle that the decision was taken to keep the excavations open and partially accessible to

194 top *The interior of the Bohemian Registry which served as an office for the state administrators. The Bohemian Registries were books that contained records of the sentences handed down by the state courts since the 13th century. The walls and ceiling are decorated with the coats of arms of the administrators.*

194 bottom *The Spanish Room was built by Rudolf II at the beginning of the 17th century to house sculptures from his collections. The ceiling plasterwork was carried out by Italian masters. The last important renovation to the room took place in the 19th century.*

the public. The area in question has since been walled and lined by cement covered with granite tiles. Today, this archaeological area is probably the most extensive in central Europe.

Not far away stands the oldest church in the complex, the Basilica of St. George. This is one of the few Roman churches that keeps the remains of the previous stone building inside. Since it was built, the basilica has contained the relics of the Premyslid princes and members of their family in addition to those of the first saint and national patron, St. Ludmilla.

The Benedictine convent founded in the Basilica of St. George at the end of the 10th century has also played an important role in the country. This is where the female members of the Czech royal line were raised and educated. More than one became an abbess with the right to crown the kings of Bohemia. Many books of high artistic and literary value were written in the famous Scriptorium of the convent during the Middle Ages. In the rooms of the ex-convent, culture still reigns: its silent corridors and large rooms

are the home of the National Gallery dedicated to Gothic and Baroque Czech art.

The Alley of Gold is a tiny world all to itself between the magnificent and enormous palaces. It is a row of small houses literally glued to the walls of the castle. It was here that the castle's fusiliers lived and, later, the goldsmiths from whom the alleyway took its name. The poor lives of the inhabitants of the Alley of Gold must have contrasted dramatically with those who lived in the luxury and pomp of the nearby imperial court. For four centuries, each little house has witnessed a daily existence filled with effort and privation, though just as interesting as those of the courtiers. More recently, these houses were taken over by Czech writers and poets looking for, and frequently finding, inspiration for their literary creations. The most famous is number 22, where Franz Kafka spent a year of his life. Today the Alley of

Gold has been transformed into a kingdom of crafts and souvenir shops.

The splendid gardens frame the whole of the castle. Beautiful trees, lawns and a huge variety of flowers vie with the elegance of the castle buildings. The union of art and nature, beauty and quiet, creates an atmosphere of intense peace. One of the loveliest corners is the small garden with a Singing Fountain in the middle of the Royal Garden. The gushing melody of the jets of water is literally in harmony with the fragile beauty of the Royal Gazebo. This building is one of the most elegant and stylistically pure examples of northern Italian Renaissance architecture north of the Alps.

The Royal Garden was created in the first half of the 16th century as an Italian garden (one of the first in Prague), but over time many exotic plants like cedars and fig trees were added to the decorative vegetation. The cultivation of tulips caused a sensation when the ambassador of the Sultan of Turkey brought bulbs to Prague in 1554. The Royal Garden was where red, white and yellow tulips first bloomed in Europe before spreading across all the continent, in particular to Holland.

194-195 *The Rudolf Gallery in the castle's north wing was built by Emperor Rudolf II at the end of the 16th century. Famous paintings from the emperor's collections were hung here. The rich bas-reliefs date from the second half of the 19th century.*

195 top The Hapsburg Room is also in the south wing of the castle. The walls were decorated with portraits of the numerous members of Maria Theresa's family. The room is often used during official visits of heads of state.

195 bottom left This is the late-Gothic Vladislav Room in the Royal Palace. It was originally used as the king's reception room; the election of the President of the Republic has been held here since 1934.

195 bottom right The Brozik Room is in the south wing of the castle. The wall paintings are by the 19th-century Czech painter Vaclav Brozik, who took his inspiration from the embassy of the Bohemian king Ladislas to the French court in 1457.

The Palace of Wilanów

THE PROUD SYMBOL OF POLAND

196 top left This detail, taken from a fireguard, depicts the Polish royal eagle, which wears a crown and grasps a sword and a scepter in its claws.

196 bottom left This portal framed by two Corinthian columns opens onto the left gallery. A bas-relief shows the triumph of King John III (Jan Sobieski), and the two statues represent Fame and Strength.

WARSAW

*I*f the battle of Lepanto in 1571 signaled the last great Venetian victory and the first success of the Christian armies in stemming the thrust of the Ottoman empire (which had until then been considered invincible), then the siege of Vienna in 1683 was the last desperate Ottoman attempt to break through the encirclement and expand its borders westward. Christian Europe was reliving a nightmare that had pursued it for three centuries: the flag with the crescent moon which had fluttered since 1453 over Constantinople (the previous capital of the eastern Roman empire) was about to be raised over Vienna, capital of the west and of the Holy Roman empire. The Polish armies led by King John III (Jan Sobieski) broke the siege and crushed the infidels. After 1683, the Ottoman empire began a slow decline, due to economic crises and the progressive stripping away of its territories; it was definitively dismembered in 1918. The joy and sense of liberation felt throughout Europe in 1683 were inversely proportional to the earlier anguish; and all over the Christian world the deeds of the king of

196 top right Jan Sobieski, seen here in a painting dating to the end of the 17th century, had a major role in the development of the palace of Wilanów.

196-197 The central section facing onto the main court is the most authentic part of the palace. It is a rectangular structure flanked by two pavilions that extend forward and are decorated with little towers on the top.

197 top The celebratory aspect of the palace is emphasized by the plasterwork and bas-reliefs that adorn the facade, like this triumphant pair over the central door.

197 bottom A battle scene is represented on the balustrade over one of the portals in the left-hand wing. The portal is framed by two pairs of Corinthian columns.

Poland were celebrated. As adulation was bestowed upon him. Sobieski, the savior of Christianity, decided to celebrate his triumph in his own country in the manner of the great Christian monarchs.

Poland's political and ideological model was republican Rome, whereas for Russia it was imperial Rome; but to imitate Rome properly meant that the ruler's residence, whether in Poland or Russia, had to be at least equal to its model. Just as strongly as Peter the Great after he took Narva and blocked Swedish expansion toward the east, Jan Sobieski, immediately having halted the Ottoman advance toward the west, felt the need for an architectural setting which would be worthy of his glory and act as a warning—through its extreme refinement and elegance—to old and possible new rivals. Consequently, both Wilanów in Poland and the Winter Palace in Russia were intended from conception to house art collections that were to grow constantly over time, and to be the shrine of the country's memory (despite the numerous political turnarounds that have taken place in both countries over the last three centuries). Curiously, both houses were of modest dimensions, though in the case of Wilanów it

*198 top and 198 center
Numerous decorations embellish
the facade on the east side of the
central body fronted by a massive
balustrade. One of the most
elegant and liveliest is a bas-relief
that represents four putti holding
up a drape displaying a mosaic
Sybil (below)*

was partly because the king had to fund the
building at a moment when military
requirements absorbed all the country's
resources and his own. Nonetheless, they were
soon transformed by their creators and were
added to, modified and remodeled by their
those men's successors. But there are at least
two differences between Wilanów and the
Winter Palace: Wilanów is a country residence
and was built outside a city that had existed
for centuries, while the Winter Palace was
designed to be at the center of a city that was
still being constructed.

In addition—and more relevant—Wilanów
was built on the wishes and at the expenditure
of the king, and it remained his personal
property, so that after Jan's death his son
Konstanty could sell it without causing a
scandal; while the Winter Palace has always
belonged to the state, whatever its form
(because in Russia, unlike Poland, the
sovereign has always considered himself
synonymous with the state).

The Wilanów complex was created as a
monument to the glory of Jan Sobieski: a Latin
inscription on the entrance notes that what the

*198 bottom The portal on the
front of the pavilion to the left of
the east facade of the building is
topped by a sculpture depicting
a warrior on horseback (in
memory of the glorious battles of
Jan Sobieski) and allegorical
medallions. Almost all the
sculptures on the facade are the
work of Italian and Polish
artists.*

*198-199 This is the east facade
of the central section of the
palace, facing onto the Baroque
garden.*

*199 top On the side of the squat
pavilion that flanks the central
section of the east facade, the
God of Time holds a sundial
bearing the symbols of the
zodiac.*

old town once had now belongs to the new town; the front of the house is decorated with a series of bas-reliefs celebrating the exploits of the victory at Vienna. The 17th-century name for the city, the Classical Roman-sounding Villa Nova, was then transmuted into Wilanów for assonance with the earlier place name, Milanów. (The land had belonged to the Benedictines from the mid-12th century but passed to the Milanowski family in the 15th century and took the name Milanów.) In the mid-17th century, Boguslau Leszczynski, uncle of King Stanislaw and Vice-Chancellor to the crown, had commissioned a palace, but its construction was halted when the foundations were being laid. It was finally bought on 23 May 1677 by the newly elected King of Poland, Jan Sobieski. Later, after the sale by Konstanty Sobieski in 1720, the palace belonged to a succession of the most important Polish magnates: the Sieniawski, Czartoryski, Lubomirski, Potocki and Branicki families. In 1805, Wilanów became one of the first Polish public museums, on the initiative of Stanislaw Kostka Potocki, and in 1945 it was bought by the Polish state and officially designated a branch of the National Museum of Warsaw.

Immediately after his purchase, Jan Sobieski commissioned the palace from the Italian Agostino Locci, a secretary at court and Chief Engineer. The first residence was a

modest single-story palace with a symmetrical internal layout: there was a central salon which also served as a dining room; a small room behind it for receiving guests; and two pairs of small square rooms at either end.

The criticism heaped upon the building for its modest dimensions prompted a second phase of construction, begun in 1681 once again on the design of Locci, who was a fervent admirer of Roman Baroque. The use of pilasters and false columns divided the facade of the central section into three parts, while the front was topped by a gallery with triumphal arches in the Roman style. In terms of structure, its nearest model is that of Villa Pamphili in Rome, designed by Francesco Grimaldi and decorated by Alessandro Algardi.

In the years between the battle of Vienna and the death of Sobieski, the house was expanded and embellished enough to make Wilanów a second Versailles—a recurring reference point in the ambitions of eastern European rulers in the 17th and 18th centuries.

After the death of the king at Wilanów in 1696, the building passed to his sons Aleksander, who died in 1714, and Konstanty,

The Proud Symbol of Poland

200 bottom left In 1826, during the Romantic period, Aleksander Potocki commissioned architects Enrico Marconi and C. Hegel to build a mausoleum for his parents. this English Gothic style building stands out in the garden.

who sold it in 1720. The new owner, Elzbieta
Sieniawska, continued the expansion started by
the Sobieski family; it was directed first by
Giuseppe Fontana but completed after 1729 by
Zygmunt Deybel according to the design of
Giovanni Spazzia. Painting was entrusted to
Giuseppe Rossi and the stucco moldings to
Francesco Fumo and Pietro Comparetti.

In 1730 after long negotiations Wilanów
was purchased by King Augustus II, but after his
death it passed to the Czartoryski family. In the
second half of the century, Szymon Zug was
commissioned by the daughter of August
Czartoryski, Izabela Lubomirska, a passionate art
collector, to build a new pavilion, an *oficyna
kuchenna* (kitchens) and a guardhouse. In

and exotic styles. His son Aleksander-August
the Younger commissioned architect Francesco
Maria Lanci to restore the north wing that
contained the Gothic Gallery, and to build
some small service buildings in the park.

Rebuilding work was continued after 1855
by Enrico Marconi, who created a chapel and a
library in the central section of the building.
The library was decorated with moldings by his
sons, who also established an Etruscan Cabinet
in the north wing which held collections of
ancient art, and a Lapidarium in the south wing.

At the end of the 19th century the widow of
Aleksander Potocki, not having any direct heirs,
bequeathed Wilanów to her cousin Ksawery
Branicki, whose family remained the owners of

*200 top, 200-201, 201 top The
Baroque garden to the west of
the palace has two terraces
bounded by a balustrade and
connected by a double
stairway. The balustrade is
decorated with whimsical
statues of putti and grotesque
figures from the first half of the
18th century.*

*200 bottom right The Baroque
church of St. Anne was built in
1772 by August Czartoryski on
the design of architect Jan
Kotelnicki. This was one of the
buildings characterizing the
time when Wilanów belonged to
the Czartoryski family. August's
daughter, Izabela, built a new
pavilion, new kitchens and a
new guardhouse.*

1799, ownership of Wilanów passed from
Izabela to her daughter, Aleksandra, wife of
Stanislaw Kostka Potocki. As an art historian,
archeologist and collector, he was a
representative figure of the Polish
Enlightenment, and it was he who opened
Wilanów to the public for the first time. He
commissioned Peter Aigner to organize what is
known as the Gothic Gallery in the north wing
to hold his collections of Far Eastern art,
graphics, books and the antique pottery he
collected during visits to Italy. Between 1799
and 1821 Potocki and Aigner designed a
romantic park that mixed classical, Neo-Gothic

the property until World War II. During the
Nazi occupation, all that could be transported
was taken away; later the house was
transformed into a barracks during the Warsaw
uprising. The entire property was nationalized
in 1945; nine years later the restoration of the
palace and the park was begun. This work
took ten years. The criterion for the restoration
was to recreate as much as possible the
atmosphere of Wilanów's most splendid
moments: those of Jan Sobieski, Augustus II,
Izabela Lubomirska and the Potocki family—all
the glories and contradictions of almost 300
years of Polish history.

*201 bottom Among the conical
and pyramid-shaped trees on
the upper terrace of the Baroque
Italian style garden stand 18th-
century Neoclassical statues
brought from Slesia after the
Second World War to replace
the originals from the Sobieski
era.*

202 bottom left Elzbieta Sieniawska appears in this oil painting by Louis de Silvestre that dates to the beginning of the 18th century.

202 top right This splendid ebony and ivory secrétaire stands in the royal antechamber. It was given by Pope Innocent XI to Jan Sobieski after the liberation of Vienna.

202 bottom right The family painting with Jan Sobieski and his queen, Maria Kazimiera, dates to 1693 and is framed by a rich gilded Baroque style frame, an element of which is reproduced in the detail above.

The images of the owners of Wilanów are especially significant. Among the most important are the superb statue of King John on horseback crushing a half-naked man wearing a turban; the portrait of the king by Jan Tricius, in a style like that used in the Sarmatia region of Persia; the similarly Sarmatian portrait of the Sieniawski family that contrasts with the equally Roman Baroque portrait of the Sobieski family by an unknown court artist; the portrait of Izabela Lubomirska by Marcello Bociarelli in a rather clumsy imitation of the French style; and the pre-Romantic picture of Stanislaw Kostka Potocki by Anton Gaff.

The art collections were started by Jan Sobieski: the general inventory of 1696 mentions pictures by Jerzy Siemiginowski, silver pots from Danzig, rich curtains made by Zolkwa, and kilim rugs, not only those imported from Persia but also locally-made rugs. Carefully chosen agents of the king searched abroad for pictures, sculptures, furniture and objets d'art, particularly in Italy, Holland and France. The king was especially keen on Dutch paintings which were bought for him in Nijmegen by his trusted agent, the Marquis de Bethune. Thanks

The Proud Symbol of Poland

to his relations with the Jesuits, who were active at the time in China, the king succeeded in procuring various examples of Chinese art: statuettes, caskets, fabrics and furniture. And through Armenian merchants who had been settled at Leopolis for some time he was able to purchase objects of Islamic art from Turkey and Persia.

Izabela Sieniawska distinguished herself for her purchases of velvets and brocades and objets d'art from Slesia, Augsburg, Berlin, Brussels, France, Holland and England.

Augustus II added works from the factories he founded in Dresden. After his death, objects that were then in fashion in Poland started to flow to Wilanów: Regency, Louis XV and Queen Anne furniture, Bohemian glassware and Meissen porcelain. Although Izabela Lubomirska loved 17th and 18th-century European paintings and antiques, it was Stanislaw Kostka Potocki, the husband of Izabela's heir Aleksandra, who was responsible for the greatest additions to the Wilanów collections. Perhaps he sought comfort in beauty and in historic objects in the face of the humiliation his country was forced to suffer when it was divided up between three empires; he made known his own feelings— both didactic and consolatory—in the essay

202-203 The Crimson Room on the ground floor is the largest room in the north wing. Its name is derived from the color of the damask on the walls. Its current appearance follows restoration work started in 1805 by Stanislaw Kostka Potocki and finished by his grandson August. It was during this period that the room became a permanent home for exhibitions of paintings.

203 bottom left The bedroom of Queen Maria Kazimiera, wife of Jan Sobieski, is on the ground floor , central section; it is famed for the large canopied bed and high-quality period damasks.
203 bottom right The small Ceramic Room is situated in the right corner of the central section garden-side. Yellow and blue ceramic tiles, some of which are Delft, cover the walls.

204 top and center left The painted decorations in the small frescoed study on the first floor of the central section of Wilanów are dense with allegorical symbols and were executed by Giuseppe Rossi for Elzbieta Sieniawska.

204 bottom left A view of the Bishop Bedchamber, dating from the 18th century, and the little adjacent cabinet. This room is situated in the north wing of the palace and was formerly a guest room.

204 top right The equestrian statue of Jan Sobieski stands in a passage below the south tower. It was produced shortly before the king's death by an unidentified court artist.

204 bottom right In the bathroom of Izabela Lubomirska, a charming and cultured collector, the bath is modestly built into the wall.

The Proud Symbol of Poland

204 center right John III's bedroom, similar to that of his wife, but separated from it by the Dutch Room, is richly decorated with paintings and plasterwork inspired by Virgil's Georgics. The theme of this room is summer, while the Queen's is spring.

205 At the end of the low gallery in the north wing hangs the portrait of Stanislaw Kostka Potocki painted by Jacques-Louis David in 1791. The wall frescoes of 1688 portraying themes from Apuleus are by the Italian artist M.A. Palloni.

O sztuce u dawnych ("On Art from the Past"). But he did not neglect great European paintings in Renaissance and Baroque styles: he purchased Italian works by Giorgione, Domenichino, Raphael, Correggio, Guercino and Carracci; French works by Le Brun, Le Sueur, Mignard and Lorrain; and Dutch and Flemish works by Rubens, Van Dyck, Jordaens and Frans Lucas Peters. He also collected valuable manuscripts like Queen Bona's prayerbook with miniatures by Sigismondo Sigismondi from 1497, the *Horae intemeratae Virginis Mariae* by J. Philippe from 1497, and two masterpieces from northern France: a 13th century psalm book and the *Horae Beatae Virginis Mariae*. Potocki's descendants continued unstintingly to enrich the art collections of the palace of Wilanów; but it was the last owner, Adam Branicki, who had the merit of donating Wilanów's library of 50,000 volumes and 2,000 prints and engravings to the State Library.

More than 300 years have passed since Europe was saved from the Turkish threat. The Western world has almost totally forgotten the name of the liberator it so liberally heaped with praise at the time. Poland, which has never ceased considering itself Western, and which now is asking for the political right to be part of the West, has never ceased to remember its heroes—recently in the era of Jaruzelski and Gomulka, or with Marshal Pilsudski, or under Russian bondage. Regardless of the succession of owners and political regimes, for over three centuries Wilanów has remained a shrine to the glory of arms and a monument to the Muses.

206 top Christian IV, one of the most beloved monarchs of Danish history and the builder of Rosenborg Castle, is here portrayed by Pieter Isaacz. The painting is housed in Rosenborg.

206-207 The aerial view shows Rosenborg Castle set in the pleasant greenery of the King's Garden and still partly protected by its moat.

206 bottom left One part of the King's Garden was laid out in the 1960s as a Renaissance garden with cut hedges in formal style and thousands of rose bushes.

206 bottom right The southern façade of Rosenborg Castle. Even though the decoration is Dutch Renaissance, the house itself is still medieval, with its steep roofs and its towers containing the staircases and topped with fantastic spires.

Rosenborg

CHRISTIAN IV'S LAST RESIDENCE

Denmark

COPENHAGEN

The Castle of Rosenborg, one of the most fascinating buildings in Copenhagen, is connected to King Christian IV more than is any other Danish castle. He is still the most beloved of Danish kings, even though he lost most of the wars he took part in, made the country poor, and reduced its grandeur by yielding up parts of the territory to Sweden. A connoisseur of the fair sex and of good houses and nice towns, and fond of music, for which he had a trained ear, Christian IV reigned as king for 60 years.

Just outside the moat of medieval Copenhagen the king bought a number of small gardens which originally belonged to the citizens of the town, and had them transformed into one large garden, still known today as the King's Garden. It was laid out as a formal Renaissance garden with hedges and alleys. Some parts were for growing vegetables and fruit for the royal household, while other were for pleasure and had small houses. One of these houses, larger than the others, was destined to become the Rosenborg castle. Its construction was started in 1606, with the original one-story building measuring only half the length of the present castle. Very soon, between 1612 and 1615, it stretched to its full length, and a second story was added and the two small towers were built. The Great Tower and the third story were added in 1624; and the present stair turret was built in 1634. The king and the queen had their private apartments on the ground floor. Each one consisted of a living room, a chamber in the tower and a bedroom. Between the apartments were the toilet and the bathroom. Today only the rooms of the king are preserved, and unfortunately none of them has been left untouched. Nevertheless, both the Living Room and the Writing Closet in the tower still give an impression of Renaissance-style interiors. (The living room in particular is considered to be the best preserved royal Renaissance-style interior in Denmark.) In those apartments Christian IV spent much of his daily life, together with his family. His queen, Anna Catherine of Brandenburg, died young in 1612, but together they had three living children. Even

before her death he fathered two natural sons by other women.

In 1615 he met Kirsten Munk, a maiden of noble family from Jutland, whom he immediately fell in love with. In the many letters he wrote to her, she is often called his "most beloved little mouse." Together they had seven children, of which the best known was Leonora Christina, who married the prime minister Corfitz Ulfeld (he was later was charged with treason and exiled, whereas she was imprisoned for 22 years). The relationship between the king and Kirsten Munk—who never officially married—was dissolved in 1630 because of infidelity. At that time the King was deeply involved in the Thirty Years' War, which cost him such a lot of money that he had to sell the crowns of his parents and, in 1643, to mortgage his own crown—made in 1596—to a merchant in Hamburg. Christian IV

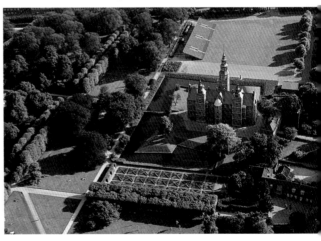

207 top left The crown of the absolute kings was made in Copenhagen, originally for the coronation of Christian V in 1670. It is embellished with two splendid blue sapphires (the largest is 144 carats), two red garnets and about 2,300 diamonds. The last coronation took place in 1840, but the crown is still used at any royal castrum doloris (lying-in-state of a deceased monarch).

207 center In a corner of the King's Garden is a statue of Queen Caroline Amalie. This queen, who died in 1881, had no children; she founded several orphanages in Copenhagen.

lived his last years as an embittered man, but he found solace in the presence of a new mistress, a servant of Kirsten Munk named Vibeke Kruse, who cared for him during his final years. In spite of her devotion she was never accepted by his children, as she was a mere commoner.

In January 1648 the king was severely ill at Frederiksborg Palace in Hillerød, some 19 miles north of Copenhagen. When he felt that his last hour was coming he demanded to be taken to Rosenborg to die. His life ended in his bed in the bedroom at Rosenborg on 28 February

207 bottom The construction of Rosenborg Castle began in 1606 when one of the houses in Christian IV's garden just outside the city walls was enlarged and then transformed.

Rosenborg

Christian IV's Last Residence

1648. Vibeke Kruse too, who had cared for him during his last years, was very ill at the time; but she was literally put out on the street, and died a short time later. The successor of Christian IV was his oldest living son, known as Frederik III. He inherited an impoverished country whose crown sat mortgaged in Hamburg. He immediately sent his prime minister to Hamburg to buy the crown back, but because the king had no money, the minister had to lay out his own money for it. Finally, Frederik III was crowned on 23 November 1648; the long-contended crown is now conserved in the Treasury of Rosenborg Castle. Frederik III was poor and had to move into the old-fashioned Rosenborg because he could not afford to built a new palace. More disasters were to come. In 1658 all Denmark was occupied by the Swedish king, and only the city of Copenhagen was left unconquered. The citizens of the town desperately hurried to finish the new walls laid out by Christian IV, and with these walls Rosenborg ended up inside the circle of protection of the fortress. Copenhagen was not taken, but the peace negotiations were hard on Denmark: the king had to give up to Sweden one-third of Danish territory: the areas of Scania, Halland and Blekinge. This led to a *coup d'état* in 1660 arranged by the king, which introduced absolutism in Denmark.

Shortly after, the king redecorated several rooms in Rosenborg Castle. The king and queen exchanged apartments and the queen renovated the bedchamber of Christian IV in Chinese style—the room is probably the oldest preserved in this style in Europe. The king fashioned his bedchamber into an audience room (the oldest preserved one in Denmark), richly decorated with heavy stucco ceiling and marble-plastered walls, all

208-209 In the splendid Long
Hall are the 1665 throne of the
absolute kings made of
"unicorn horn" (or rather
narwhal tusk) and the 1730
silver throne of the Danish

queens; the two are guarded by
three lifesize silver lions from
the 1660s. The thrones have
not been used since 1840 but
the lions are still used at the
royal castrum doloris.

209 bottom left The marble
bust on top of the pedestal is
that of king Frederik IV, to
whom this room is dedicated.
Frederik IV, Christian V's
successor, was the last king
who used Rosenborg regularly
as a residence.

209 bottom right On the door to
Christian IV's study in the tower is
a painting of Christ as the Man of
Sorrows. The work depicts
Christian IV's vision of 8 December
1625 at Rosenburg. His own
handwritten description of the
vision is still preserved.

decorated with national emblems and symbols
of divine power.

The next king, Christian V, preferred to
stay in other castles, and does not seem to
have used Rosenborg Castle very much,
although he considered it to be a very secure
place, as it had its own moat, stood far away
from any inflammable building, and was now
also protected by the walls of the city. So he
moved the treasures of state and of the royal
family to the castle. The vaulted cellars were
strengthened with iron-clad doors and
complicated locks. On the second floor a
special room was made to keep the regalia in;

210-211 The living room of Christian IV, also known as the Winter Room, dates from the early 17th century and is excellently preserved. The splendid ceiling by Pieter Isaacz, which was originally in another room, replaced the previous stucco ceiling.

210 top, bottom and 211 top right The paintings set in the panels of Christian IV's living room were bought in Antwerp. They are works by various painters, some anonymous and some well-known, and represent a unique collection of Netherlandish art. The clock is a version of the astronomical clock in the cathedral of Strasbourg.

three different keys were required just to enter the room. One key was kept by the keeper of the castle, another by the court marshal; the last was in the king's own hands. Today, 300 years later, the regalia are still kept at Rosenborg Castle—not in the same room, but in a subterranean vault made of reinforced concrete.

The succeeding king, Frederik IV, was the last king who regularly used the castle as a residence. He rearranged the rooms on the first floor, but unfortunately very little of them remains: only the extravagant mirror cabinet, with its mirror-clad walls, ceiling and even a part of the floor (giving the king a chance to get a glimpse of what was underneath the dresses of young women). The greatest work

of art from his period is the stuccoed ceiling of the Long Hall, depicting important political events, military orders and royal symbols. Together with the 12 tapestries ordered by his father, Christian V, to commemorate the Scanian War (1675–79), the Hall was transformed into an impressive monument of the young absolute kingdom.

Royal life at Rosenborg ended during the time of Frederik IV because the king could afford to build new, luxurious palaces to create the proper frame around the absolute monarch.

The last member of the royal family who lived here regularly was one of the king's sisters, who had rooms in the castle until about 1725. After that the castle was only

211 top left The elegant crown of the Danish queens was made in 1731. The piece is by the court jeweler Frederik Fabritious.

211 center The crown of Christian IV, made in Odense for the coronation of 1596, is a magnificent piece of Renaissance jewelry and the most precious object in the Treasury of Rosenborg. Set with enameled figures, pearls and diamonds, it weighs about six pounds.

211 bottom The tapestries of Christian V's room were made expressly for this room around 1690. Set against one of the beautifully covered walls is the large Japanese cupboard that belonged to his queen, Charlotte Amalie, who used it for her collection of souvenirs and curiosities.

very innovative in its exhibition technique, proposing a chronological exhibition covering the successive royal families. A walk in the museum would thus be a pleasant journey through the history of Denmark from Christian IV onward.

The museum opened to the public in 1838 as the first publicly accessible museum in Copenhagen, and when King Frederik VI died in 1839 a room dealing with his reign was arranged. Rosenborg thus became the first museum of contemporary times in Europe.

After the abolition of absolutism in 1849 the palace became state property. But the private collections of the king were allowed, by Frederik VII's royal order of 1854, to become entailed property passed on from king to king. Frederik VII, the last king of the Oldenburg dynasty, died in 1863, and with relics of the history of his life the displays at Rosenborg were complete. To continue the tradition, further rooms were later prepared at the castle of Amalienborg to celebrate the latter monarchs.

used on very few occasions, such as royal birthdays and a few parties. It was, however, a tradition that visitors to the king and other people of the royal family were invited to see the regalia. In this way the castle kept its most important function as the treasury of the kingdom. At the same time it got a new function: it served as the royal attic! Indeed, furniture and other objects that were out of style but too good to be discarded were put into the castle. The Royal Collection of Coins and Medals, which had been established in the castle in 1783, moved to the Nationalmuseum in the 1830s.

At the beginning of the 19th century it was suggested that Rosenborg should be opened to the public. The plan created was

212 top The statue of the founder
of the castle, Karl Johan, appears
about to come down towards the
city on horseback; he gestures
with his right hand in the
direction of the old royal fort of
Akershus.

212-213 The large ballroom is the
most impressive room in the
castle. Two stories high, it is
circled by white and gilt columns
and reflects the majestic
character of the events it hosted.
Those heading for the large

dining room used for state
banquets pass though the
ballroom where one dances
afterwards to the accompaniment
of the orchestra seated at the far
end of the room.

212 bottom left The castle
chapel, which is open for services
every Sunday, is dominated by
the tall pillars that give the
interior a vertical, sacred effect.
The apse at the far end of the
room is covered by a flat roof
painted to make it seem vaulted.
The chapel is used by the royal
family for baptisms and
confirmations.

The Royal Palace in Oslo

A MONUMENT TO THE MONARCHY

For Norwegians there is only one castle. It stands in Oslo atop the Bellevue elevation at the end of the avenue named for Karl Johan. The castle has stood here since 1848, when it was built for King Karl Johan by a Danish military engineer, Hans Ditlef Frants Linstow.

The castle and Karl Johan Avenue evoke images of crucial moments in the history of the country. Even the structure of the building represents an image: it embodies ideas and concepts which have roots in ancient Greece and Rome. With its bright simplicity, the construction is built in Empire style. The name refers to the empire of Napoleon, who drew inspiration from the Roman empire. The Empire style was not only "gentle," but also revolutionary. Following the French Revolution of 1789, simple bourgeois virtues were once again embraced after the pretty artificiality of Rococo. Architecturally, the preferred solution

Externally, two themes are primarily used to project the idea of royalty. One is the fact that the castle is built on a rise, the other is the rigid symmetry around the castle balcony.

It was the king himself who chose the location of the castle. As early as 1822 Karl Johan had decided to build his residence—his Kongelige Slott—on a solitary rise outside the town that had been the capital since 1624. The word *slott*, from German *Schloss*, meaning a closed area, suggests that a royal residence should be built on an isolated site. (The English word *palace* derives from the Palatine, namely a hill in Rome where the emperor built his palace.) The elevated location was underscored in the design of the building, which seems to project upward with its three floors and smaller attic. The vertical central columns and the pointed pediment also seem to reach toward the sky. The most important element is nevertheless the ground floor, which was

213 top Ever since the 13th century, the coat of arms of the Norwegian royal family has shown the gold rampant lion on a red background, the crown and the ax.

212 bottom right The small ballroom with its cool green walls and Ionic columns is used for smaller receptions and gatherings. It is like a portrait gallery with busts and paintings, especially of the English royal family, relatives of Queen Maud. She was married to King Haakon VII, the first king after Norway won independence in 1905 and grandfather of the country's current monarch, Harald V.

lay in the heroic content of Greek and Roman ideals for which patriots fought and died according to a 19th-century Romantic spirit. The style of the castle therefore came to express both monarchic and heroic traits. The latter reflected the Norwegians' fight for freedom after 1814, while the former reflected the function of the castle.

As the king's residence, everything aimed to make it a suitable residence for the head of state, worthy of his rank and the nation whose fate he determines. Using Empire style as an instrument, the concept of royalty was to be conveyed by both interior and exterior.

designed to resemble a high plinth raising the building into the air. Following the style of the period, the base was considered part of nature: gray in color, with round arches framing the windows and plasterwork marked into squares to resemble stone blocks, it was designed to give an impression of solidity and massiveness. On the next, main, floor, the wall is bright and smooth with tall, crowned windows. The second-floor windows are smaller; above, a light band of wrought iron circles the building like a transition between castle and sky.

Stillness and equilibrium have always been considered important aspects of the royal

213 bottom The castle's main facade has a tall ground floor and a majestic appearance. The building is in strict Empire style and was completed in 1848. The balcony with the temple front represents the visual termination of the main street, Karl Johan Avenue, which leads up from central Oslo.

function. Since the Renaissance, castle architecture has tended to reflect this equilibrium. In Oslo it is the castle balcony that makes the facade symmetrical. The balcony is designed like Greek and Roman temples with tall columns and an imposing pediment. The building extends for an equal distance on either side and terminates with somewhat projecting corner elements. The main purpose of the castle balcony is nevertheless to represent a visual termination of Karl Johan's avenue. As the destination of a street procession from the city at the foot of the hill, it represents the climax to the triumphal parade. The steps in front of the square (completed in the 1870s) draw the eye to the columns and are the same width as the balcony when seen from the bottom of the slope. With Brynjulf Bergslien's equestrian

The castle is divided into three floors, each with its own purpose, in accordance with a scheme dating from the Renaissance. The second floor, which was supposed to have low, simple rooms, was at that time intended for servants, but is used today for guest accommodation. The rooms on the ground floor were meant to be used for the court, in accordance with the old idea that the ground floor was to be practical and useful. Its rooms are simple, massive boxes with the exception of two sumptuous royal apartments which were installed on this floor due to lack of space. The architect intentionally gave this area a massive appearance to underscore the fact that this floor carried the whole building. The corridors have vaulted ceilings to evoke grottoes, while the windows have arches and

statue of Karl Johan positioned here, it is as if the king himself comes to meet his people.

Over the years the rooms of the castle have undergone a number of changes, especially after each change of king, but the original plans are nevertheless relatively intact. The upward projection of the facade has its counterpart in the interior in the theme of views on all sides: the main rooms on the second floor have views in all directions.

The symmetrical arrangement around the castle balcony is offset by a solemn processional scheme in the interior. It starts from the main staircase behind the balcony, continues to the first floor, and from there into the main rooms.

are embedded in deep niches. In many points the walls are decorated with a grid to resemble stone blocks, just as are the outside of the ground-floor walls.

The rooms on the first floor were designed very differently from the ones below. This was the piano nobile housing all the royal representation rooms such as ballrooms, dining rooms, halls and audience rooms. This is where the monarch was to appear in all his splendor, surrounded by tall windows and lofty ceilings. However, the element which most effectively emphasizes this majestic atmosphere is the row of columns along the walls. These are either free-standing or

arranged in rows; sometimes they are placed against the walls as separating pilasters and sometimes simply painted directly on to the plasterwork. The columns give the walls an illusion of openness—the massiveness seems to dissolve and one sees out between the columns as if the surface did not exist.

This is the kind of open view one has in the Bird Room. This waiting room before the king's audience room is painted to represent an airy pavilion with wooden columns and no roof. Wild vines wind around the construction, small birds dart in and out of the foliage and a large eagle flies across the middle of the room. The eagle has been a symbol of royalty since time

214 top *King Olav V, the popular monarch who died in 1991, was surrounded by private keepsakes both from England and Norway. His living room is dominated by family photographs, comfortable furniture and a mixture of old and modern paintings.*

214 center and bottom *The Bird Room is the antechamber to the King's audience room. The room is surrounded by a scene of Norwegian mountains and valleys painted by Johannes Flintae, and a royal eagle*

hovers in the ceiling, attentively watching the visitors. The room was meant to inspire nationalistic sentiments in visitors as they prepared to meet the king, and is considered a masterpiece of Norwegian decorative art.

214-215 *The Mirror Hall takes its name from the mirrors in the door panels and is one of the most splendid rooms in the castle. With tall mirrors, crystal chandeliers and gilt furniture, it is rich and varying in character.*

This is where English-born Queen Maud's own piano is located, and in the corner is a bust of her consort, king Haakon VII. He was elected king by the people in 1905 after termination of the union with Sweden.

215 bottom left *The red sitting-room on the ground floor houses furniture in majestic early Baroque, while the walls are covered with portraits of the Bernadotte family; above, the ceiling decoration extends like a sail.*

215 bottom right *The white drawing-room adjoining the red room is characterized by a lighter Rococo style with carved and gilt panels. This is the antechamber of the cabinet ministers' room, which the King used to cross on his way to meet the government.*

216 top left The crown prince's audience room, also called the Arcade Room because of its row of gilt arches and delicate Empire decorations, adjoins the large ballroom. It was formerly used as a chambre separée where party guests could withdraw for conversation and rest. It is now used by the crown prince as an office and audience room.

216 bottom left On one's way to the king from the stair hall with its row of columns, one passes into the king's antechamber before reaching the audience room proper. Since olden times such sequences of antechambers have been designed to heighten the visitor's expectation before meeting the monarch.

A Monument to the Monarchy

immemorial. All around the room we see uninterrupted scenery of imposing Norwegian mountains and valleys. Behind the castle balcony we find Norway's most impressive staircase leading toward the royal apartments. The source of inspiration was the Baroque *scala regia* which had already in the 17th century become a part of the vocabulary of royal architecture. The staircase endows the simple act of ascent with a significance underscoring that the visitor is reaching the king.

Just inside the gate the path from outside divides into two identical courses which wind along the wall to a mezzanine where they are reunited. From here a large staircase continues up to the first floor and to the balustrade that overlooks the castle square and Karl Johan Avenue. If one has an audience, one walks from the balustrade either to the right and straight to the king, or to the left and to the crown prince. The path leads in a straight line through a row of rooms facing onto the castle square and to the "holiest" room, where the royals wait. Since olden times, such rows of antechambers have been intended to heighten one's anxiety. If one is visiting the castle not for an audience but for a party, one first enters the small ballroom which faces the park located behind the balustrade. One continues to the right, through the large ballroom, and from there into the dining room above the low northern wing. The dramatic effects increase and the rooms become more and more splendid as one approaches one's destination. Below, by the main gate, the character is heavy and massive. This is the ground floor, with its vaults and stone block walls, and we are surrounded by rigid and simple Doric columns. We encounter this type of column once again at the top of the stairs, but here they are gentler

and more slender with soft rings around the base and small decorations around the capitals. If we continue into the small ballroom we find Ionic columns. These are much more delicate than their Doric counterparts, still more slender and taller, and have spiral patterns in the capitals and rows of pearls near the floor. The walls of the room are painted cool green, the columns are creamy yellow and along the ceiling is a colorful band of small palms and ribbons. Yet the small ballroom gives an expectant air. Only when we enter the ballroom does our expectation reach its climax in an explosion of magnificence and splendor. The room occupies more than two floors, reaching up toward a ceiling with crossing beams expanding in all directions. Solemn columns stand in rows around the parquet supporting a gallery which circles the room with lit chandeliers above. The columns are now Corinthian, and are crowned by lush foliage in white and gold. This order was used in antiquity for triumphal columns surrounding market squares in towns. The ballroom is also a kind of *agorà* which opens not only upward but outward, as the walls are covered by mirrors right down to the floor. A door in a corner of the ballroom opens to the banquet room. The ceiling is lower here, and the walls are covered by a pattern of intertwined slender vines. The room is intimate compared to the spacious ballroom. This is how architect Linstow emphasized the different functions of the rooms: the ballroom, where one danced, should be splendid, open and expansive, while the dining room should be focused on gathering around the table. The castle of Oslo is therefore a typical example of formal architecture, entirely aimed at exalting the public functions of the head of state and, in some way, leaving privacy aside. Thus the castle is not simply a residence but a symbolic building, conveying the sense of Norway's equilibrium, rigor, power and opulence, in present days as well as in the past.

The architecture is conceived to suit this role. Only when the trumpets sound and the limousine glides into the main gate do the rooms acquire a meaning and Norway can rest.

Sweden

STOCKHOLM

The Royal Palace in Stockholm

A THOUSAND YEARS OF ROYAL TRADITION

218 top In this painting housed in the Cathedral of Uppsala, King Gustav Vasa, the first Swedish monarch, is portrayed as he proclaims hereditary monarchy.

218 bottom The western entrance of the royal palace is seen here from the outer courtyard. The palace architect Nicodemus Tessin the Younger designed this facade in Roman Baroque style after the fire of 1697.

Stockholm, the capital of Sweden, is situated at the meeting point between the Baltic Sea and Lake Mälaren, where a vast archipelago with thousands of islands stretches both inland and out to sea. The capital is located right in the center of this unique environment and the Royal Palace is situated at the exact meeting point of the sea and lake.

A visitor today will find a gigantic palace in Roman Baroque style, but the history of this royal residence is much older than the facades indicate. The origin of the palace is uncertain but interesting. Some time circa A.D. 950–1000, the Vikings living in the area pulled huge tree trunks down into the water outside the location of the present palace to create a narrow entrance for ships entering Lake Mälaren from the Baltic. The purpose was to give the Vikings the chance to check whether the arrival was a friend or foe. This was crucial, as the Mälar valley was economically the most important area in the kingdom. And because villages and cities along the lakeshore were unprotected, control of the lake area was fundamental for national security. Although no remains of a fortress from this early period exist, it is certain that the entrance had to be protected, so there were probably some wooden buildings on the site.

Around the year 1240, Birger Jarl, regent in Sweden, started to construct a huge stone fortress with a round keep. The defense walls were between 20 and 25 feet thick, which made it the strongest fortress in the Baltic area. It consisted of two main parts, called the castle

218-219 The White Sea Ballroom is furnished as a large salon where the king and queen entertain guests in connection with a state banquet. The painted framework of the ceiling was painted by the Italian artist Domenico Francia around 1735 and contains a skilful trompe l'oeil perspective.

219 top left The Hall of State is the throne room of the royal palace. The silver throne was made in the German city of Augsburg. For centuries this hall has functioned as a session room for the Swedish Parliament.

219 top right Queen Lovisa Ulrika's Audience Chamber is a combination of Swedish and French design. The interior is a creation of the Swedish architect Jean-Eric Rehn who also made the drawings for the throne. The

tapestries, depicting scenes from the tale of Cupid and Psyche, were woven according to designs by Boucher and were produced at Beauvais. The overdoor panels are painted by the Swedish painter Johan Pasch.

219 bottom Tessin's engraved drawings for the new palace show the north and south entrances. The northern entrance is inspired by the entrance to Palazzo Farnese in Rome. The majestic southern entrance leads to the hall of state and the royal chapel.

and the Economy Yard. Tradition says that the merchants in Stockholm had the opportunity to store their goods in low buildings around the Economy Yard. Times were uncertain and Stockholm had developed into an important trading city where goods were unloaded from tall ships sailing on the Baltic onto smaller ships that plied Lake Mälaren. The importance of the fortress increased together with that of the city.

During the Middle Ages the castle was primarily a military fortress and secondarily one of the more important royal residences. The Stockholm fortress was given the name of the

Castle of the Three Crowns, which indicates the the significance of the place: the Three Crowns were, and still are, the national symbol of Sweden. This symbol has a religious and a political background. The religious meaning is clear: the crowns represent the three biblical kings who journeyed to pay their respects to the newborn Jesus. The political background, however, has been more difficult to investigate. Probably the symbol dates back to King Magnus Eriksson, who reigned in the middle of the fourteenth century. At one period in his career, he was king of three

independent nations—Sweden, Norway and Skåne. It may be that each crown represented a kingdom, and that King Magnus Eriksson's personal coat of arms later became the national symbol.

From 1297 until 1521 Sweden was forced into a union with Denmark and Norway called the Kalmar Union. During this period, Copenhagen became the political center of the Nordic countries and Stockholm was just an important city. In 1521, the young Swedish nobleman Gustav Vasa broke this medieval union and the modern state of Sweden was

formed. Two years later Gustav Vasa was elected king of Sweden. Under his reign Stockholm started to develop into a modern capital and the old medieval fortress became the prime residence of the Swedish monarchy.

Naturally it was impossible for the kings of the Vasa dynasty to live in a medieval castle, so the building was slowly transformed into a Renaissance palace. The old Economy Yard was turned into a ceremonial courtyard with an Italian loggia, and a new wing was added containing the throne room, which was called the Hall of State.

One of the new interiors very representative of this time was an audience room with lovely tapestries made in Sweden in the 1560s. The tapestry decorations were an allegory of the origin of Sweden; they showed the Paradise described in the Book of Genesis as being situated in Sweden, and the Swedish kings as being direct descendants of Noah.

After the peace of Westphalia in 1648 Sweden became one of the great powers of

Europe, and it was decided that the palace should once again be modernized. The palace architect, Nicodemus Tessin the Younger, started the project in 1692. Sweden's great seat of power called itself Roma Nova, and the architect had been educated in Rome as a pupil of Gian Lorenzo Bernini; it would have been quite natural for him to decorate the building as a Roman Baroque palace. But Tessin disliked Roman interiors and the Roman way of arranging an apartment so instead he designed the palace in the French style.

In 1692 the first step was taken and the northern wing of the palace was rebuilt. Three years later the exterior was completed and work began on the interiors.

On 7 May 1697 a fire completely destroyed the palace except for the newly rebuilt northern wing. Some six weeks after the catastrophe Nicodemus Tessin presented his plans for a new palace, and the royal family and the Swedish government accepted them. The new palace was a complete Roman city

220 top right Gustav III's State Bedchamber combines a splendid Baroque ceiling with wall decorations in Neoclassical style. The King's writing table is a 1778 work by the Swedish cabinet-maker Georg Haupt.

220-221 There has been a chapel inside the palace walls since the end of the 13th century at least. The present chapel was inaugurated in 1754. The court parish is made up of court employees and their families.

221 top Gustav III's State Bedchamber contains three elaborately decorated cabinets in ebony, which were made in Paris in 1784 by the renowned cabinetmaker Adam Weisweiler.

221 bottom The Audience Chamber of the State Apartments contains a canopy embroidered in Milan around 1500 at the request of the Sforza family. Its female figures recall the work of Sandro Botticelli.

palace, probably one of the largest of its kind in Europe.

The plan was that it should take about five years to complete the new complex, but history decided otherwise and Sweden's many wars, especially those with Russia, made it impossible to build at all. In the end, the royal family did not move back to the palace until 1754.

At the time of the fire in 1697, work on the royal apartments had started and Tessin created drawings for different interiors. At that time Sweden did not have enough skilled artists to fulfill the architect's designs for the interiors, so a group of French artists was invited to Stockholm. The combination of Swedish design and French quality produced excellent results, of which the Gallery of King Karl XI is a good example. From the beginning the gallery was used as a promenade where the courtiers could talk and stroll. Today its function is quite different; the gallery is used for state banquets when a 145-foot-long table is laid and about 160 guests can be seated.

Building at the new palace practically came to a halt between 1707 and 1727. But the Swedish parliament took the decision to restart work and in 1754 the palace had reached the point where the royal family could move in.

In 1727 the palace architect Tessin wrote a letter to a young Swedish architect, Carl Hårleman, asking him to come home from a long education in France and Italy to assist Tessin in his work of completing the palace. A few months later Tessin died and Hårleman became artistically responsible for the completion of the palace. At the beginning of the 1730s it was necessary to start on interior decoration. Hårleman came to the same conclusion as Tessin had, some decades earlier, saying that the design should be Swedish—but that he needed French and Italian artists to give the new interiors the required quality. Hårleman had been educated in Paris during the period when French taste moved from the heavy Baroque of Louis XIV to the light and elegant Rococo style; therefore it was quite natural for him to use this new French fashion in his interiors for the Stockholm palace. It is said that Hårleman was probably the first architect outside France to use this new style, and his Rococo interiors are the best example of French style outside of France itself.

During the Neoclassical period at the end of

Giuseppe Verdi wrote an opera about this tragedy, called *Un Ballo in maschera*, which starts with an audience in the State Bedchamber.

The desire to create some sort of a national memorial to the king resulted in the founding of a national museum in June 1792, one of the first public art museums outside Italy. The heart of this new institution was the king's own collection of ancient Roman sculptures. The museum opened in the palace in 1793 and the two galleries that house the antiques are still preserved in their original state, making them unique historic documents.

222-223 The Bernadotte Gallery was decorated in the 1730s, as demonstrated by the decoration on the ceiling. Some decades later it was transformed into a painting gallery. Today the gallery houses a collection of family portraits of the Bernadotte dynasty.

the 18th century, King Gustav III was on the throne. From a cultural point of view, he was one of the most important kings to have reigned in Sweden: most of the country's national cultural institutions were founded by this king. Some examples are the Royal Opera House, the Royal Theatre of Drama and the Swedish Academy, best known today for the Nobel Prize in literature. The king dominated culture to the extent that Swedish Neoclassical style is called the Gustavian Style. A remarkable interior from this period is the king's State Bedchamber. In was in this room that the king died after being shot at a masked ball at the Opera House in 1792. The Italian composer

In 1810, the French field marshal Jean Baptiste Bernadotte, one of Napoleon's generals, was elected crown prince of Sweden. Eight years later he ascended the throne with the name Karl XIV Johan. The Bernadotte family has reigned in Sweden ever since, making it the longest reigning dynasty in Swedish history.

For centuries the royal palace in Stockholm has been the official residence of the monarchs of Sweden; the king and queen also have their offices there. All official ceremonies are held in the palace and visiting heads of state are accommodated here. All offices of the court are also located within the walls of the palace.

223 top This overdoor panel painted by the French Rococo painter François Boucher is found in the Don Quixote Room. Swedish craftsmen fashioned the sculpted frame after a design by the architect Jean-Eric Rehn.

223 bottom The State Bedchamber of Queen Sofia Magdalena was decorated in the 1770s in the Swedish version of the French Louis XVI style. The overdoor panels were painted by the French artist Charles Joseph Natoire in 1743.

The Kremlin

THE HEART OF RUSSIA

*I*n the cities of ancient Rus' (as the Moscow region was called) the term *kreml'* meant an enclosed complex, a sort of citadel or acropolis, inside which the residence of the prince, the cathedral, the houses of important people and the seat of city administration were found. The first examples had wooden palisades or clay walls with towers placed at intervals.

Ancient Russian culture was essentially a culture of wood; stone was only used for extremely symbolic buildings. It was no accident that the first stone building in *Rus'*—or the first to appear in written accounts—was the church of the Madonna of the Tithes (Bogorodica Desjatinnaja). The first stone *kreml'* was built in Moscow in the 1580s when its princes organized the various lands of Rus' and made Moscow the capital of the Orthodox empire. They wanted a successor to Rome and Constantinople—the "new Rome."

For non-Russians today, the dark walls of the Kremlin, seat of Soviet power, conjure up the fear of Communism. They contrast with the image of the Moscow of White Stones (Belokamennaja Moskva) which for centuries evoked greatness for Russians; but here the emphasis was on the material, not the color.

Moscow became the uncontested capital of the Empire, and from the second half of the 16th century new enclosure walls began to be built, or wooden ones to be replaced, with brick and stone in the other main cities. (These included Novgorod—known as Gorky during the Soviet era—Pskov, Tula, Kolomna, Kazan, Astrakhan, Rostov, and others.) But in the 18th century an edict from Peter the Great forbade construction of new buildings outside of the "city of stone"—St. Petersburg.

225 top left This map, taken from a 17th-century Dutch atlas with Latin inscriptions, shows the layout of the buildings of the Kremlin during the reign of Boris Godunov (1594-1605). It is dedicated to Tsar Aleksei Mikhailevich (1645-76).

225 right V.M. Vasenev (1848-1926), one of the most appreciated Russian historical painters, painted this imaginary portrait of Ivan IV "the Terrible," the first Russian emperor crowned in the cathedral of the Dormition, in 1547. In the photograph beside the imposing head of Ivan the Terrible can be seen all parts of the Kremlin visible from the far side of the Moscova River.

224 center The two-headed eagle is set in the center of the backrest of the gilded and inlaid wooden throne of Catherine II, which is covered with red velvet.

224 top The Tower of the Savior (Sposskaja bashnja) and the colored onion domes of the small church of St. Basil are among the symbols of Moscow.

224 bottom The imperial insignia (the crown and scepter reproduced here, and an orb) were produced by the imperial workshop for Tsar Mikhail Fedorovic. They are absolutely unique in the delicacy of their workmanship and in the quantity and quality of precious stones that adorn them: emeralds, sapphires, rubies, and pearls with polychrome enamel.

224-225 The domes of the cathedral of the Dormition, a mixture of Italian and traditional Russian Orthodox styles, stand out among the other buildings. The coronation of all Russian rulers from Dimitri Ivanovic, grandson of Ivan III, to Nicholas II, took place here.

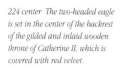

The first mention of the Kremlin in Moscow dates from 1156, when Prince Yuri Dolgoruki had a wooden palisade built on Cape Borovicki, a rise at the confluence of the Neglinnaya and the Moscova Rivers, from which it was possible to control the road to Vladimir and Suzdal.

In the 1320s, Ivan Kalita widened and strengthened the palisade made of oak trunks over three feet thick, built the stone cathedrals of the Dormition (Uspenskij Sobor) and the Archangel (Archangel'skij Sobor) and also constructed his own house in wood. At the same time, Cathedral Square (Sobornaja Ploscad) was laid out.

The hero of the first Russian victory over the Tatars, Dimitri Donskoi, built a stone wall that enclosed an area almost equal to that of the current Kremlin. In 1404, the first clock appeared on a Russian tower here.

The golden age of the Kremlin was the second half of the 15th century, the period identified with the long reign of Ivan III (1462–1503). On the initiative of Pope Paul II and Cardinal Bessarione, Ivan in 1472 married Zoe (renamed Sophia in Russian) Palaeologus, niece and presumed heir of the last Roman emperor of the East. In 1480 he freed himself of the Tatars under whose dominion Moscow had suffered since 1240. With the submissions of the republic of Novgorod and the principality of Tver, he took control of all of northern and western Russia by the end of the 1480s. Men of letters who had fled from Serbia and Bulgaria at the time of the Ottoman invasion gathered in Ivan's court; these were nobles who wanted to put themselves at his service. Nobles also arrived from the crumbling Tatar khanate and even from Lithuania, as its sovereign (who was also king of Poland) controlled southwest Rus' and was contending for primacy over all of Rus'.

Artists came to Moscow mostly from Milan and Rome, and especially from Venice (or via Venice), perhaps on the advice of Sophia, who had contacts with that city. In the space of little more than twenty years, these artists transformed the Kremlin into what Gutkind has defined "an architectural picture worthy of a

226 top The cathedral of the Archangel was designed by Alvise Novyj (1505-9) and was used as a pantheon of Russian rulers. The Venetian architect perfectly synthesized Renaissance elements with the traditional, five-domed Russian architectural model.

226 bottom In Orthodox churches the people do not see the celebrants during services, but they hear their voices on the other side of the iconostasis, as in the cathedral of the Archangel.

226-227 The magnificent interior of the cathedral of Archangel is the best example of horror vacui or horror of empty space that pervades holy Russian architecture: the columns are completely covered with frescoes, the iconostasis is divided into panels, each containing an icon, and the "royal doors" are covered with embossed images.

227 top A celebratory inscription in pseudo-ancient Cyrillic characters runs around the base of the tallest dome of the Belltower of Ivan the Great.

227 center right This detail of the busy and colorful facade of the cathedral of the Dormition also demonstrates the horror vacui of holy Russian architecture.

227 bottom left The Belltower of Ivan the Great (named for Ivan III, 1462-1505) was erected in 1505-8 and completed in 1600. It dominates the Kremlin and the city of Moscow and has the double function of lookout tower and symbol of the grandeur of the state.

227 bottom right The magnificent cathedral of the Dormition stands, with other buildings, in Cathedral Square in the southeast area of the Kremlin.

sovereign." Worthy of a sovereign, moreover, linked to the house of the Byzantine emperor and therefore the prospective heir to his universal throne.

As with the artists 250 years later in St. Petersburg, those in Moscow were asked to use their talents and experience in observance of the rigid rules that governed the "liturgy" of the power celebrated in Moscow, and to propose technical solutions that were innovative in form but deeply conservative in substance.

The first Italian architect invited to Moscow was the Bolognese Ridolfo Fioravanti. In Russia he was nicknamed "Aristotle" for the breadth of his technical knowledge; he was also a military engineer and became responsible for Ivan III's artillery. Fioravanti received the commission for the reconstruction of the church of the Dormition in place of Ivan Kalita's original version, which had been destroyed by an earthquake.

Once the foundations had been laid, Ivan sent Fioravanti to Vladimir to study the canonical forms of the holy architecture of Rus', which could be seen in the cathedral there. The combination of the Italian's own experience and his exposure to

Russian architecture created what is still today the most attractive building in the Kremlin. This peculiarity is noted by Lazarev who tells how the fundamental forms of the cathedral of the Dormition at Vladimir were adopted by Fioravanti in a structurally different context, resulting in a monumental and finely proportioned complex. In line with Italian tradition, Fioravanti made wide use of the golden ratio for both the external and internal designs. As the interior did not include the gallery used in traditional Orthodox churches, it was divided into 12 units that support five domes. The slenderness of the columns and walls, which strongly contrasts with the height and width of the open space, created a

completely new look in Russian architecture: that of a large room punctuated by columns that decorate but do not encumber it.

The cathedral of the Dormition is often mistakenly called "of the Assumption," a reference to the Roman Catholic belief in the Assumption (ascent) of the Virgin's body and soul into Heaven. But Orthodox Christians believe that only the soul of the Virgin Mary rose to Heaven after her death, or Dormition (sleep). Greek and Slav icons show the Virgin laid out on a bed while her soul, a small white mark in the center of the icon, seems to rise toward the figure of Christ Pantokrator. Mary has always been worshipped in Rus', particularly by its rulers who—in one of the

229 bottom left A view through the splayed portal of the cathedral of the Annunciation, with its rich Oriental decoration, shows the iconostasis decorated with icons by Feofan Grek and Andrei Rublëv.

229 bottom right Low vaults and darkness characterize the traditional interior of the cathedral of the Annunciation, built in 1484-89. It later became the private chapel of the Russian emperors.

230 top The beautiful portal
leading to the Tzarina's Golden
Chamber dates to the 16th
century and is richly decorated
with gilded carving. The
doorway offers a glimpse of the
frescoes inside the Golden
Chamber, which appear in the
photograph below.

230 center and bottom left Low
vaults and darkness characterize
the residence (Zolotaja palata) of
Irina Godunova, widow of Tsar
Fedor Ivanovic and sister of his
successor, Boris Godunov. The rich
marquetry, gilding and religious
frescoes qualify this palace as an
empress's personal space.

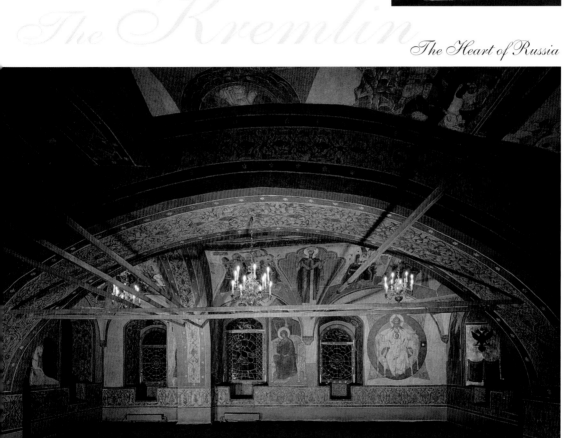

most frequent scenes in the chronicles—invoked the Virgin Help of Christians (Zastupnica) before battle and, in general, before taking important governmental decisions. It is not accidental that all new cathedrals built in the 16th century follow Fioravanti's model nor that, when Ivan III decided to "restore" the Constantinopolitan ritual of imperial coronation, never before practiced in Rus', the cathedral of the Dormition was chosen for the celebration. The first to be crowned was the grandson of Ivan III, Dimitri Ivanovic (who was never to reign) and the last was Nicholas II. The rite was celebrated 22 times in all, even after the capital had been transferred to St. Petersburg: 11 times with the ecclesiastical Slav name of *venčanie*, which was used until the joint coronation of Peter the Great

and his half brother Ivan V, and 11 times with the Latin-like name of *koronaciya*, starting with Catherine I, wife of Peter.

It is in the church of the Dormition that the throne of Ivan IV is conserved. Ivan was crowned in 1547 as the first Russian emperor. On the sides of the throne is engraved part of the Motto of the Princes of Vladimir (Skazanie o knjaz'jach vladimirskisch) in which the genealogy of the Moscovite rulers is shown from the Viking Rjurik (Rørik), who was in turn descended from Prus, who was the legendary blood relation of the Roman emperor Augustus.

After "Aristotle" Fioravanti, many other Italian architects arrived in Moscow from Italian states, including Pietro Antonio Solari; two others known by the name of Alvise; and another two, referred to as Marco and Antonio,

230-231 The large salon on the first floor of the Palace of Facets has a striking shape: the frescoed, typically Muscovite vaults seem to grow out of the single square central column.

231 bottom The vestibule on the ground floor of the Palace of Facets is also impressive, although a fire in 1682 led to heavy restoration.

232 left and 233 top right
The form of the columns and decorative motifs at the Golden Threshold (Zolotoe kryl'co) of Terem Palace show the transposition of woodworking methods to stone.

232 top right Terem Palace includes the oldest part of the Kremlin. Construction of the palace over the existing building was completed in the 1630s. It was to become the private residence of the imperial family.

232 bottom right Terem Palace became almost the only model for Russian civil architecture during the whole second half of the 17th century. In 1635 the architects Bashen Ogurzov, Trefil Sciarutin, Antip Konstantinov and Larion Usciakov were asked by Mikhail Feodorovic to raise the existing building (from the previous century) by two floors. Two further orders and an attic were built over the cellar. The gallery though the attic known as the Teremok (or little Terem) was a real fifth floor originally fitted out with bedrooms and relaxation rooms.

232-233 This is the northern face of the Kremlin's Great Palace. The domes of Terem church and the cathedral of the Dormition can be seen in the center background. The profile of the tall Belltower of Ivan the Great is further to the right. The dominant feature of the northern face of the Kremlin are the magnificent colors of Terem Palace on the left, which emphasize the impression given by the design of the building—that each floor grows out of the one below.

who were indicated in the accounts with the epithet "Frank" meaning Catholic or westerner.

They were commissioned with the rebuilding of the Kremlin, a project which was doubtless framed within a general plan taking account of military as well as artistic and architectural considerations. The precise demarcation of the Kremlin triangle, the positioning of the towers, their shape and relationship with the central buildings all indicate the hand of a true maestro. That would be Fioravanti, who is supposed to have had a hand in the execution of this massive project, made all the more complex by the rebuilding of all the churches within the Kremlin. All the works were carried out in the Russian or, more precisely, the Muscovite tradition, within the walls and following the layout of the internal buildings set by the works dating back to Ivan Kalita and Dimitri Donskoi. (Russian and Soviet critics made a point of emphasizing that "the Italian maestri were inspired by the national Russian tradition.")

The works dragged on with a few interruptions from 1485 to 1516, when the dike

that connects the Neglinnaya with the Moscova was finished, making the Kremlin isolated and inaccessible. The isolation was further increased by the erection of the second enclosure wall, the one facing the square known since the 15th century as Red Square (Krasnaja Ploščad') when the adjective *krasnaja* meant "beautiful" and not "red."

Between 1487 and 1494, Solari and Marco Frank built the Palace of Facets (Granovitaja palata) which has a facade, seemingly unique in Russia, of diamond-shaped ashlar. (The current exterior was created during restoration after the fire of 1682.) The linear, Renaissance appearance of the facade contrasts strongly with that of the salon on the first floor, a large quadrangle with a square pillar in the center supporting typically Muscovite frescoed vaults.

In 1505–9, the Archangel cathedral built by Ivan Kalita was reconstructed to the design by the Venetian Alvise Novyj (meaning "the New"—another Alvise had preceded him). From a compositional point of view, Alvise followed the model of the cathedral of the Dormition fairly closely; but in the decoration of the facade he made broad use of Lombard-style motifs derived from those popular in Venice in the early Renaissance. The new

Archangel cathedral became the pantheon of the Russian rulers. Its high priest (*protopop*) became the confessor of the Tsars, starting with Ivan III.

During the 17th century, the period when Russian culture was perhaps most heavily influenced by the West, the decorative elements of the Kremlin were redone in a style that might be defined as Baroque. Most importantly, various towers were embellished. The Tower of the Arsenal (Arsenal'naja bašnja), built in 1492 by Solari, was nearly doubled in height, and a domed triumphal arch was built in the 1620s above the Savior Tower (Spasskaja bašnja) through which the main entrance to the Kremlin passes.

234-235 *Affairs of state were discussed in the Parliament (or Duma) Room where many disputes were resolved between the Russian nobles at the time of the Tsars. Note the large, inlaid 17th-century table with gilded legs, and the ceiling fresco of the Madonna and Child.*

The Kremlin

Between 1635 and 1636, the stone residential section of the imperial palace was built by A. Konstantinov, B. Ogurcov, T. Šarutin and L. Ušakov. Today the building is known as the Terem Palace (Teremnyj dvorec). The term *terem* is derived from the Turkish for apartment or place of habitation. The terem were modeled on ancient wooden residences and had an intimate, welcoming appearance, which made a strong contrast with the reception rooms.

In this century, the Ministry of Arms (Oružejnyj prikaz) was remade into the Armory Palace (Oružejnaja palata) containing the imperial workshops, the craft schools and the collections of Russian antiquities.

During Catherine the Great's reign

(1762–96), large projects of urban rebuilding were carried out at the Empress's request in both the new and the old capitals. In Moscow, especially, the layout of the Kremlin had to be reinterpreted to fit the role it was given in a city plan that was to equal the Paris of the Sun King. But the commission set up to deal with it (Komissija o kamennom stroenii) was too busy thinking about the new plans for St. Petersburg. Consequently, a new department was specially set up by decree on 14 March 1774 for the "drawing up of the general plan for improvement of the constructions in Moscow;" it was headed by P.N. Kožin, with L.L. Legrand as chief architect. Legrand's decisions largely coincided with those made by V.I. Baženov—who was with M.F. Kazakov one of the torchbearers of the Classicism that was so loved by Catherine—in the design of what is known as the Kremlin Great Palace (Bol'shoj Kremlëvskij dvorec). Baženov's plan was to rebuild the Kremlin as an integral part of the overall creation of a new city layout which meant that a section of the walls and two towers overlooking the Moscova river had to be demolished. The demolished walls were soon rebuilt, but the Great Palace was unable to avoid the Napoleonic exploding mines.

The only great construction of the 18th

234 bottom The Tsarina's bedroom is dominated by a carved wooden four-poster bed. There are few remains of the original 17th-century decorations; those to be seen today were executed by T. Kissilov in 1836-38 from drawings by F. Solnzev, an academic who tried to recreate the previous floral motifs using oil paints.

235 left Large ceramic stoves stand in two corners of the vestibule on the fourth floor of Terem Palace.

235 top right The decoration in the Throne Room in Terem Palace is all red, the color of power. The two-headed eagle sits on the keystones.

235 bottom right The vaguely Gothic paired windows are one of the innovative features of Terem Palace. The light that filters into the rooms is refracted by the splendid colored windows, a rarity for the period, that accentuate the richness of the frescoes, floral and animal motifs and acanthus leaf ornaments covering the vaults, pillars and beams.

236 center left Catherine's room, the main room in the west wing of the Great Palace, takes its name from the Order of Saint Catherine, whose emblems appear on the wall decoration. The soft color and the Empire furnishings give the room a harmonious atmosphere.

236 bottom left The St. George Room, named in honor of the Knights of St. George, is considered the best example of interior architectural design in Russia. It is the most vast and impressive room in the Great Palace.

236 top left The Kremlin is surrounded by thick walls studded with massive towers. The fortifications were built beginning in the 15th century, starting from the southern side of the Kremlin facing the Moscova River, as this was the side most exposed to enemies.

century in the Kremlin was the Palace of the Senate, built in 1777–88, designed by Kazakov. It is a triangular building with a circular room at its center crowned with a dome.

Before his retreat in 1812, Napoleon had mined the Kremlin, just as the Nazis were to do, more scientifically, at Karskoe Selo before abandoning their siege of Leningrad.

Restoration after Napoleon lasted more than 30 years, but many buildings were destroyed for ever. In their place, K.A. Ton designed the new Great Palace (finished in 1849) and the new Armory Palace (completed in 1851), in which all the imperial arms collections were displayed.

The two-story Great Palace topped by a fourfold dome in imitation of ancient Russian churches has reception halls on the first floor. The largest is St. George's room, with decorations dedicated to victories by Russian armies and to important people in the order of St. George. Using the former rooms of St. Alexander and St. Andrew, I.A. Ivanovič created the Palace of Congresses in 1922, which served as a shrine to Soviet and international Communism for almost 70 years.

This huge complex, the Kremlin, is the result of continuous enlargement, reconstruction, restoration and adaptation according to changing tastes and politics, and can be seen under two aspects: formal and ideological. A historian of English art identified three phases in the history of the Kremlin: the original wooden version; then the "Italian" model of the age of the Renaissance; and, last, the modern version to which Catherine II added buildings in Neoclassical style (in particular the Senate) and which Nicholas II disfigured with the erection of the awkward mass of the pseudo-Russian Great Palace.

But interpretation of the history of the Kremlin cannot be broken down on the basis of criteria, however correct, of the history of art, nor of the nationality of architects or the taste or lack of taste on the part of the rulers. The history of the Kremlin is the history of Moscow, and Moscow, Russia, for good or ill.

The history of the Kremlin and Moscow is that of ancient Rus', the Grand Principality of Moscow, the Russian Empire, the Soviet Union and, presumably, the newly born Russian Federation, even if it is too early—after only seven years of precarious existence compared to seven hundred years of history—to hypothesize on the future of the bastion of continuity that is the Kremlin.

The Heart of Russia

The Kremlin

236-237 and 237 bottom right Past and present merge in this picture: a traditional dome is seen in the foreground, with the Great Palace of the Kremlin, and a building from the Stalinist era in the background. Today the

Kremlin is famous not only for its splendid Old Russian golden-domed churches, and for the magnificent palaces and the precious collections in its museum; it is still the heart of the country's social and political life.

237 top This room was formerly the bedchamber of Catherine II. The empress's alcove has been moved elsewhere, but the original 18th-century furnishings remain, including a lovely French clock. The columns in this room are the largest monoliths in Russia.

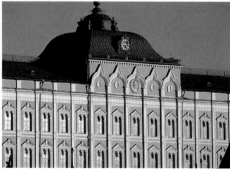

237 bottom left The outside of the Great Palace in the Kremlin, the Tsars' Moscow residence, is imposing but simple and elegant. The main facade faces the Moscova River; the Cyrillic letters CCCP stand for the Union of Soviet Socialist Republics.

238-239 This passageway
between two rooms in the
imperial residence of the Great
Palace is both majestic and
original. The panels with floral
motifs on a red background are
vaguely Pompeiian in design. The
lovely carved wooden frames are
held up by perfectly restored
wooden columns that rest on two
painted supports that run the
entire length of the corridor.

239 left Unlike the other rooms in
the Tsarina's apartment, the
small drawing room shows the
influence of Neo-Rococo style. The
main features are the
combination of light colors
(white, gold and blue) and the
original layout of the room
around a central pillar which
divides the transit area from what
is called the Welcoming Corner.
The large porcelain lamp in the
background was made by the
imperial manufactory in the first
half of the 19th century.

It has been violated only a few times but that has not meant there was ever a break in continuity: the Tatar Khan Tokhtamysh massacred men and destroyed its buildings but once he retired, the damage was quickly repaired and Russian revenge was planned from inside the citadel. Twice at the beginning of the 17th century, the Poles placed an "usurper" in the Kremlin and twice fresh forces came out of deepest Russia to chase the invaders out—it was then the turn of the Poles to be oppressed by Russia. Napoleon left the Kremlin injured to meet his Waterloo.

All decisions relating to international politics are taken inside the Kremlin. Ivan Kalita (*kalita* means "bourse") was appointed by the Tatar Khan to collect all the tributes of Rus', which began the fortune of Moscow; this was imitated by successors who accumulated amounts of money large enough to build a power able to liberate them from ancient

239 top right The Large Reception Room is pure Baroque, with gilded furniture and wall decorations, and large gold and green brocades.

239 bottom right This suite of seven rooms in the south wing of the Great Palace is truly magnificent. The passage is dominated by the large drop-crystal chandeliers and upright gilded candelabra/vases in Neo-Rococo style.

dominators and finally erase them from historical memory. The Kremlin Palaces of the Prince and the Metropolitan faced one another, and later the Palaces of the Tsar and the Patriarch. After 1922, the various branches of the Communist Party and the Soviet Government existed together there; the Congresses of the Third International, the Komintern and the SUCP were held in the Great Palace, and it was there that in 1936 the constitution of the USSR was approved. It was also the setting in which Krushchev announced his plan of de-Stalinization and Gorbachev announced *perestroika*.

Karskoe Selo

CATHERINE'S PALACE

Russia

ST. PETERSBURG

A sort of "Versailles complex" took hold of rulers across central and eastern Europe in the 18th century. The Russian monarchs seemed to suffer from the most intense spasms of it: if the construction of St. Petersburg was a challenge, that of the large suburban residences such as Karskoe Selo, Peterhof, Pavlovsk, Oranienbaum and Gatchina was the royal response to the impelling desire for self-aggrandizement, using the indispensable tools of the arts, chiefly architecture, to do so.

The "Russian Leonardo da Vinci," M.V. Lomonosov, wrote in his discourse for the inauguration of the St. Petersburg Academy of Fine Arts that Russia, vast and glorious after its victories, deserved the finest works of art to celebrate its greatness.

However, Lomonosov was simply restating the idea that had inspired the work of rebuilding and expansion of the Kremlin in

240 top This Enlightenment portrait of Catherine II in the Temple of Justice (hung in the Tret'jakovskaja Gallery in Moscow) was painted by D. Levicki (1735-1822).

240 center The statues of Atlas holding up the globe alternate with the wide windows of the facade of the Great Palace to create a vertical contrast to the massive horizontal form of the building and to balance the tones of white and blue.

Moscow between the end of the 15th century and the beginning of the next. The idea that the greatness of the state should be clearly reflected in the magnificence of its architecture runs continuously right through the history of imperial Russia and, without interruption, through that of the Soviet Union.

The most significant example of celebratory magnificence—even to the point of excess—is the complex of palaces and parks at Karskoe Selo (Village of the Tsars). The place was renamed Detskoe Selo (Village

of the Children) with Soviet demagogy after 1917, and then again renamed as Pushkin in 1937, on the centenary of the death of the poet who has always been considered Russia's most genuine representative by all the regimes to have ruled since his time.

The long and complex work of construction and organization of Karskoe Selo has one further thing in common with the other great Russian residences: it was originally a palace of modest dimensions that was progressively expanded and connected to other buildings, before the whole complex was rebuilt according to an overall design which was then watered down in a series of modifications and additions. In the St. Petersburg area this process lasted more than 200 years, from the start of the 18th century to the era of Stalin.

The varied countryside of the site chosen for Karskoe Selo was unusual compared to the general flatness that is Russia. The location was known as Sarskaja Myza (Island Farm) and was first mentioned on a Swedish map in the 1670s. After the victory of Narva and the transfer of part to Swedish Estonia to Russia, Peter the Great gave six farms in the region, one of which was Sarskaja Myza, to his wife Catherine, who was to succeed him to the throne (1725–27).

Catherine set up her own private chapel dedicated to St. Catherine in a wooden building where the Great Palace (Bol'shoj Dvorec) now stands. The church of the Dormition was built later, also in wood. From that time, Sarskaja Myza began to be indicated in documents as Sarskoe Selo which then developed into Karskoe Selo.

Unlike Peterhof and Oranienbaum, the residence of A.D. Menshikov (Peter's favorite and Catherine's lover), the first wooden buildings at Karskoe Selo were not what is now called the "castle of pleasure" but just a modest "villa" in traditional ancient Russian style.

Thousands of families of peasants *na vecnoe zitie* (those condemned by caste to remain peasants for the whole of their lives) were brought from different parts of the crown territories, often thousands of miles from their new compulsory residence, to

240 bottom The current appearance of the Great Palace is partly the result of work carried out in the 1740s by A.V. Kvasov and S.I. Chevakinksi, but mostly due to Rastrelli's contribution of 1752-56. The building's 325-yard perimeter and the rich sculptural decoration make the it the undisputed Baroque masterpiece of Russia.

240-241 The imposing facade of the Great Palace is the result of work by several generations of architects, craftsmen, and artists from various countries. The domes of the annexed church can be seen in the background.

241 top This portrait of Bartolomeo Rastrelli was painted by Pietro Antonio Rotari. The painting is held today in the Russian Museum of St. Petersburg.

241 bottom left The central section (Srednij dom) of the facade that overlooks the old garden of the Great Palace, as the Soviets called the building once known as Catherine's Palace. This the oldest part of the building: it was constructed in 1718-24 by architect I.F. Braunstein.

241 bottom right The traditional five golden domes crown the church designed by S.I. Chevakinski on the extreme right of the central section of the Great Palace. Chevakinski succeeded Trezzini as Kvasov's assistant. He later took full responsibility for the project, a post which he held until 1760, with the Italian Rastrelli as his assistant.

242-243 The sumptuous Large
Gallery was the hall where parties
used to take place. Rastrelli chose
intaglioed stone instead of plaster
and stucco for the serial decoration
of this room, as he probably

considered that use of the cutting
knife created minimal differences
between one panel and the next,
and produced a single
unrepeatable output rather than a
monotonous series.

243 top left The Agate Hall was
designed by Charles Cameron
(1740-1812), an undisputed
master of interior decoration
known for his exceptional use
of colors and the wide range of

materials he deployed,
including the semiprecious
stones with which Russia
abounds, glass, majolica,
Chinese lacquer and precious
fabrics.

construct the first stone buildings at the
beginning of the 1720s.

Scarce and fragmentary information on
Karskoe Selo and no drawings survive from
this first phase. The only thing recorded is that
a few buildings were constructed and the first
gardens or park were designed and laid out
around them.

The first systematic plan of the area was
drawn up by the architect Zemkov in 1742–43
while Elizabeth, daughter of Peter the Great,
was on the throne (1740–62). As early as 1743,
Catherine I's stone palace—which had been
built by Braunstein in 1722—was rebuilt and
connected to the central section by galleries.
Zemkov was succeeded after his death by his
pupil A.V. Kvasov, who worked in association
with the Swiss Giuseppe Trezzini, and then by
S.I. Chevakinski. When Kvasov was
transferred to the Ukraine, Chevakinski was

left to oversee the works until 1760 in
association with Rastrelli.

Rastrelli had already worked at Peterhof
and was later to design the church of St.
Andrew in Kiev and participate in the
rebuilding of the Winter Palace; his
exceptional talent was particularly suited to
the design of interiors. Rastrelli's favorite style
dictate was that a palace's main stairway
should be placed at the side of a building
rather than in the center, and that an *enfilade*
of rooms and studies should open out from
the main entrance. This idea was used in the
Great Palace at Karskoe Selo with persuasive
conviction. Rastrelli, a wonderful designer,
was personally responsible for all the internal
decorations, which were full of color,
movement and lighting effects. Innumerable
mirrors reflected the gilded volutes of the
marquetry, the ceiling frescoes and the floors

that were so elaborate they seemed like
lacework.

Rastrelli refused Kvasov and Chevakinski's
design for the Great Palace: three sections
connected by single-story galleries and a
general emphasis on the vertical. Instead he
created a single, compact volume over 324
yards long, a geometric succession of columns
and pilasters, windows and balconies, with an
interplay of colors: light blue plaster, white
columns and gilded statues.

Rastrelli also built many other buildings of
the *Lusthaus* type (in part using Kvasov's and
Chevakinski's designs) which were used to
accommodate guests from the court, to serve
intimate dinners, and to rest in after walks in
the countryside or hunting. Of these, only the
Hermitage and the Grotto beside the Great
Pond remain, but they lack any rich sculptural
decoration.

the bodies of water and the green areas.

The architect V. Neelov and his son were sent to England in 1770 to study gardens so that they could dedicate themselves on their return to the work that was so dear to Classicists—forcing nature to seem more natural, more similar to a work of art.

In 1773, work on the Great Pond began. Its originally straight banks were altered to make it seem like a real lake. Two small islands were created in the western part, Wild Island and Stony Island, and a third at the eastern end, Small Island. The existing Big Island was enlarged.

Neelov was assisted by two master gardeners, J. Busch and T. Il'in, in his organization of the garden areas. It has been

243 top right Rastrelli's portrait gallery is dominated by the large Dutch ceramic stove. The portrait of Empress Elizabeth by Heinrich Buchholz hangs on the left. The parquet was recently restored according to Rastrelli's design.

243 bottom right Two tall ceramic stoves standing opposite one another divide the Art Gallery of the Great Palace into two halves. The paintings on the walls, separated only by thin gold frames, became simply part of the furnishings.

Catherine's Palace

In the 1740s and 1750s, a large plan to organize the gardens was undertaken. The most beautiful statues were transferred from the St. Petersburg gardens to Karskoe Selo. The oldest trees were also transported and pruned so that they looked like pieces of bizarre architecture. Thousands of workers and craftsmen (stone masons, stucco decorators, engravers and gardeners) worked for over a decade to complete the grandiose project.

Then Catherine II, the Semiramis of the North, came to the throne. She wanted to link her name with rebuilding projects for Moscow and St. Petersburg which had until then been unimaginable and, naturally, she wished the same for Karskoe Selo, the history of which had from the start been linked with that of the nearby capital.

So began the third phase of construction of the site and countryside of Karskoe Selo. The first was linked with Catherine I and an intimist, "old Russian" model; the second was associated with Elizabeth and a wild Rococo style; the third was to be the work of Catherine II in a purified and rarefied Neoclassicism not always compatible with what had preceded it.

Two of the most debatable alterations in this phase were the construction of two wings that stuck out widely from either side of the Great Palace facade, and the moving of the official entrance to the center of the main facade. All this distorted Rastrelli's design, which in itself was a great success, and did not help to create coherence with the new taste of the age.

The greatest achievements during Catherine's phase of construction were the leveling of the land and the arrangement of

calculated that over 200,000 trees had been transported to Karskoe Selo for planting before 1772.

Neelov had already designed the first of the buildings in the park, the Palladian Bridge (Palladiev Most), in 1769. Columns and memorial arches were erected in the early 1770s to celebrate Russian victories in the war against the Ottoman empire (1768–74): the *Ruina* designed by Velten, the rostral column by Rinaldi and the Gatchina Gate topped by a triumphal arch.

Domenico Quarenghi—the most Russian of the Italian architects or the most Italian of the Russian architects—and the unequalled master of Russian Neoclassicism, also had a central role during the third phase of construction of Karskoe Selo. He was originally called by Empress Catherine II in 1779 to St. Petersburg, where he had previously worked on the Winter Palace and designed many palaces and interiors. He had returned to Italy in 1810 for family reasons and there he was surprised by the decree of Viceroy Eugène Beauharnais that ordered

Neelov to build a "stone house with 14 floors" for the hereditary prince Paul. This building was later to house the lyceum where Pushkin studied.

During the 19th century, work on the site continued uninterrupted. Service buildings, pavilions, columns and artificial ruins were all built, as well as a Turkish bath with minaret and golden dome designed by I.A. Monighetti in 1850–52. This last feature reflected the taste for the exotic, so fashionable in the previous century, which had never gone completely out of favor.

After 1917, Karskoe Selo was transformed into a museum complex, also to be used as a holiday village.

During the siege of Leningrad which stretched for 900 days from September 1941 to January 1944, Karskoe Selo suffered serious damage, first from bombardments and then from the German occupation.

Immediately after the war ended, restoration began, on the principle of each element returning how it was and to where it was, although some buildings had been lost

244 top The Green Dining Room (Zelënaja stolovaja) and all its decorations were designed by Cameron, who worked also on decorations. This two-tone door panel features gryphons, stylized plant figures, and putti.

244 center The magnificent parquet with geometrical and plant-shaped patterns and the Pompeii-style ceiling are the major attractions in the Blue Drawing Room, designed by Cameron. It can be considered his masterpiece in Karskoe Selo.

244 bottom This section of ceiling in the Blue Drawing Room is typical of Cameron's taste. It is painted in panels and medallions with gryphons, putti and scenes based on classical motifs.

all Italian residents in Russia to return home. Placed in a dilemma, he decided to return to his second homeland where he was to die seven years later.

At Karskoe Selo, Quarenghi planned and directed the work on the palace, later named the Alexander Palace, and worked with Cameron on the design and construction of a new city, Sophia, which Catherine wanted built in the park. Quarenghi built a church/mausoleum in the cemetery of Sophia in which stood the funeral monument of A.D. Lanski, one of Catherine's favorites.

In 1778, the Empress commissioned

for ever. At the same time, the task of recovering the stolen treasures was begun with patient investigation and difficult diplomatic negotiations. Everything that was recovered was replaced as closely as possible in its original position.

Now the wounds have healed. Karskoe Selo is still enchanting—more for its magnificence and overall coherence than for the beauty of its individual details. Its attraction also lies in the work of those who have preserved "a thing of beauty" that is a "joy forever," regardless of the regime that produced it.

244-245 This white marble stairway is a typical example of a Neoclassical interior. It connects the ground floor to the first floor in the central section of the building.
The brilliant white of the marble and of the stuccoes creates an intense brightness that eliminates the need for much outside light, which is filtered here by the red window drapes.

245 top These stucco medallions showing mythological scenes were produced by I.P. Martos, the most famous craftsman of the period.

245 bottom left Cameron's skill is evident in this view of Marija Fëdorovna's bedroom with its splendid parquet flooring made from different types of wood and its slender columns, both fluted and spiral.

245 bottom right Apart from the delicacy and variety of materials used, the Green Dining Room is notable for the sobriety of its design in comparison to the tastes of the period, and the harmonious combination of horizontal and vertical features.

Peterhof

✦ ST. PETERSBURG

Russia

THE KINGDOM OF FOUNTAINS

246 top right The imperial coat of arms and the monograms of the sovereigns appear as a brass decoration on the cover of The Book of the Coronation of their Majesties Tsar Alexander II and Tsarina Marija Alexandrovna, published in 1856 by the Imperial Academy of Sciences of St. Petersburg. Inside, 17 lithographs and watercolors illustrate the stages of the ceremony.

Peterhof is the realm of fountains symbolically expressing the realm of waters and the wash of the foamy waves against the shore. This place seems as though it was brought to life by the will of the powerful King of the Seas, who made it his residence. With these thoughts the famous painter Aleksandr Benois (1870–1960), one of the main exponents of the world of art, described the fascinating "Russian Versailles," which he often painted in his watercolors. Peterhof was the first and most beautiful summer residence in the area of St. Petersburg. Stretching along the Gulf of Finland on a strip of land over a mile

long, it was built by Peter I the Great. The Tsar wanted Peterhof to be closely linked to the gulf, for the sea was a source of fascination to him and he considered it an element of his destiny.

In 1703, he had founded the new Russian capital on the shores of the Baltic. This difficult enterprise had been undertaken for strategic and commercial reasons. The marshy, unhealthy and almost uninhabited area seemed just right as a new point of access to the sea, and as the site for a naval base against Sweden. Russia's traditional marine outlets were cut off: the White Sea by ice for many months of the year, and the Black Sea by the Turkish enemy. So Peter, realizing that the Fort of Saints Peter and Paul at the mouth of the river Neva did not have a good location, began to build another at Kronštadt on the island of Kotlin in the Gulf of Finland, 20 miles from the St. Petersburg. The Tsar, who was fond of carpentry and other manual activities, rowed out from the nearest point on the coast to oversee the works. So it was that a small wooden house called Peterhof ("Peter's Court" in German) was built here where he could hear the murmur of the waves. On 13 August 1705 it was mentioned in the field journal of the Tsar for the first time. Nine years later a pavilion called Monplaisir was built in its place, in the Dutch style favored by the emperor. In the capital the court indulged in all kinds of excess with the approval of the bizarre and extravagant emperor; at Peterhof there was even less restraint.

The opportunity to turn Peterhof into a luxurious residence for receptions occurred after the victory of Poltava (over the Swedes) in 1709. It is documented that the emperor took part in drawing up the first plans of the parks and palaces destined to "celebrate Russia as a grand maritime power." The Tsar had traveled around Europe and, wishing to create a complex that could rival Versailles, he invited famous foreign painters, gardeners, engineers and other specialists to Russia. Architects like the Frenchman Jean-Baptiste Alexandre Leblond, the pupil of Le Notre who had created the gardens at Versailles, the Italian Nicolò Michetti and the German Johann Friedrich Braunstein created a large park with avenues, views and terraces on the basis of the king's sketches. The

246-247 A curtain of trees pulls open to reveal the central section of the Baroque Great Palace of Peterhof and before it the Grand Cascade, the Grotto and the Samson Fountain reflected in the waters of the Maritime Canal.

247 top The portrait of Peter the Great, kept in the Hermitage, was painted in 1717 by Jean-Marc Nattier. Peter's scepter demonstrates his power as sovereign and his shining armor his power as military commander. One hand is ready to grip the hilt of his sword and the other rests on his helmet.

246 top left and 247 bottom right Two shining details from the fountain in the Upper Park called Me žeumnyj or Neopredelěnnyj—"uncertain"—due to the changes made in its decorations. The definitive version made in 1958 by the sculptor Gužij shows a monster surrounded by four dolphins.

246 center Peterhof's main fountain, the Samson Fountain, stands before the immense Grand Cascade with green marble steps, the north face of the Great Palace above it, and the Pavilion of the Chapel on the left.

246 bottom A closeup view of the Grand Cascade also shows the Maritime Canal. The original function of the 430-yard-long canal was to provide access to the palace by water. On the right stands one of the two Neoclassical pavilions designed by Voronichin in 1803 with gilded domes, columns and fountains on the roof.

248 top The Cascade of the Golden Mountain in the Lower Park falls nearly 40 feet with steps decorated with balustrades and white marble statues. The large fountains at the bottom are called Menažernye (from the French "mènager"—to save) because, although they have a 50-foot spray, they use little water.

248-249 A general view from the south of the summer residence of Peterhof and the Gulf of Finland. The Great Palace divides the two parks, the Upper and Lower Parks. The latter, seen in the foreground, used to be an orchard but was turned into the palace's main court. Today it is a French garden with symmetrical flowerbeds, fountains and statues made from marble and gilded bronze.

Great Palace was designed in Baroque style by Leblond and Braunstein and situated like a fulcrum between the Large and Small Parks. It overlooks the Grand Cascade, the loveliest of a series of fountains and small lakes.

At Peterhof there are no hidden pumps: the water reaches the site from the Ropšin hills, 11 miles away, using a system designed on Peter's directions by the engineer Tuvolkov. It includes 11 artificial and natural tanks, canals and locks.

On 15 August 1723, the official inauguration of the residence took place and, although it was not finished, everyone was delighted by the beauty of the setting and the profusion of fountains. Again it was the Tsar who had inspired Peterhof's most extraordinary feature—the Grand Cascade in front of the Great Palace. A canal bordered by steps and fountains starts

biblical hero forces open the lion's jaws from which a jet of water shoots 65 feet into the air.

After Peter the Great's death in 1725, his niece Anna Ivanovna, his daughter Elizabeth I, and then Catherine II further embellished Peterhof, which had become famous throughout Europe as the "Versailles on the sea." The Great Palace was enlarged by the Italian architect Francesco Bartolomeo Rastrelli: maintaining the Baroque facade intact, he raised the central section by one floor and added two lateral wings which terminated in pavilions with golden domes—the Pavilion of the Chapel to the east and the Pavilion of the Imperial Eagle to the west. The symmetrical north facade was 295 yards long and faced the sea. Its design was enlivened by the inclusion of protuberances and indentations and by the different heights of the various sections of the

249 top The Monplaisir Palace is the architectural center of the eastern Lower Park. The north face, made from brick and crowned by the white, pavilion-style roof, can be seen among the trees and the jets of the 1721 fountain made from tufa, called the Sheaf Fountain.

248 bottom left The Baroque-style Pavilion of the Imperial Eagle of the Great Palace was designed in 1745 by Rastrelli. The name comes from the golden coat of arms on the onion dome, the symbol of the Russian monarchy.

248 bottom right A general view of the facade of the Orangerie. In the foreground appears the round fountain with the Triton, where the powerful jet of the monster is echoed by the lesser sprays of the four gilded turtles.

from the Cascade's tank and pours out into the sea. The Baroque Grand Cascade designed by Leblond, Braunstein, Michetti and Zemcov boasts 64 fountains and 225 gilded bronze sculptures of sea gods and goddesses, and allegories of Russian rivers and the maritime vocation of the empire, in a majestic glorification of Russia's access to the Baltic and its victory over Sweden. The battle of Poltava had taken place on the nameday of St. Samson, and so the Samson Fountain in the tank at the bottom of the Cascade symbolically dominates the whole composition. (Peter, moreover, was often celebrated as "the Russian Samson.") The

building. It was painted yellow with white window settings. The tall attics and chimneys were typical of the houses and palaces of St. Petersburg. The interiors were modified by Rastrelli into a scintillating parade of rooms embellished with gilded marquetry, mirrors, frescoes and inlaid parquet.

Over the following years, famous architects were called to make alterations and modifications according to the taste of the period so that very little of the original work by Rastrelli, designer of the magnificent Winter Palace, remains. One lovely example is the Gala Stairway created in 1750 (and entirely redone

249 bottom The Neptune Fountain is the most spectacular in the Upper Park. The statuary was purchased in 1798 by Paul I at Nuremberg. Nymphs symbolizing Bavarian rivers, the Pegnitz and the Rednitz, riders on sea-horses and four putti on dolphins and sea-dragons disport themselves at the base of the pedestal of the King of the Seas.

250 top and bottom The Audience Room from the mid-18th century was designed by Rastrelli in Baroque style with white walls decorated with pilasters and gilded plasterwork. The large mirrors that face one another enlarge the dimensions of the room to infinity.

250-251 The Neoclassical Throne Room (measuring over 3,500 sqare feet) is decorated with portraits of the royal family. Nicholas I's coronation throne stands in the background. The crystal chandeliers are Russian-made, from the factory of Prince Potēmkin near St. Petersburg. The delicate amethyst shading is obtained by adding gold to other metals during casting.

251 top The pair of Sèvres porcelain vases (1807) were a gift from Napoleon to Alexander I. They are kept in the Empress's Room in the Cottage in Alexandra's Park. The vases are 21 inches high, cobalt in color and finely decorated with gold. They boast magnificent grisaille medallions showing scenes from mythology.

in 1985) which shines with gilded inlays in lime wood and with trompe l'oeil paintings. The Česme Room (once an antechamber), dedicated to the great victory in the war against the Turks (1768–74), was redone by Yuri Matveevič Velten in the more sober Russian classical style to house 12 large paintings by Philipp J. Hackert commemorating the naval battle of Česme. The huge throne room was decorated by the same architect in 1777–78 with particular elegance given by the matching of gold and white and luminosity from the reflections of mirrors and glass panels.

The portrait of Catherine II on horseback by the Danish artist Virgilius Erichsen stands

out from those of the other Russian rulers. Velten enlivened the walls of the White Dining Room in 1774–75 with refined stucco decorations inspired by banquets and feasts and featuring flowers, fruit, hunting trophies, quivers of arrows and musical instruments.

Jean-Baptiste Vallin de la Mothe also worked for Catherine the Great and in 1763 designed the two Chinese Studies, which are decorated with lacquer panels from the early 1700s and high quality parquet. In the Portrait Room, the French architect commissioned 368 portraits of women from the Veronese painter Count Pietro Rotari (in Russia from 1756) which produced a great ornamental effect. The legend

goes that Rotari was charged by the Tsarina Elizabeth to search out the most beautiful girls in the 50 Russian governorships, but in fact he used only 8 models in different dresses and poses. The sweet, smiling faces seem to be multiplied into infinity by the mirrors placed over the mantelpieces. The room is especially light due to the large windows that open onto the two gardens. The Living Room next door is small but elegant; it is also called the Partridge Room for the birds that appear in the silk tapestry from Lyons. The Ottoman Room, designed by Velten with painted Chinese silks on the wall and a large Turkish divan with embroidered cushions, was a tribute to the Oriental vogue of the period. From

251 bottom left The elegant amaranth and gold porcelain fruit bowl from the Gur'evskij dinner service. It is 16 inches high and has an engraved cup held up by two girls in Russian dress. In order to exalt the power of the empire, all the pieces in the service were decorated with scenes inspired by Russian life and costumes.

The Kingdom of Fountains

the age of Peter the Great, the founder of the palace, there remains the Oak Study, a sober but interesting room that is a statement of the emperor's tastes and attitudes. The study, lined with a magnificent oak *boiserie* engraved by the Frenchman Nicolas Pineau in 1718–20, houses some books and a table clock and many other objects that belonged to Peter. In the center a globe recalls that the Tzar liked navigation and was an experienced seaman. Pineau also engraved the Oak Stairs and the Vestibule; the latter is also decorated with the fresco *Aurora on a Carriage* and a portrait of Peter the Great by Danish painter Benoit Coffre, for which the emperor sat in 1716.

The Great Palace was for receptions, not for daily life: the Tzar preferred other palaces and pavilions in the park such as Monplaisir, the Hermitage, Marly and the Cottage. The splendor and magnificence of the interiors of the Great Palace leave the visitor amazed, and it is difficult to believe that so much beauty was reborn from ashes, like the phoenix, after its dramatic recent history. During the siege of Leningrad in World War II (September 1941 to January 1944), the front line ran south of the city along the Gulf of Finland, right near Peterhof and the other residences. Consequently, the Great Palace and other buildings were looted and partly destroyed, while the park was

251 bottom right The Gur'evskij dinner service (1809-17) stands on a table in the Yellow Room in the Catherine Wing of the Monplaisir Palace. A gift to Alexander II, it was ordered by Count Gur'ev from the Imperial Porcelain factory in St. Petersburg. A fine portrait of Alexander hangs on the wall.

252 top left Peter I's oak-lined study contains a traveling pen and inkpot and an English globe. The set is completed by two elegant "cabinets," small chests/safes similar to miniature palaces.

252 bottom left The Portrait Room, designed by Leblond and Rastrelli, is located in the center of the palace. Magnificent bronze French clocks of the 18th century stand on the mantelpieces. The andirons, also French, are true works of art and show the figures of Venus and Vulcan.

252 top center This ship's sundial (London, 1716) is finely worked in brass and silver. It was a gift from the English king, George I, to Peter the Great. It stands in the oak-lined study in Marly Palace.

252 bottom center Catherine II bought the 368 pictures that portray the grace and beauty of Russian women from the widow of Pietro Rotari, the court painter of Elizabeth I of Russia. To remind the viewer of the transitoriness of beauty, the face of an old woman appears every now and again.

mined. Of the 4,000 valuable objects in the complex, perhaps more than 2,000 were carried off; furniture, carpets, paintings and bronzes were hidden in the cellars, and fountain statues were either camouflaged or hidden in ditches. Nevertheless, the damage was incalculable. In January 1944, Peterhof was freed and renamed Petrodvorets (Russian for "Peter's Palace"). Only recently has the original name been reinstated.

Reconstruction began immediately and much of what we admire today is the result of meticulous restoration work based on plans, descriptions, photographs and fragments of original pieces, sometimes from shreds of material.

The uniqueness and attraction of Peterhof, which in the perfection of its restoration seems to have returned to its golden period, lies in the

Peterhof
The Kingdom of Fountains

252 right When the court was at Peterhof, the royal insignia were kept in the Crown Room on the small table designed by Brenna. The walls and interior of the bed alcove are lined with an 18th-century Chinese silk of very rare design: it shows the secret process of preparing Chinese porcelain. The richly carved bed in gilded wood is Italian.

253 The walls of the Gala Staircase are covered with extra-fine decorations, garlands of flowers, vases, mythological figures, false niches and two real ones housing the gilded wooden statues of Autumn and Winter. The graceful figures of Summer and Spring stand opposite. The wrought iron banisters are decorated with gilded elements.

theme of water. As though in intimate conversation with the expanses of the gulf, gushing waterfalls and fountains are the real distinctive feature of this residence, spectacularly set in the immense park (laid out afresh in 1779 in Neoclassical style by Giacomo Quarenghi. The majority of them are in the Small Garden, but the most beautiful is the Neptune Fountain in the center of the French-style Large Garden. Also striking is the Chessboard Fountain, in which the water runs over marble chessboards observed by ferocious dragons who spout water from their mouths. Over 500 jets of different heights make up the Pyramid Fountain; the two Roman Fountains echo those in St. Peter's Square; and the Sun Fountain, with 12 gilded dolphins, radiates spray in rotating disks.

The prankster Peter the Great followed 18th-century fashion with amusing "surprise" fountains, like the Umbrella, the Three Firs and the Oak Fountains that occasionally soak visitors, and with paths unexpectedly sprayed by jets of water. Just as the character of Peter I shines through in this magical place, the sad end of his nephew, the weak and extravagant Peter III, is linked to Monplaisir, his favorite retreat. While celebrating his nameday there on 28 June 1762 he heard that his wife Catherine, whom he had relegated to Peterhof, had escaped to St. Petersburg and had been proclaimed Empress. A few days later Peter was assassinated. This was the beginning of the long reign of Catherine II the Great, the German princess who proved to be the true heir and continuer of the work of Peter I.

Magnificence and Power in the
Oriental Palaces

In the East as in the West royal or noble residences are designed as the visible expression of power over territory: they must therefore embody a character of maximum "monumentality" and combine the very best that the architecture and art of a country are able to produce.

There are two different and contrasting conceptions of "monumentality" on the Euro-Asiatic continent: there is the Western and central-Asiatic version, which with many variants reached eastward to the border of the lands covered by Chinese civilization, and there is the Far-Eastern interpretation. In the former, which includes Europe, the Middle East, central Asia, India and Tibet, a monument is thought of in terms of amplitude and, more importantly, in terms of height. The resulting structures are often huge, multistory buildings which are sometimes heightened further by being placed on a platform or plinth. An example in India is the *prasada*, the archetype of the palace and temple, a compact multistory structure which inclines inward as it rises and which is seen in the rajput fort at Amber.

The second, Eastern concept, found in China and the other countries to which Chinese influence spread—Korea, Japan and Indochina—often interprets "monumentality" in terms of distance between various elements of a complex; these elements are preferably only one story high, but many are placed on a tall plinth. The various sections of a palace (reception, residential and service areas) are not situated in a single building or contiguous structures; they generally stand as single entities in a hierarchical arrangement with regard to the central north-south axis, the magnitude of the courts, and the height of their dais or roof coverings, as can be seen in the Forbidden City in Beijing.

The architectural concepts of palatial monuments in the two geographical areas are also distinguished structurally: in Europe and western and central Asia, the design produces multistory and polyfunctional constructions with solid load-bearing walls and roofs that generally are flat or have overhangs. The *dian* in the Far East, on the other hand, is usually a single-story pavilion generally used for a single function. It is formed of three parts: a dais, some wooden bearing sections and an overhanging covering made of glazed tiles supported by a typical bracket system or *dougong*. The nonbearing walls serve exclusively for purposes of division and are sometimes moved back to the second span of columns to form an external porch. This model is ordered in terms of importance around a series of courts along one or more north-south axes on a symmetrical and specular layout: the more important pavilions are sited on the central axis of the entire complex.

In Indochina, the "Western" Indian and "Far Eastern" Chinese architectures are combined and overlaid. In the royal palace in Bangkok we see single-story pavilions (*prasat*), similar to Chinese designs, next to bell-shaped *stupa*, typical of India. The *prasat* have a dais, wooden colonnade and glazed tile covering and are used as religious and civil meeting

rooms. Of course heavy Chinese immigration into Thailand has influenced certain architectural solutions, transforming the Chinese architectural vocabulary into a completely local parlance. The typical curvature of eaves on Chinese roof coverings has been transposed into sharp acroters turned to face upward, while the Chinese order has been replaced by robust columns with brackets derived from Indian designs. The coverings are piled on top of one another in a manner as original as the brightly colored, animated and often gilded external decorations.

The influence of Mongol and Turkish invaders who had assimilated elements of Far Eastern architecture in their homelands, produced a fusion of these two opposing interpretations of "monumentality," as is demonstrated in the Red Fort in Delhi and in Topkapi in Istanbul. The elevated position and compact appearance of the Red Fort gives the

impression to an external viewer of west Asian architecture whereas, on the inside, several pavilions with porches, like the *diwan-i-am*, recall the Far Eastern concept of space. The *diwan-i-am* is situated on the central axis of the complex at the far end of a wide court and displays an Indo-Islamic architectural vocabulary (polylobate pointed arches, twin columns, cornices supported by brackets, a flat covering with *chattri*—kiosks on columns—at the corners), but its location, single-story structure and low dais with steps are reminiscent of the Chinese *dian*.

In Topkapi, however, the kiosks are clearly Islamic in appearance, with a strong Persian influence. Surrounded by porches with pointed arches and set amid gardens, their external apertures and discordant arrangement recall the imperial summer palaces in China. Even the majolica tiles from Iznik which decorate them are decorated with motifs, often blue and white, derived from Chinese porcelain, of which the Ottoman emperors had a valuable collection. (The Turkish word for

glazed pottery is *chini*, from the same root as *China*.)

In every large palace, whether in the East or the West, the approach to the center of power, represented by the throne room, audience room and council chamber, took place gradually and according to a precise ceremonial which has an effect on the construction of the rooms and division of the spaces. But in Asia as compared to the West, the monarch was considered holier and the ritual that accompanied a meeting with the king or emperor was more complex and selective, so more time was required to complete that ritual, with the effect that the layout of rulers' residences was more functional. In Topkapi in Istanbul, the Red Fort in Delhi and the palace at Amber in Rajasthan, the building was designed so that the slow approach to the ruler led through a succession of rooms, often separated by courts, until one reached the throne room. This architectural conceit reached its peak in the Forbidden City in Beijing. The route to the Son of Heaven, guarantor of earthly order and reflection of

256 top Wall inscription in Topkapi Palace, Istanbul.

256 bottom left View of the Red Fort of Delhi and its massive walls.

256-257 The Pavilion of Baghdad and Sultan Ibrahim's canopy in Topkapi Palace.

Magnificence and Power in the

Oriental Palaces

cosmic order, was gradual, long and selective to the utmost degree. The entire city of Beijing was designed on the orders of the Ming dynasty at the start of the 15th century as a single large complex which permitted a correct and ritual approach nearly four miles long to the Emperor via the Yongding men (the southern gate on the north-south axis). It was necessary to pass through external walls, cross the entire Outer or Chinese City (Wei Cheng), pass through the defensive walls of the Inner or Tartar City (Nei Cheng), then cross the Imperial City or bureaucratic area (Huang Cheng), and pass under the famous Tian-an men (Gate of Heavenly Peace) to reach the Meridian Gate

that entered the Forbidden City. Here the three audience pavilions on the same north-south axis (San-ta dian) were a succession of concentric screen walls and monumental gates and passages across wide courts that sharply reminded privileged visitors of the power and holiness of the Emperor.

A similar ceremonial walk, though less complex and symmetrical, was seen in the succession of three courts at Topkapi—the same number of courts, palaces and temples as prescribed in China. Let it not be forgotten that the ancient Turks had contacts, disputes and exchanges with the Chinese civilization during the early centuries of our era, and that the great

Turkish empire during the 8th century imitated Chinese architectural models in its monuments and tombs of the Khagan in Mongolia.

A common destiny has come to most of the loveliest mansions and palaces in Europe and Asia where rulers and aristocrats accumulated works of art for the love of collecting or for reasons of patronage. Now that monarchical power has disappeared from nearly all countries, new regimes have transformed the monumental houses into museums so that all citizens can enjoy the extraordinary artistic treasures that were gathered over the centuries.

257 top left Inside view of the Red Fort of Delhi.

257 top right Decorative detail of Ahmad III's Dining Room, Topkapi Palace.

ISTANBUL

Turkey

Topkapi Palace

THE SCINTILLATING DOOR TO ASIA

opkapi Sarayi, or Topkapi Palace, in Istanbul is an extraordinary architectural and cultural projection of the Ottoman empire, of which it was for centuries the moving force. When Mohammed the Conqueror took Byzantium on 29 May 1453, a new phase of urban development began for the city which had once been known as Constantinople and which had recently suffered from a period of decline. Having taken the city at last, it was important for the Muslims to signal their presence on its most important areas, starting with the church of St. Sophia, which was soon transformed into a mosque. To begin with, the victorious sultan, who belonged

could be a place where Ottoman architectural style was freely expressed.

As the residence of the sultan from about 1470 to 1839, the palace was subject to innumerable alterations and additions, besides being the victim of two large fires, in 1574 and 1665. Such a long and tormented life does not hide the fact that the essential and constant feature is the organization of the space into four large courts, each one leading to the next. In this design, the decisive contribution was from Sinan, the greatest Ottoman architect, who acted after the 1574 fire.

About Sinan's life and particularly his youth, information is scarce: he was certainly

258 top right The portrait of Mohammed II (1451-1481) is by Sinan and hangs in Topkapi. Mohammed was a great administrator and protector of the arts; it was he who conquered Constantinople and made it the capital of the Ottoman empire.

258 bottom Like other Moslems, the Turks prize gardens which, in the Koran, symbolize Paradise. The gardens at Topkapi are still well-kept, like this one in front of the Treasure Rooms.

to the Ottoman dynasty founded at the end of the 12th century by Osman I, had a residence built around what is now the university. Soon, however, he changed his mind and opted for the tip of the Golden Horn, a spot of incomparable beauty and security where the ruins of the palace of Constantine had stood since it was sacked by the Crusaders and abandoned by the Comneni dynasty. Unlike other buildings in the city, which were reused in some way (St. Sophia, for example, and the large water cisterns from the Roman or Justinian eras), the palace was not therefore a modification of a previous building and so it

Christian, born in 1491, and enrolled like many of his brilliant co-religionists in the corps of Janissaries or the imperial guard. After conversion to Islam, the new recruits received strict military training. Although many revolts occurred, the sultan could always count on their support, and he rewarded the best with high honors often forbidden to Turks. (This is a clear demonstration that the Ottoman administration had an open character and was primarily concerned with efficiency.) After broad military experience in which Sinan saw combat in Austria, Mesopotamia, Apulia and Corfu, he was appointed palace architect in

258-259 This panorama reflects the character of Istanbul: the ancient maritime city displays the traces of several civilizations and forms the bridge between East and West and old and modern. The rounded roofs and minaret-type chimneys of the Harem contrast with the modern buildings of the new city in the distance.

258 top left and 259 top *The miniature of, and for, Murad III (1574-95) is taken from a manuscript held in the Istanbul Museum of Turkish and Islamic Art. It was produced in 1583, during the years of political balance after the defeat of the Turks at the Battle of Lepanto (1571). Ottoman miniatures are the direct equivalent of the great Persian artistic tradition; they impress with their ability to idealize reality.*

259 bottom This miniature from a 17th-century manuscript housed in the Correr Museum in Venice shows a view of Topkapi. The artist succeeded in making the domes and minarets the characteristic element of the palace, but his arrangement seems medieval and is does not succeed in portraying the airiness of the complex.

260 top This building houses the fountain of Sultan Ahmad III (1703-30) who was deposed by the Janissaries and died, perhaps poisoned, some years later. The fountain stands in the first court. Construction began in 1728, replacing a Byzantine building.

260 bottom This detail of the Harem room, built by Sinan for Murad III, demonstrates its grandeur. The dome, the largest in the palace, originally rested on stone arches. The large salon gives access to the apartment of the sultan's mother and to those of his concubines.

1538 and subsequently began a brilliant artistic career. The works of Sinan and his many pupils left their mark on the face of Istanbul and many other cities in both civil and religious architecture.

One of his tasks at Topkapi was the rebuilding of the Harem within its original walls but with the addition of new rooms. The court of the black eunuchs, the lodgings of the concubines and the large reception hall which was built for Murat III were without doubt all the work of Sinan. The reception hall's great dome (the largest in the palace) embodies the taste for simplicity and the monumentality of the large dimensions that characterize the spaces built for this sultan, in particular the covered swimming pool. Other designs by Sinan are the Harem hospital and the colonnade on the north side of a room of the holy relics where a tooth, a cloak and two swords belonging to Mohammed are kept. This last area, which was also built during the reign of Murat III, has been heavily restored.

This brief summary following the steps of the most important Ottoman architect at Topkapi allows us to draw some general conclusions about the history and importance of the palace. In the first place, this was conceived as a living building designed for the execution of multiple functions; it was built essentially to be the citadel of power. This explains the clear distinction of the areas in the physical, and increasingly selective, approach to the sultan from court to court until the third, where Bab-i Saadet (the Gate of Happiness) opens into the audience rooms.

The private areas were clearly separated from the public areas; putting aside any legendary and exotic reconstruction, the Harem corresponded to the private apartments

in any large European palace. Living in the Harem were the sultan's concubines (sometimes as many as 300), his wives (never more than 4, as prescribed by the Koran), his mother (with her own apartments) who was the *éminence grise* of the harem, and his children, who until the 18th century were segregated in the so-called *kafes* (cages) which in reality were splendidly decorated rooms. The purpose of the *kafes* was to keep the children separate from the world (as the sacralization of the sultan increased with the decline of the empire) and above all to keep them away from the temptation to participate in palace plots.

An important consequence of all this was the necessary functionality of the building, which had to satisfy the daily requirements of approximately 5,000 people efficiently and with varying levels of elegance. As Sinan showed, there was no hierarchy involved in the design of the Ottoman architecture, and to build a bathroom or barracks (of which there were plenty at Topkapi) was no less dignified than to build a mosque. Above all, the same degree of importance was granted to functionality (which was essential also for the mosque and its annexes) and stylistic considerations. The hand of the architect and his expressiveness are noted no less in a bridge than in a *türbe* (an Ottoman mausoleum). It is not by chance that the kitchens in the second court, with their lovely vent ducts and a number of fire-prevention

260-261 The elegant porch outside the Kubbealti still has its original marble, porphyry and granite columns topped by muqarna capitals that reproduce stalactites. The Kubbealti (the room below the dome) behind the Harem in the second court is divided into three separate sections. One was for meetings of the ministers, another was used as the palace archive, and the third was the grand vizir's study.

261 top The picture shows the Court of the Favorites onto which faced the apartments of the women who were successful in giving the Sultan a son. Also facing the court were the apartment of the princes and the accommodation reserved for concubines, the young girls educated at court, from whom the ruler chose his wives.

261 bottom left This view of the Harem from the third courtyard is a good indication of the structural complexity of the palace. The minarets, windows and balconies lend variety and dynamism to the building.

261 bottom right A long covered gallery leads to the Pavilion of the Sacred Cloak. It was built in the 15th century and used to contain the most valuable reliquaries, one of which was Mohammed's cloak.

features (reduced use of mortar, abundant use of stone and strategic distancing from any other building) are one of Sinan's most interesting designs. In this case the great architect derived his inspiration from the old palace of Edirne.

Comparison with the Escorial may be enlightening: the Escorial was the huge pantheon/monastery that Philip II of Spain built in the Guadarrama mountains, which represented the Spanish monarchy no less than Topkapi represented the sultan. The comparison is not far-fetched: consider the compelling parallel drawn by Fernand Braudel

between the Hispanic empire of Philip II and the Ottoman empire, in which the structures were much more similar than might be suggested by their century-old opposition—which became a long-term cohabitation after the battle of Lepanto (1571). Certainly, the first thing we notice is the different geographical setting: on one hand, a distant, austere and almost wild location; on the other a separate but urban setting. (The fourth court of Topkapi offers splendid views of the Bosphorus and its traffic, right where the two lovely recreation pavilions celebrating the victories linked to the cities of Erivan and Baghdad were built in 1635 and 1638; the second is especially attractive for the elegance of its decoration.)

The second thing to be noticed is the surprisingly different role of the religious element, which was essential at the Escorial but secondary at Topkapi. This fact demonstrates the nontheocratic and nonfanatical character of the Ottoman dynasty and the distinction between religious belief and the apparatus of the state. Many large mosques were built in the city and certainly the fact of shared religion, without radical intolerance, was one of the most important features of the empire. But it was no more important than political submission to the sultan: freedom of worship for Jews and Christians was guaranteed by the Koran. The rigid military organization whose tradition has lasted to modern times seems to be the essential instrument of unification that permitted the Ottomans (non-Arab Muslims) to offer political unity to the Islamic world right through the 19th century.

Where the Escorial and Topkapi share a strong parallel is in the taste for art collections. Both complexes are also important museums that house the objects collected by generations of rulers. Topkapi has remarkable collections of furniture, clothes, glassware, porcelain, weapons, carriages, jewelry, books and miniatures (the palace contains several libraries) and what is displayed is only a part of what the museum holds in total: it is just a selection of the most precious items. The display of richness relating to the everyday life of the palace must not, however, be thought of as equal to that of the present treasure rooms. The aesthetic pleasures of most of the palace inhabitants were surely far more modest; and even the sultan must have had to derive much of his pleasure from contemplation of the sea, of the gardens full of tulips (a flower that spread from the Istanbul court north through

262 top The niche, a traditional element of Islamic palace art, can be seen in many of the Harem rooms.

262 center The Imperial Room in the Harem was begun during the reign of Suleiman the Magnificent and completed by Osman II in the late 18th century. This room is mostly European in style but has a long quote from the Koran over the canopy.

Topkapi Palace

263 top left A courtyard in the Harem, which is a separate and well-defined section of the palace. It contains other courtyards and open areas designed for group use. The various sets of inhabitants of the Harem—the concubines, the eunuchs, the princes, the mother of the sultan and the sultan himself—shared the space it contained on a hierarchical basis.

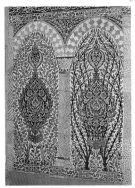

263 top right As in all areas of Topkapi, use of majolica tiles was also common in the Harem. Like miniatures, the tiles often reproduce architectural motifs. The precision and care expended on each decorative element in the various compositions is evidence of the love of harmony of forms and colors that is typical of Arab art.

262 bottom Preceded by the waiting room of the grand vizir and other dignitaries, the Room of the Sacred Cloak is the religious heart of Topkapi. It is entered by a door inlaid with mother-of-pearl. Lovely 16th-century majolica tiles surround a kiosk with silver gratings half-covered by heavy drapes. Apart from the cloak, the kiosk contains the swords and bow of the Prophet and an ancient hand-written Koran.

262-263 Completely lined in wooden panels painted with floral motifs alternating with magnificent bowls of fruit, the Dining Room of Ahmad III is one of the best examples of the philosophy that has pervaded architecture of Arab interiors for centuries: the exact, geometric volumes of the room are concealed by decorative elements that, from an aesthetic viewpoint, make the presence of furniture unnecessary.

264 top left This 16th-century binding in gilded leather encrusted with precious stones contained a divan or collection of poems belonging to Murad III. It is decorated with stitching, motifs of leaves, Arab inscriptions and an amazing quantity of emeralds and rubies. It is kept in the Topkapi Museum.

264 top right This parade helmet dates from the late 16th century. Its iron frame is lined with a sheet damascened with gold. The base is inscribed with some verses from the Koran; rubies and turquoise stones are used for decoration.

264 bottom The Celebrations Throne got its name from being used during religious holidays. It is one of the major attractions of the Treasure Rooms. It dates from the late 16th century and is made from wood of the walnut tree. It is lined with gold and encrusted with 954 gems.

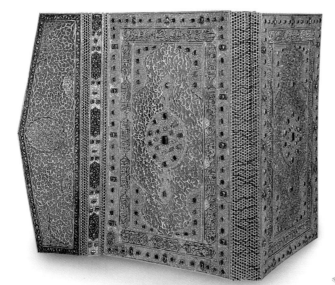

Topkapi Palace

The Scintillating Door to Asia

264-265 This painting from the end of the 18th century is kept at Topkapi. It shows a court reception of Suleiman III in the setting of the Az Odasi, the Audience Room, where the Sultan received foreign ambassadors and high dignitaries. Every year, Mozart's opera The Abduction from the Seraglio is performed here. The Western term "seraglio" used to signify Topkapi is derived from the Turkish word saray, meaning palace.

265 bottom left This turban ornament dates from the 17th century. The beautiful design and the colors are no less impressive than the value and number of pearls and gems. The Topkapi collections are evidence of the sultans' taste for precious objects, often from the Orient.

265 bottom right *The throne and canopy of Ahmad I (1603-17) are splendidly decorated. "Ordinary" materials like mother-of-pearl, ivory and semiprecious stones are mixed with precious gems of all sizes. The canopy, a triumph of gold, rubies and emeralds, is topped by a feather made of rock crystal. Inside hangs an incredible emerald and pearl ornament.*

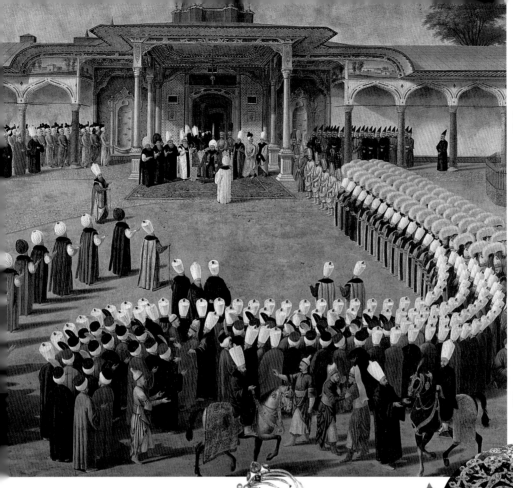

265 top right *Topkapi Museum contains many treasures whose fame spread throughout the West from the late 18th century onward. One such example is this 86-carat diamond called the Kasikçi Diamond. It is set among 49 smaller diamonds.*

Europe), and of the splendid majolica tiles in different rooms—especially in the Harem but also in other rooms such as the Baghdad Pavilion. With their blue, green and red floral decorations on a white background, the majolica tiles at Topkapi were nearly all produced in Iznik, the manufacturing center not far from Istanbul that dominated production during the 16th and 17th centuries. The museum inside the beautiful Çinili pavilion, near the palace walls, houses a lovely display of them.

Topkapi museum is of such excellent quality that it could be taken as example for any country in the Near East or Middle East; it is moreover symptomatic of the typical characters in recent Turkish history. The capital and the point of reference for the whole Muslim world for centuries, the symbolism and exercise of power in Istanbul was focused on Topkapi, which experienced its greatest moments and then a slow decline in the 17th and 18th centuries. During that decline the sultan increasingly resembled an invisible queen bee; royal power was exercised

266 top and 266-267 Close-up details demonstrate the beauty of these superb majolica tiles from Iznik. Products from Iznik, which previously had been white and blue, were after 1540 characterized by polychrome designs.

266 bottom left A majolica panel and the Sultan's monogram are shown side by side. The Islamic prohibition on representing living beings encouraged the use of geometric and floral decorations and of the adoption of calligraphy as an ornamental motif.

266 bottom right This room in the Harem features a large chimneypiece with golden reflections against a wall dominated by a geometric layout of majolica tiles that mirror and multiply the shape of the windows.

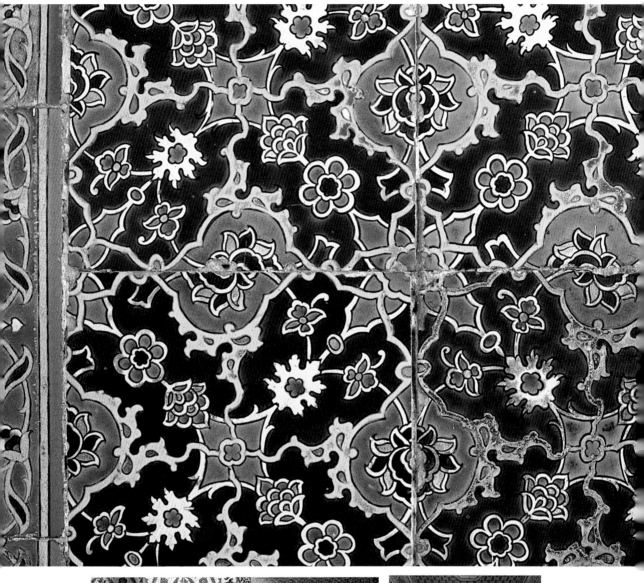

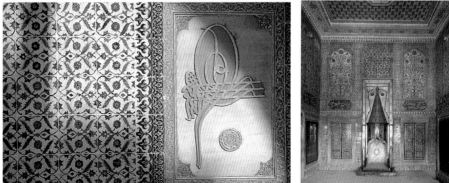

267 top The majolica factories in Iznik increased their output after the conquest of Constantinople by Suleiman the Magnificent (1453). The boost given to the construction industry in Istanbul increased the demand for religious as much as for civil architecture. The Ottomans may have prompted a jump in demand for majolica, but only because such factories already existed from Byzantine times.

by courtiers and the intrinsic weakness of the Ottoman empire was caused by its creation of not a nation, but rather an administration dedicated above all to the levying of taxes without bothering to offer a unifying project to its different peoples in their varying situations. The empire's subject peoples became increasingly restless and foreign interference became constant, but Turkey did not experience the humiliation of the protectorate or of colonial domination, as did many other Muslim countries.

The Scintillating Door to Asia

267 center The wonderful contrast of the turquoise and the blue colors typical of Iznik style is noteworthy in this beautiful majolica panel.

267 bottom The majolica tiles in this room of the Harem furnish it and also create calligraphic decorations. The panels are clearly defined. The high quality boiserie and the play of light on the tiles create a lovely effect. The symbolic images to be seen on Iznik tiles originated in Persia and China.

Although it was of no use in avoiding the breakup of the empire, the push for modernization of the country came from within. As a symbol of the Turkey that was to be left behind, Topkapi was abandoned and the sultans built other, more modern and more European palaces such as the Dolmabahçe, constructed between 1843 and 1856. At the same time, a culture of archaeology and museums was developed with a German positivist influence which encouraged conservation and care of the legacy of the past. The new Turkey—created in 1922 with the establishment of the Republic of Turkey by the untiring efforts of the reformer Mustafa Kemal Atatürk—continued to regard its past with pride and attentive action. This attitude is eloquently demonstrated by the displays on view in Topkapi and its museums, as well as in the museums of pottery, archaeology and the Ancient East, an anthology of the archaeological riches of the territories which once made up the Ottoman empire. Given the uncertainties of the present, this attitude may offer us an assurance for the future.

Amber Fort

THE COURT OF THE SUN GOD'S STOCK

286 top right While the form of the floral marble panels that decorate the Shish Mahal are inspired by Islamic art, the motif expresses the central importance of flowers in Hindu rituals of homage to the king and the gods.

and of strong flavors and colors, so arid and steppe-like that it was given the name of Marusthali, "the land of death" and yet able to transform itself into an expanse of flowers on those rare occasions when the monsoon blesses it, Rajasthan is the reflection of its inhabitants, the glorious *rajaputra* (sons of kings) who are capable of the greatest bursts of energy and the worst excesses.

The Rajput—to use the most common name for the peoples of the "Land of Kings"—were responsible for the knightly legends of Indian folklore. Their magnificent forts, massive and chaotic, extravagant but delicate, reflect their character.

Their mixed origins created a series of feudal kingdoms based on clans each ruled by a *raja*, a king assisted by powerful landowners. Linked to the king by blood-ties, the landowners were fairly independent and were obliged only to pay him a part of their own tributes and to supply troops in times of war.

War was their main occupation: extremely able horseback warriors, the Rajput structured their existence around a complicated chivalric code which focused on battle. Considered sacred, combat became a sort of ritual; but its inflexibility had the effect of impeding the development of war tactics. Battle became stuck in a sort of huge chess game that left the Rajput unable, when the moment came, to prevent the invasion by the more agile and imaginative Islamic knights.

Beside their courage, it was the customs of the Rajput that struck other Indian peoples most. They practiced female infanticide, used and abused opium and alcohol, ate every type of meat except cattle, and above all they observed the ceremony of *jauhar*, an extreme test of courage: when a stronghold had no means of resistance or escape, the cornered men would put on their wedding clothes and make a last charge, shouting *jay* (victory) and hoping for death on the battlefield. The women and children voluntarily threw themselves on the men's funeral pyres.

The valor and strength of the Rajput led the Brahmins to welcome them into the caste system at the second level, that of the warrior. A grandiose rite of fire was traditionally held on Mount Abu, in which the existence of the *agnikula* (the fire lineage) was sanctified. The four largest Rajput clans were part of this lineage: they were the Pratihara from southern Rajasthan, the Chalukya from Gujarat, the Paramara from Malva and the Chahuan from eastern Rajasthan.

The Kachhavaha of Amber and Jaipur, on the other hand, claimed their descent from the sun via Kusha, son of Rama. Rama was the incarnation of the god Vishnu and protagonist of the great Indian epic poem, *Ramayana* ; he made the ideal prototype of the chivalric ruler. The foundation of Amber in the 10th century, on a strategic site on the caravan route between Delhi and Rajasthan, is wrapped in legend. It was ascribed to the prince, Dhola Rai, who was hidden as a baby among the aboriginal people of Mina from his dethroned mother. The story is indicative of the ambiguity of the Rajput world:

268 top left The Singh Pol (Lion's Gate) is a compulsory passage to gain access to the fortified complex. The highest part of Amber, the Jaygarh (Victory Fort) lies at a strategic position overlooking the caravan route between Delhi and Rajasthan. Amber seems to have been founded in the 10th century.

269 top left The Amber hill is surrounded by imposing walls with towers that protected not only the palaces and temples but also the small town. Access was controlled by numerous gates protected by barbicans.

269 top right The splendid Dalaram ka Bagh (Dalaram's Garden) on a small island is named after the architect who planned the nearby city of Jaipur in 1727.

268 bottom left The ramps leading to the rock, controlled by gates and bastions, made access possible only by a tortuous path strategically controlled from the rock, affording the opportunities of blocking access at several points along the way.

268-269 The oldest part of the complex of Amber dates back to Man Singh I (1590-1616), who built the Mansinghgarh, the fort named in his honor. But it was Jay Singh I (1622-1668) who built the beautiful palaces on the rock.

269 bottom Proximity to Delhi and the excellent relations between the Kacchavaha rulers of Amber and the Moghul court contributed to cultural exchanges. The influence of Islamic architecture is obvious in this crowning kiosk.

270 top *The gardens of the
private apartments of Jay Singh I
repeat the classical Moghul layout
of the* Char Bagh *or "four
gardens" built around a central
fountain and featuring canals in
the shape of a cross.*

270-271 *The picturesque Ganesha
Pol, named after the elephant-
headed god, provides access to the
private quarters on the rock. The
quarters feature a harmonious
and elegant layout without
sacrificing defensive structures.*

Dhola Rai killed the king of the Mina who had welcomed him as a guest, thus founding his kingdom on blood; but local ballads remember him also as a great and noble warrior, and celebrate his amorous deeds with the beautiful Maru. Amber became the capital of a powerful state thanks in part to the alliance between its rulers and the Mogul emperors. The first to create this bond was the *raja* Bhagwan Das who married his sister, Maryam Zamani, to the emperor Akbar in 1562. It was to Maryam that Akbar's heir, Jahangir, was born. Man Singh I was showered with prestigious military honors by the Moguls and modeled the life of the Amber court on that of Delhi. Jay Singh I was given the governorship of Deccan province by Shah Jahan and received the title Mirza Raja (noble sovereign). The main buildings in the Amber fort were constructed by Jay Singh I.

The excellent relationship between the Kachhavaha clan and the Moghul court allowed the state to prosper and gave rise to an interesting synthesis of architectural styles. These can be seen both in Amber and in the new capital, Jaipur, built by Jay Singh II in 1727. Proximity to Delhi transformed the kingdom of the Kachhavaha clan into one of the major points of artistic reference when, once the Islamic empire began its decline, the imperial court artists looked for somewhere else to go.

Amber is one of the most significant examples of the Rajput *garh* (fort) which is based around a series of fortifications—bastions, buttresses and thick walls with monumental *pol* (gateways)—which protect the royal palace. The palace contained at its center the *prasada* (the multistory residence) which

had the *zanana* (women's apartments) at the top. It seems that the separation of men from women was not so clear-cut before the arrival of the Muslims and that only more recently were the Rajput palaces divided into the *mardana* (men's apartments) and the *zanana*. The ground plan of the palaces became more articulated, though still regular, with the *rajabhavana* (the buildings used for receptions and audiences) facing onto an external court and the *rajaniveshana* (royal apartments) arranged around a series of internal courts.

The Rajput fort tried to combine the compact structure of the multistory *prasada* with one- or two-floor pavilions either isolated or built as wings. There were therefore three blocks to the *mahal* or *mandir* (palace): first, a service court with stalls, storehouses, kitchens, armory and a temple in front of the main court with the *diwan-*

The Court of the Sun God's Stock

i-am (the pavilion that included the *darbar*, or audience, hall). The second block had one or more courts overlooked by the ruler's apartments with the *diwan-i-khas* (a private reception room), the treasury and a small, private shrine. Third was the *zanana* with its terraces and gardens.

The small size of the rooms, particularly in the women's section, is an indication that life took place as much as possible outdoors and on the terraced roofs. The narrow and tortuous corridors that connected the various parts of the palace were designed to block treacherous attacks on the ruler by his courtiers or relations.

The residential area of Amber, first capital of the Kachhavaha clan, stands around an artificial lake within a solid enclosure wall. In the middle of the lake is a small island called the Garden of Dalaram (the name of the original architect of Jaipur) which is denominated the Jaygarh (Victory Fort). To enter the fort, the visitor passes through the Suraj Pol (Gate of the Sun) and enters Jaleb Chouk, the service court with barracks and stables added by Jay Singh II. The Chandra Pol (Gate of the Moon), leads out of this court to the temple of Narasimha, the leonine incarnation of the god Vishnu, and to the Jagat Shiromani (Gem of the World), a temple with an enormous prayer hall.

Passing through the Singh Pol (Lion Gate) framed by two towers featuring *chattri* (kiosks supported by columns and topped by small domes) and designed to force a right angle turn, one passes the palatine temple dedicated to Kali (the terrible face of the consort of the god Shiva) and enters the courtyard of the *diwan-i-am*. This is an imposing hypostyle building constructed by Jay Singh I with a central hall supported by

272 *The vault was first introduced to India by Muslims; Hindu artists started using it relatively recently, with an abundance of splayed jambs often transformed into decorative niches.*

gray marble columns and surrounded by a double series of red sandstone pillars with elephant capitals. The public audience hall is shaded by wide overhangs and ends in a terrace with decorative grilles; its design was inspired by the architecture the Mogul emperor Akbar's time.

The entrance to the private quarters of the fort, the Ganesha Pol (the gate of the elephant-headed god), has an attractive facade with arches screened by *jali* (fretted screens) and a *bangaldar* roof (with curved overhangs like a hut). It is topped by pinnacles with water jars. From the Sohag Mandir on the top floor, delicate grillework allowed the unseen women to follow the events in the public audiences. The Bhojan Shala (Banquet Room) is situated on the same floor; it is decorated with scenes taken from Hindu mythology and with reproductions of India's holiest cities.

272-273 Situated above the Shish Mahal, the Jash Mandir features very rich mirrored wall decorations, mosaics and inlay work. The niche with a vase of flowers is a traditional motif.

273 top The Shish Mahal covered with glass tesserae and small mirrors is one of the most unforgettable halls of the palaces of the period; the refraction of light creates a very particular atmosphere.

273 bottom Simple and linear in layout, the rooms feature rich decorations that completely cover the walls, using both painting (a Hindu element) and inlay work (an Islamic contribution).

The garden courtyard of the *diwan-i-khas* opens on the other side of the gate, with the elegant Sukha Nivas or Sukha Mandir—the "place of delight" in Jay Singh's apartments—on the right. Here, the main hall with beautiful doors and sandalwood and ivory knockers is cooled by a water channel in the floor decorated with white and black marble zigzag strips. The channel is fed by a hydraulic machine and flows into a small waterfall in the *char bagh* (the traditional Islamic garden designed in four parts). The Jay Mandir stands on the left in several sections. It was influenced by the elegant design of the pavilions at the fort of Agra built by the fifth Mogul emperor, Shah Jahan. It has a lovely *diwan-i-khas* and *shish mahal* (Palace of Mirrors), a building that recurs in every Rajput residence. Above this is the Yash Mandir (Palace of Glory) which is magnificently decorated with glass, mirrors and golden tiles and inlaid with semiprecious stones. Higher up is a terrace with a *bangaldar* roof.

In the same courtyard is the dark *zanana* built by Man Singh I. This maze of bedrooms, storerooms, service rooms, bathrooms, kitchens and screened terraces holds the memory of various *maharani* (queens) and *kumari* (princesses) who ended their lives as *sati*— virtuous wives who followed their dead husbands onto their funeral pyres. Sixty of the 1,500 wives of Man Singh died this way.

Objects of passionate and ephemeral love affairs and pawns to be exchanged in wedding alliances, the Rajput women lived shut up inside the walls of the *zanana* , announcing their arrival with the tinkling of their anklets, their jewelry and the encrusted girdles that held up their clothes, their hennaed feet leaving red footprints on the marble floors. They wandered the magnificent gardens, now no longer in existence, playing on swings in a ritual evocative of fertility and joy which also cooled them during the summer heat. But in times of war they turned into fighters as heroic as their menfolk, and their memory is handed down in popular legends.

The facades of the various buildings in the fort are enlivened by protuberances and recesses featuring *jali* and *jarokha* (bow-windowed balconies). Together with the wide overhangs, they give the rooms a cool and faintly mysterious half-light. The polylobate arches, the *bangaldar* roofs and the *chattri* on their slender columns show the Rajput preference for curves, while the profuse decorations hiding the underlying architectural forms is typically Hindu.

The Red Fort in Delhi

PARADISE ON EARTH

274 top In the detail of a panel of the gateway of the Nakkar Khana is this symmetrical floral decoration, which, together with calligraphy, is one of the favorite ornamental elements of Muslim artists.

274 center The Nakkar Khana reveals the skilful play of walled areas and open space, and the creation of contrasts of light realized by Islamic architects combining arches and loggia windows.

The atmosphere of the *Thousand and One Nights* is still present in the fabulous palaces of the Moguls, the Muslim rulers who came from Mongolia to govern India for more than two centuries. It's no surprise that the oldest complex in this assortment is of Indo-Persian origin and long predates the definitive drafting of the Arabic stories, which occurred around the year 1400. Set in gardens studded with brightly colored flowerbeds and cooled by fountains and pools, the delicate marble palaces are reminiscent of an encampment of tents. The arrangement of small one-story, or at most two-story, pavilions in courts surrounded by an enclosure wall recalls the nomadic origins of the Turkoman Timur, better known as Tamerlane, and the Mongol Genghis Khan, who were the forefathers of the founder of the Mogul dynasty, Babur. And indeed, besides their stable settlements, the Moguls always had

itinerant courts comprising huge encampments. Made of wooden walls held together with leather strips, they could be put up in just a short time. They were provided with all kinds of facilities and even had baths—not just for the king and his retinue, including his harem, but also for his soldiers.

Dispossessed of his small princedom called Fergana, Zahir-ud-Din (later to be known as Babur the Tiger) occupied Kabul, took Samarkand and decided to descend into India when he received requests for help from the enemies of Ibrahim Lodi, the sultan of Delhi. Babur defeated Ibrahim in 1526 and occupied the capital, though he found it dirty, dusty and without gardens. The Moguls remained in power for 200 years although Babur's son, Humayum, lost his throne to the Afghan usurper Sher Khan, until he took it back with Persian help.

Humayum's heir, Akbar, gave a solid base to Mogul power and, between one military campaign and another, found time to build the fort at Agra and his ideal capital at Fatehpur Sikri, both of which were partially financed by earnings from trading pepper, cloves, cloth, gems and saltpeter with Europe. Akbar's son, Jahangir, was not as skilled as his father but was able to live on his reputation thanks to his wise Persian consort Mehirumisa, better known as Nur Jahan (Light of the World). She allowed her husband to content himself with his favorite occupations of watching animals and sating himself with opium and wine, while she ruled with acumen and transfused her Persian artistic background into Indian architecture. She made the heir to the throne, Shah Jahan, marry her niece, Arjumand Banu, and he renamed her Mumtaz Mahal (Pearl of the Palace). He gave her some political responsibility in affairs of state; indeed, although confined to the harem, Mogul women always exercised great power.

Most famous as the builder of the Taj Mahal, the magnificent funeral monument dedicated to his wife, Shah Jahan also built the Red Fort in Delhi, the fairytale complex that still stands despite suffering at the hands of invaders and time. A refined aesthete, Shah Jahan himself apparently made the original sketches for his buildings and modified the wooden models made from these. His goal of artistic perfection and the custom established by his predecessors

275 top left Shah Jahan began building the Red Fort in 1638. It is protected by a mile and a quarter of walls with two gates: the Lahore Gate, shown here, and the Delhi Gate.

275 top right The elegant white marble domes of the Moti Masjid (Pearl Mosque) rise above the sandstone wall around them. They are pear shaped and reminiscent of the Hindu motif of water jars placed one on top of the other.

of founding new capitals around Delhi induced him to do the same. Eight cities make up modern Delhi: the legendary Indraprastha celebrated in the epic poem Mahabharata, the historical Lak Kota or Qila Rai Pithora of the Hindu dynasties, five cities built by Muslim rulers and the last, an Anglo-Indian city.

The Muslims besieged the citadel of Lal Kota in 1192. A little more than a century later, Ala-ud-Din founded Siri, the third city of Delhi and the first Muslim capital, of which nothing is left today. Little survives of Jahanpanah built by Muhammad Tughlaq. The fifth city, Firuzabad or Kotla Firuz

Shah, was built by Firuz Shah in 1354. Humayum founded Dinpanah, which was built around the Purana Qila (Old Fort), and Shah Jahan built the seventh Delhi, Shajahanabad, in 1638 around Lal Qila (Red Fort) and Jama Masjid, the largest mosque in India. A decade was required to finish the new city, especially the fort, which alone had cost tons of silver and gold. In general, the fort (*qila*), the mosque (*masjid*) and the mausoleum are the three great expressions of Islamic architecture. The original solid, gloomy defensive citadels evolved into open courts set in splendid

274 bottom left The huge gateway of the nakkar khana or naubat khana, the "place of the drum," a building that in the past served as a residence for the palace musicians who lightened certain moments of the Emperor's day.

274 bottom right This panel shows a symmetrical floral composition within a frame of flowered volutes and reveals the aesthetic perfection of careful inlay work in hard stone.

274-275 The walls of the fort that formed the heart of Shahjahanabad, the seventh Delhi, are interrupted by steep blue ramps and towers topped by small white marble domes that contrast with the red sandstone.

277 top left As in the other pavilions, the wide splayed windows of the diwan-i-khas used to be covered by drapes or tapestries in precious cloth that increased the shady areas inside, while the arches were screened by curtains.

277 bottom left In the Rang Mahal, which was part of the private apartments of Shah Jahan, the rooms are divided by fretted panels featuring motifs, some of which—such as the scales in the picture—are of European inspiration.

gardens. The *char bagh* was a park divided into four gardens by raised avenues through which waterways flowed; it evoked the Pairi Daeza—the "walled place" from which the Greek term *paradeisos* (paradise) derives—a floral tapestry set with fountains, cloisters and small pavilions.

Mogul forts were generally divided into three sections, each with its own mosque: the court used for public audiences with the *diwan-i-am,* the pavilion used for ceremonies; the buildings of the *daulat khana* (residence of the king) or royal apartments, set around the *diwan-i-khas,* the pavilion used for private receptions;

and the *haram saray* or *zanana,* the section reserved for women and surrounded, like the *daulat khana,* with magnificent gardens. Protected by more than a mile of walls and by the river Yamuna, the Lal Qila can be entered through the lovely Lahore and Delhi Gates. The Delhi Gate is the main entrance. The contrast between the massive red sandstone walls and the slender, white marble pavilions is one of the most charming aspects of the fort.

Once past the area where the palace bazaar used to be held, a square courtyard leads to the *naubat khana* or *nakkar khana* (place of the

276-277 *Multi-lobed arches are a main feature of the* diwan-i-khas, *the "hall of private audiences" in marble with a ceiling that was once in solid silver studded with precious stones. This hall was once the backdrop to the splendor and tragedies of the Mogul Empire.*

appeared to his courtiers each day; and the *diwan-i-khas* which contained the famous Peacock Throne later stolen in the sacking of Delhi in 1739 by the Afghan adventurer Nadir Shah. Many tales are told about this extraordinary object: it seems it was an enormous, diamond-studded, gold sofa more than six feet long, held up by 12 columns of emeralds and topped by a diamond-studded canopy. The famous peacocks were set on the canopy with a wheel of precious stones flanking a tree of life which grew out of a pot in a cascade of more precious stones. As if all this were not enough, even the cushions of the throne were quilted with jewels. Annexed to the *diwan-i-khas* were the *hammam* (baths), three rooms with mosaic floors permanently covered by a film of water and walls with reflecting glass tiles. The Moti Masjid (Pearl Mosque) which stands in front of the *hammam* is a jewel made of milky marble enclosed by red sandstone walls. It was built by Aurangzeb in 1662 with three pear-shaped cupolas and slender

277 bottom right *The private apartments in the Red Fort are connected by the Nahar-i-Behisht (Canal of Paradise) which fed a superb fountain in the shape of a lotus in the Rang Mahal. The fountain is made of marble and semiprecious stones.*

drum). This is a two-story building housing the musicians who announced the movements of the emperor. Further on, a wide courtyard opens onto the public *diwan-i-am,* built in sandstone plastered with powdered marble. It has polylobate arches and a back wall inlaid with semiprecious stone against which the marble canopy for the throne rests on a high platform. It seems that part of the inlay of the canopy was the work of a French goldsmith, Austin de Bordeaux, who carried out the work in return for his freedom after being imprisoned for smuggling.

Behind the *diwan-i-am,* private apartments line the river bank, connected by the Nahar-i-Behisht (Canal of Paradise) which carried water to the various parts of the fort: to the slender princesses' pavilion; to the Rang Mahal with the wonderful fountain in the shape of a lotus flower made from marble and precious stones, and the ceiling which was once lined in gold and silver; to the Khas Mahal, three marble pavilions built in 1639–49 as a private residence for the emperor, with the Muthamman Burj, the three-story octagonal tower from which Shah Jahan

278-279 *The high throne platform, decorated with inlay work in hard stone, crowned by a canopy and preceded by the bench of the vazir, the prime minister, rests against the rear wall in the* diwan-i-am.

278 top *This foreshortened view of the Rang Mahal reveals the essential lines of Islamic architecture, where details such as the multi-lobed curve of the arches, the trusses of the eaves, and the small kiosks at the corners make an important contribution to artistic elegance.*

278 bottom left *The* diwan-i-am *(hall of public audiences) is a pavilion of red sandstone with wide multi-lobed arches that allowed court meetings to be heard and seen from the outside as well.*

Paradise on Earth

minarets. Between the *hammam* and the mosque stands the Hayat Baksh Bagh, the Mongol garden with geometrically shaped flower beds. Accounts from the period tell us that one section of the beds used to be filled with red flowers and another with white flowers (the moon bed). Two small marble pavilions (the Spring Pavilion and the Autumn Pavilion) stand in the Hayat Baksh Bagh. The last, very important building, the Shah Burj, is the octagonal tower of the aqueduct that stretched for 50 miles to carry water to the palace.

Unfortunately, the *haram saray* has been almost totally destroyed. Western travellers such as Tavernier, Manucci and Bernier, who had direct or indirect experience of the fort, wrote of its magnificence—furniture and furnishings made from precious metals, carpets and screens, silk hangings and tents, perfumed water splashing in the gold fountains. The gilded existence of the Moguls was summed up by a famous phrase engraved in the *diwan-i-*

Jahandar Shah and his favorite, the low caste dancer Lal Kumari, the Sayyid brothers bloodied the court, nominating and killing various rulers. So when Nadir Shah swooped down on Delhi in 1739, no one could stop him. The population was massacred and the invaders left with incredible booty, including the famous Grand Mogul diamond, renamed the Koh-i-noor (Mountain of Light). A few years later Delhi was struck again when the Afghan Abdali sacked the capital, reducing it to a ghost city. The fort was now a place of horror. The puppet emperors were prisoners and their women died of hunger in the harem. When the English took control of India, Lal Qila was conceded to the Moguls as their residence, although they were emperors only in name. Nothing of value was left: even the gilded ceilings had been stripped. But the final act had not yet taken place. The Indian Mutiny in 1857 induced the last emperor, Bahadur Shah, to declare war on the English, but he was defeated and a year later the English

279 top The hard stone inlay work that decorates the wall of the throne of the diwan-i-am *also features unusual animal and human motifs, apparently by the French artist Austin de Bordeaux.*

279 center Another magnificent decoration of the throne wall of the diwan-i-am: *graceful arches frame flowered stems with corollas that seem to sway in the breeze: the refined engraving work is emphasized by the monochromatic color scheme.*

278 bottom right The Moti Masjid or (Pearl Mosque) lives up to its name with the mother-of-pearl splendor of its structure. Spaces for prayer carpets are marked on the flooring all around the water tank provided for ablutions.

khas: "If there is a paradise, it's here, it's here." Although Shah Jahan's successor, Aurangzeb, was crowned in the Lal Qila, he spent very little time there. Instead Jahanara—beloved daughter of Shah Jahan, the image of her mother Mumtaz Mahal—held court.

At the start of the 1700s under Bahadur Shah, the Red Fort became a sort of gilded prison for the imperial princes, who were confined there to prevent their mixing in politics. The splendor of the palaces began to fade as the number of imperial branches of the family grew and the fort became increasingly crowded. After the assassination of emperor

destroyed a good part of the fort. Yet the fascination of Lal Qila remains. The vandals were not able to destroy its lovely rooms completely. The pure architectural lines are still intact, semiprecious stone inlays still exist in some hidden corners and delicate decorations that escaped the eyes of the wreckers can still be seen. The intangible romantic atmosphere of the court of the Grand Mogul still hovers over the fort: its perverse and refined emperors, beautiful, mysterious women and incredible riches—a slice of cruel and fascinating history has been transformed into myth.

279 bottom This detail of one of the rooms in the Khas Mahal shows the extreme refinement of Mogul architecture: the profile of the polylobate arches is accentuated by the border, which ends in a flower motif above.

The Forbidden City

BETWEEN HEAVEN AND EARTH

280 top right The most important gates to the palace usually had an upper section of wooden mesh design, perhaps lined on the inside with paper, and a lower section made of one or more solid panels richly carved and decorated. Here is a detail of such a decoration.

280 center The stylized form of the two bronze lions in front of the Gate of Supreme Harmony, and others in the Forbidden City, resemble real animals less than mythical ones.

280 bottom This is the plan of the Imperial City from an 18th-century Chinese manuscript held by the British Library in London.

Situated in the heart of Peking, the Forbidden City—also known as the Imperial Palace—is the most extensive and best conserved complex of buildings from the imperial period in China. It is a miniature city with roads, temples, libraries, gardens and residential quarters. The emperors, empresses, members of the imperial aristocracy, concubines, and eunuchs of the last two dynasties, the Ming (1368–1644) and the Qing (1644–1911), lived here for about 500 years until the end of the Chinese Empire and the foundation of the Republic in 1911–12. For all that time, the Forbidden City was inaccessible to the majority of Chinese people.

Construction of the Forbidden City dates to the first decades of the 15th century during the reign of Yongle, third emperor of the Ming dynasty. Works began around 1417 and were

mostly concluded three years later. This was an exceptionally short period considering the complexity and magnificence of the city; but it was made possible by the physical strength of more than 1 million workers and the intellectual skills of over 100,000 craftsmen and engineers.

Construction of the Forbidden City was only the most valuable gem in a larger process of the rebuilding and the architectural renovation of Peking, which culminated in 1420–21 with the transfer of the capital of the empire from the "southern" city of Nanking.

Today this architectural masterpiece comprising a thousand different buildings (magnificent palaces, pavilions, towers, all decorated with exquisite skill) must be very different from how it appeared in the 15th century. There have been numerous additions and reconstructions in various phases.

Most of the costly periodic reconstruction projects followed fires, which were often devastating due to the wide use of wood in the buildings. The fire of 1421, just a few months before construction was expected to end, was particularly serious. Often fires were caused by lightning bolts and sometimes by fireworks which were used to celebrate the New Lunar Year.

A fundamental material in traditional Chinese architecture, wood used for construction purposes was chosen with extreme care and according to rigidly defined criteria. In the case of the Forbidden City, it is said that Emperor Yongle sent a number of emissaries to various provinces so that they could personally select the materials to be used. One particularly valued type of wood, generally used for fixtures and decorations,

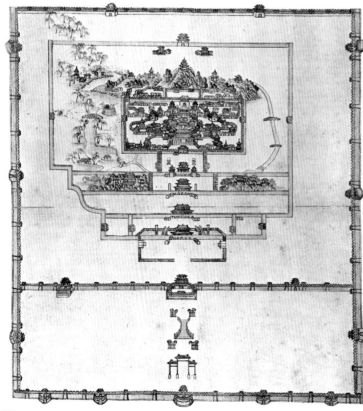

281 top right *The expression "Forbidden City" in Chinese is created from three terms: zi jin cheng. The first refers to the Pole Star, which is fixed in time and space: it is here that the supreme divinity lives surrounded by other gods on other stars. The second term signifies "prohibited" and therefore not to be approached by the masses. The third term indicates a fortified city surrounded and defended by walls.*

280-281 Chinese architecture placed great emphasis on the shape and decoration of roofs. The shape was determined by the function and importance of the building, the decoration by the shape of the roof. The decorations mainly consisted of dragons, lions, sea-horses, winged horses, phoenixes and other mythical creatures that had a propitiatory and protective function.

281 bottom This 19th-century engraving by the Frenchman Adolphe Rouargue shows a view of Peking from the south.

281 top left The widow Empress Ci Xi (1835-1908) began to emerge at court in 1856 when she bore a son to the Emperor Xianfeng, to whom she was a simple, low-caste concubine. In a few years, however, she managed to increase her position and her influence, and in 1862 on the death of Xianfeng she became the regent for the young Emperor Tongzhi. Ci Xi consolidated her power and bore an increasing though discreet influence on the decisions of the emperor until her death.

only grew in internal mountainous areas of the province of Sichuan, nearly 1,000 miles south of the capital. The area must have been especially rough and inaccessible, to judge by a saying of the era: "If one thousand men enter these mountains, only five hundred will come out again."

The selected wood was sent to the capital by water, in particular via the Imperial Canal. Similar routes were used for bricks and floor tiles which mostly came from the neighboring province of Shandong and from Suzhou in the southeast. These were used in massive quantities; for example, the large courtyards were often covered with three, or as many as seven, layers of floor tiles.

Roof tiles were generally produced in Peking outside the Forbidden City in what is

now the southwestern quarter of Liulichang. In fact the name Liulichang is a shortened version of "liuli wa chang" meaning "workshop for the production of glazed tiles."

The planning of the Forbidden City is a clear indication of another essential characteristic in traditional Chinese architecture: cosmology. The residence of the Emperor and seat of imperial power was considered a microsymbol of a larger, universal cosmic order. The theories of *yin* and *yang* and the *wu xing* (five elements) had particular relevance in this context.

According to tradition, every single object in the world could be divided into two opposite and independent elements, yin and yang. Everything "in heaven and on the earth" originated from the interaction of these

opposing elements; for example, the earth was yin and the heaven yang. Yin was synonymous with negative, female, cold, dark, below and even; yang was positive, male, hot, light, above and odd.

The five elements (wood, fire, earth, metal and water) represented the five categories into which all known phenomena were classified and with which man was constantly in contact. The life of an individual—and consequently that of society—became part of a complex system of interactions and correspondences in which every phenomenon had its own defined place. A correct and harmonious cyclical combination of these elements (e.g., water produces wood which is in turn destroyed by fire) was able to bring happiness and well-being; erroneous combinations could, on the

282 top left The Hall of Supreme Harmony was strictly reserved for the most important occasions, such as the celebration of the New Year. On that day the officials of the Minister of Rites led the procession in front of this hall, to the beat of a drum, while the emperor, carried on a sedan to

the pavilion, ascended the throne to the sound of ceremonial music.

282 top right The three reception pavilions, the Hall of Supreme Harmony, the Hall of Middle Harmony and the Hall of Protective Harmony, are all on the same terrace.

282-283 After passing through the Meridian Gate, the visitor reaches a large court where the Golden Water flows beneath five marble bridges. The Gate of Supreme Harmony, standing in the middle, is 77 feet high and was originally called the Gate to Serve Heaven. It was given its

current name at the start of the Qing dynasty. The construction we see today dates to the second half of the 19th century.

282 bottom This photograph shows one of the bronze incense burners next to the throne in the Hall of Middle Harmony.

Between Heaven and Earth

The Forbidden City

283 center left The size, number and sequence of the animal-shape decorations on the roofs were strictly related to the importance of the building and had to conform to precise rules.

283 top right The imperial throne in the Hall of Protective Harmony is on a north-south axis like those in the adjacent Halls of Middle Harmony and Supreme Harmony, in observance of Chinese principles of geomancy.

283 center right Inside the Hall of Supreme Harmony, the imperial throne occupies the center of the room. Pilasters stand on either side of the gold throne; the six central ones are painted with dragons in two shades of gold, the others in red lacquer. Incense containers stand on the right and left of the throne.

283 bottom right The steps of the Imperial Way in front of the Hall of Supreme Harmony are carved with clouds and dragons. Below, the waves breaking against the rocks symbolize the earth. The imperial dragons in high relief flying through clouds are a dominant decorative aspect of the Imperial Way.

contrary, be responsible for unhappiness and malaise.

Numerous combinations of other groups of five were linked to each of the five elements, giving rise to complex correlations: the five directions (four cardinal points of the compass plus the center); the five colors (red, green, yellow, white and black); the five phases of life; the five emotions; the five atmospheric elements, and so on. Wood, for example, was associated with east, green, birth, anger and wind.

This complex cosmic symbolism is constantly reflected in the Forbidden City. The city was divided into two sectors, the Outer and Inner Courts. The Outer Court was where the rulers attended to their duties as administrators of the empire and received

ministers; it was associated with *yang* and situated in the south. The Inner Court, where the emperor lived with the imperial family, was associated with *yin* and situated in the north.

With regard to colors, green (or blue) was the symbol of growing buds, the start of life and the east; it was widely used as the color of roof tiles on buildings where young princes studied. Similarly, the residence of the widowed empress was usually situated in the western part of the Forbidden City, which was associated with the idea of the final phase of life and with the color white (the color of mourning). Red was a symbol of happiness and was widely used to color the walls, windows fixtures or columns of palaces.

taken from the excavation was heaped behind the city to form the Hill of Longevity (later called the Panoramic Hill, and more generally known as Coal Hill) on which pavilions were built in the 18th century. In the meantime, water channels were dug inside the city and named the Golden Water.

Similar works were motivated by aesthetic and practical requirements. The surrounding countryside was beautified and the drainage of rainwater improved. Cosmological considerations were also included: the river was channeled so that its waters flowed from west to east in accordance with the principles of Chinese geomancy.

The Inner and Outer Courts of the Forbidden City were surrounded and

Yellow was linked with the center and the concept of glory and honor—it was often used to color roof tiles on imperial palaces.

Other factors such as water and wind also had notable importance in architectural design. An ideal site for a construction normally had hills behind it and a body of water in front, while the direction the building faced was determined by the direction of the sun and wind.

Construction of the Forbidden City was accompanied by the digging of a deep ditch around the city's enclosure walls. The earth

defended by an enclosure wall. Like a Chinese box, the Forbidden City was located inside a larger area, the Imperial City, which was surrounded by its own wall and, in its turn, enclosed by what was known as the Inner City. The Inner City was the northern area of the capital and it too had its own defensive walls. To the south the Outer City extended in an area that contained commercial and manufacturing activities. This was protected by a wall only in the 16th century.

Solidly built on a rectangular ground plan, the Forbidden City covered more than 849,000

285 bottom left Terrace balustrades are usually decorated with sculpted dragons, aquatic animals, and bamboo and floral motifs. Decoration of capitals and pillars varies according to the importance of the building they are attached to: in those representing imperial power, for example, dragons and phoenixes are most common as they symbolize the Emperor and Empress respectively. Flowers, bamboo and lotuses decorate capitals in the gardens.

285 bottom right Detail of the enameled ceramic decoration with floral motifs on the walls. This kind of ceramic working, grès, gives the material particular strength and has been used in China since 1500 BC.

286-287 The dais, throne and screen inside the Palace of Celestial Purity rivals those in the Hall of Supreme Harmony for beauty, though this is less ornate. Handpainted calligraphic signs of the emperors Kangxi and Qianlong hang from red lacquered columns and Chinese symbols are engraved on the screen panels. A pair of cranes— the symbol of longevity—flank the throne.

square yards and measured 1,041 yards from north to south, and 816 yards east to west. The enclosure wall was nearly 26 feet high, was surrounded by a wide moat and had a series of gateways. The walls had watch towers at the corners and guard points that were supposed to render the Forbidden City inviolable and invulnerable.

Four large access gates stood at the four compass points: the Meridian Gate to the south, the Gate of Divine Prowess to the north and two Glorious Gates at the east and the west.

The Meridian Gate is the most splendid and was the main entrance to the Forbidden City. It had five passageways: the central one was normally reserved for the Emperor; the two flanking entrances were reserved for the aristocracy, and civil and military functionaries; and the two outermost entrances were only opened on days when the Emperor held audience. On those days, the civil functionaries usually entered through the eastern gate and the military functionaries through the western gate. Candidates being examined for the administration service in the

city (in the final stage of a long and difficult selection process allowing only the best talents to enter the bureaucracy) entered depending on the number they had been assigned: even numbers through the right entrance and odd numbers through the left entrance.

In the area next to Meridian Gate the Emperor normally accepted any prisoners of war after a victory. He would receive memorials from members of the aristocracy and functionaries on set days.

The Gate of Divine Prowess was originally built with a superstructure of a drum and bell which are now housed in the Drum Tower and the Bell Tower further north. At dusk the drum was struck first, and then the bell was rung at fixed intervals. During the last imperial

various buildings, including the imperial archives, stand on either side.

The Gate of Supreme Harmony is the largest ceremonial entrance in the Forbidden City. Opposite the gate stands a pair of bronze lions. These are the largest of the six pairs of lions inside the city. Introduced to China with the advent of Buddhism, the lion was the symbol of the splendor, dignity and solemnity of the Emperor, and pairs were usually placed to guard palaces and temples. The three pavilions just inside the gate are commonly known as the Three Great Audience Pavilions; the smaller, center pavilion is square, while the others are rectangular. When seen as a group, the three seem dynamic and uniform. Sculpted figures of dragons (the expression of imperial power), cranes and turtles (good

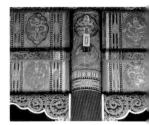

286 bottom Thuribles similar to those shown are found throughout the interior of the Palace of Celestial Purity. Incense containers are usually placed on or next to the dais.

287 top This closeup shows the fine detail and quality of decoration in the Palace of Celestial Purity.

dynasty, girls allocated to various services inside the imperial city would enter through this gate.

Entering the Forbidden City by the Meridian Gate and heading north along the Imperial Way, the visitor ascends one of the five arched bridges with a marble balustrade over the Golden Water and arrives at the Outer Court. Passing through the Gate of Supreme Harmony, the visitor finds three large pavilions: the Hall of Supreme Harmony, the Hall of Perfect Harmony and the Hall of Protective Harmony. Two other pavilions and

omens and symbols of longevity) can be seen in this area, as elsewhere in the city.

The Hall of Supreme Harmony is the largest and tallest building of its kind in China. The windows and the external doors and internal fixtures glint with gold. Inside is a central platform on which stands the imperial dragon throne of lacquer and gold. This Hall was the center of court activity during the imperial period. All the important ceremonies (ascent to the throne, celebrations of the Emperor's birthday, weddings) were held here.

287 bottom The various buildings in the Forbidden City offer great variety in the shape of their roofs. The most important have a horizontal ridge with four oblique sides and a double cornice known as a double-eaved hipped roof. Buildings of lesser importance have a double-pitched roof without overhangs at the edge, known as a pitched mountain-shape roof. There are numerous variations of both types.

288 top Dividing doors were usually used to separate the rooms into communicating sections, as in the Hall of the Union. Built in wood, they usually have a mesh upper section and a bottom part carved with decorations—in this case with dragons and phoenixes.

The Hall of Perfect Harmony was a sort of stopover point for the Emperor on his way from his private apartments in the north part of the city to the Hall of Supreme Harmony. Here he would usually read reports and receive the homage of various ministers.

Further north, one reaches the third pavilion, the Hall of Protective Harmony. During the Qing dynasty, state banquets and imperial examinations were held here.

Situated in the north of the city, the Inner Court is much more compactly arranged than the Outer Court. Its pavilions, palaces, kiosks

288-289 and 289 bottom left The Gate of Nourishment of the Mind opens onto the court where the palace of the same name stands. An arch in front of the court screens the view of the pavilion from outside. The arch has a double function: to prevent curious passersby peering in, and to block access to malignant spirits.

where the widowed Empress lived; the residences of concubines of previous emperors; and the residences of the imperial princes.

The most important buildings here are the Palace of Celestial Purity and the Palace of Earthly Peace. As both house the residential quarters of the Emperor and Empress, they are situated centrally. Together with the three large pavilions of the Outer Court, they form the heart of the Forbidden City. The choice of names (celestial, earthly) clearly reflects the will and auspices of the Chinese emperors that

289 top There are many articles to be seen inside the Hall of the Union besides the imperial sedan chair: a copper water clock to the right of the throne, a large striking clock at the left of the throne, and the 25 imperial seals, made mostly from jade or metal and used to authenticate documents, which are kept here.

288 center The Hall of the Union, the Palace of Earthly Peace and the Palace of Celestial Purity are known as the Three Rear Palaces. In the first, shown here, the imperial court paid homage to the Empress on important celebratory occasions such as the Spring Festival and the Winter Solstice.

and gardens are closely grouped. A series of ceremonial entrances, walls, galleries and raised walkways bring life to an intricate layout of buildings that is typical of traditional Chinese architecture.

The main entrance to the Inner Court consists of the Gate of Celestial Purity, which is divided into six sections: the Three Rear Palaces which include the residences of the Emperor and Empress; the Six Eastern Palaces and the Six Western Palaces, residences of the imperial concubines; the Hall of Nourishment of the Mind, residence of the Emperors from the mid-18th century; the Palace of Longevity,

Heaven and the Earth existed together in peace and harmony. Renovated several times, the Palace of Celestial Purity was used by the Ming dynasty and the early Qing dynasty as the Emperor's residence.

During the first decades of the 18th century, Emperor Yongzheng moved his residence to the Hall of Nourishment of the Mind, and the Hall of Celestial Purity became the hall where foreign emissaries were given an audience.

The Palace of Earthly Peace is similar but slightly smaller than the Hall of Celestial Purity. It was the residence of the Ming empresses

289 bottom right The main room of the Hall of Nourishment of the Mind is focused on the throne; above it is a caisson ceiling. Two bookcases stand against the north wall flanking the lacquered screen. The two peacock-feather fans on either side of the screen were used for ceremonial purposes.

290-291 and 291 bottom right
Bronze statues of animals are a
recurrent motif opposite or on
either side of gates, palaces and
pavilions. Their function was
mainly protective or ceremonial.
Generally, statues were made in
pairs and represented male and
female. Proud and powerful, the
female whose paw is visible in
the large detail also shows her
maternal nature as she plays with
her young one.

290 bottom Turtles and cranes
were the symbols of longevity. The
turtle in the picture is an incense
holder: the shell is actually a
cover which can be lifted off to
place the incense inside. Incense
holders were usually used during
important ceremonies to add
further mysticism and solemnity
to the occasion.

and the first Qing empress. Toward the mid-17th century, a few years after the foundation of the Qing dynasty by the Manchurians, the pavilion was significantly renovated and became a place of worship for Lamaism, the religion practiced in Manchuria. The eastern section of the building used to accommodate the Emperor's wedding chamber.

The Hall of Nourishment of the Mind stands to the south of the Six Western Palaces. The Emperor would receive his ministers in the heated rooms on either the eastern side or (depending on the historical period) the western side of the pavilion. It was from the room on the eastern side that the celebrated Empress Ci Xi guided the Empire during the later 19th and early 20th centuries, in the names of the young emperors who succeeded to the throne during that period. She would "advise" the emperor on how to manage state affairs from behind a yellow curtain placed in front of the imperial throne.

Between Heaven and Earth

291 bottom left The gardens of the Forbidden City are an integral part of the pavilions and palaces in the Inner Court. One of the most important is the Imperial Garden, which measures 87 yards north to south and 151 yards east to west. Several buildings stand in its grounds. One of these is the exquisitely decorated Kiosk or Pavilion of the Thousand Autumns with its conical roof.

291 top right and 291 center right This bronze elephant stands by the north gate to the gardens. The elephant was considered a symbol of power and longevity in ancient China. In the upper photograph, a detail of the decoration of the caparison on the animal's back shows a dragon in bas-relief.

The Royal Palace
in Bangkok

Thailand

BANGKOK

IN THE CITY OF THE ANGELS

292 top right This beautiful embroidery adorns the cushion on the Chakri Maha Prasat throne. It represents the Garuda, the mythical mount of Vishnu, and symbolizes the sky.

292 center left A detail of the Dusit Maha Prasad's roof shows it is made of small tiles of red and green glazed ceramic. The 12 sloping overlaid roofs of this building are divided by gilded decorations; they represent a stylized naga, the divine serpent that protected the Buddha while he was meditating.

292 bottom right In the foreground stands the small and elegant raised pavilion, the Thinang Aphon Phimok. Behind it, the side view of the Dusit Maha Prasad allows us to admire the beauty of the tall and slender gilded spire above the traditional sloping roofs.

292 bottom left The buildings of the Royal Palace are surrounded by a pleasant park. The layout of the Western-style gardens alternates open spaces with views of the main palace buildings.

292-293 The view of the overall site shows several of the architectural styles to be found in the Grand Palace that stands next to the royal temple complex of Wat Phra Keo. The blue-tiled pavilions of the Amarinda Vinichai contrast with the green tiles of the Dusit Maha Prasad which stands over the Thinang Aphon Phimok Prasad.

293 top left This ancient map of Bangkok clearly shows the artificial canal built on the river Menam by Rama I at the end of the 18th century to create the island of Rattanakosin, the place chosen by the king to create his residence.

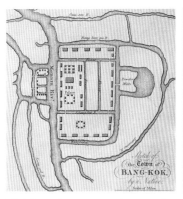

*I*n 1917, Conrad in *The Shadow Lines* gave a valuable description of the appearance of Bangkok, the capital of the East, washed by the waters of its river. Even today, from the banks of the Mae Nam-Chao Phraya, the "Mother of the Waters," the pointed corners of the temple roofs with their little jingling bells and the golden glint of the pagodas that stand out against the tropical blue sky create an atmosphere of interior and exterior harmony.

In April 1767, Ayutthaya (Ayudhya), capital of the kingdom of the same name from the 13th to the 18th centuries, fell after a long siege by the Burmese army. The city was put to the

Taksin began the reconquest only two months after the sack of the capital. As he conquered city after city, his reputation grew in leaps and bounds. In October 1767 he had reached Thon Buri, where he settled to unleash the final attack on the Burmese forces and liberate the country. In just seven months, Phya Taksin had reconquered Ayutthaya. The reward for his success and, above all, for the liberation of the ancient capital was the royal title; but the city had been destroyed, exhausted by sieges, fires and looting. Despite its newfound unity, the city did not have enough resources to rebuild itself. The new capital was moved south to the city of

293 top right Wat Rajapradit, built in Bangkok by King Mongkut (Rama IV), is small but extremely elegant. Inside the Bot or main chapel, fine examples of wall paintings dating from 1864 can be seen. The picture shows a detail of a view of the palace area. The mural is part of the cycle dedicated to the Ceremonies of the 12 Months which, up through the reign of Rama IV, were performed to mark the passing of the months.

flames and whatever could be carried away as booty was stolen. Almost nothing was spared from the destructive fury of the enemy.

Everything seemed lost as the Burmese slowly extended their jurisdiction to the Gulf of Siam; but to the southeast, on the eastern shores of the Gulf, one of the greatest generals of the kingdom of Ayutthaya had put himself at the head of a group of loyal and armed troops. Phya

Thon Buri on the west bank of the Chao Phraya. The end of the reign of Phya Taksin was overshadowed by his premature and dangerous insanity when he was only 48 years old. The instability of the king favored the rise to power of one of the country's most successful generals during the reconquest of Siam. This was Chakri, who became the true leader of the nation. In 1782 at Thon Buri, General Chakri was

293 bottom Inside the Chakri Maha Prasad is located the Throne Room, still in use when foreign ambassadors are received. The British architect who designed and built the palace— today the most famous building in the complex—in 1876-82 must have based his ideas on Italian Renaissance architecture.

294 left The only areas still in use in the Chakri Maha Prasad are the reception rooms where the splendidly decorated Throne Room is found. The wooden throne is lined with gold and silver and crowned by a nine-layer umbrella. The throne is placed on a platform. The magnificent crystal chandeliers were presented by European kings.

294 top right The mother-of-pearl throne in the Dusit Maha Prasad complex is one of the most elegant in the palace. The room it stands in, like the building in its complex, is a perfect example of first period Rattanakosin style.

294 bottom right This large and sumptuous room in the Chakri Maha Prasad complex is a typical example of King Chulalangkorn's westernizing influence. A long red carpet takes the visitor through the Neoclassical style room, with marble walls and western windows, toward the large door that leads to the Throne Room.

295 Inside the Maha Monthien complex, a doorway through which only members of the royal family can pass leads to the Amarinda Vinichai room, the only section open to the public today. This is where the Throne of Thrones is placed, the Phra Thinang Busbok Mala, which dates to the reign of Rama I. It is made from sculpted wood in the form of a boat and completely covered with gold. It stands on a raised platform, also covered with gold, to give the visual effect of a throne suspended in the air. Today, the ashes of the kings of the Chakri dynasty are kept here.

crowned king of Siam with the name of Rama I. Rama I was the founder of the Chakri dynasty that still rules in Thailand, and with his ascension the modern capital of the country was also created.

The king chose as his residence a small harbor village called Bang Khok ("village of wild olives") on the east bank of the Mae Nam-Chao Phraya opposite Thon Buri. The narrowest section of the river was considered most easily defendable and most suitable for the construction of a new royal residence, so a canal was dug here to create an island called Rattanakosin, "the abode of the Emerald Buddha." The new city was given a long official name which was abbreviated to Krung Thep, "city of the angels."

In 1782 construction of an enclosure wall began, which Rama I ordered built of Ayutthaya bricks, almost as if he wanted to invest the new residence with the same holiness enjoyed by the old capital. The wall was 2,000 yards long with 14 guard towers and was to see the new capital of Siam grow from the reign of Rama I (1782–1809) through that of Rama V

(1868–1910).

The new royal residence in the City of the Angels was called the Grand Palace. The Grand Palace is like a city within chaotic, modern Bangkok. It covers 624 acres and is filled to bursting with tourists—foreign and domestic—on all days of the year. The gilded roofs that seem to grow up towards the sky, the hot smell of incense and the reverent, holy atmosphere induce the visitor to walk in silence among the buildings that have been the home of the "lords of life" for more than 200 years. The layout of the large, walled palace complex can be divided into three sections: the oldest is Dusit Maha Prasad, followed by Maha Monthien and by Chakri Maha Prasad, built during the reign of Rama V, King Chulalangkorn (1868–1910). The residential area where the women's apartments used to stand, the service pavilions, the Sivalaya gardens and the temple complex or royal chapel of Wat Phra Keo stand around these buildings.

Shortly after the enclosure wall was completed, Ramathibodhi began construction of Wat Phra Keo (1784–85). This temple was to contain Siam's holiest image, the Emerald Buddha, which was plundered by Rama I during his war against Laos. This figure of Buddha was sculpted from a single block of emerald-green

297 bottom This corridor in the Chakri Maha Prasad is in European Neoclassical "eclectic" style, and has tall Corinthian columns and gas lights held up by soldiers in medieval armor.

In the City of the Angels

The Royal Palace in Bangkok

296 top The personal character of the modernizing king, Chulalangkorn, is apparent in this family portrait of the king, his wife and five children painted in 1897. The artist was Edoardo Gelli, an Italian, who worked at the Thai court at the end of the 19th century with many other Italian artists.

296 center The room—or study—in the Chakri Maha Prasad where Gelli's family portrait of Rama V hangs was decorated in European style.

296 bottom The Crown of the Victory, worn by the Thai kings, is also the diadem worn by the Buddha dressed in royal robes. Thus the embroidery represents the sacrality of the king thought to be a living Buddha.

296-297 The echo of 18th-century English drawing rooms is evident in this well-appointed reception room in the Chakri Maha Prasad. It is decorated with portraits of the Chakri kings and European rulers.

jade 12.2 inches high, and is today an object of great veneration and a destination of pilgrimage for worshippers from throughout the country. Little is known about this precious statue, which is said to bring peace and wealth to the country that possesses it. Its history is only known from the time when the statue was discovered in 1464 at Chiangrai in the kingdom of Lanna. A Laotian tradition says that the statue was sculpted in India on the wishes of the venerable Nagasena in the 1st century BC during the reign of Milinda (Menander). It was then moved to Pataliputra, where it remained for more than 800 years before being taken to Sri Lanka. From there the Emerald Buddha was taken to Pagan in Burma and, later, to Chiangrai.

Once the large temple had been built to hold the sacred image, Ramathibodhi began to construct the Amarindraphisek (audience hall) where the throne was installed. It was here that political life in the new capital finally began to take shape. But the Amarindraphisek was made entirely of wood and in 1789 a disastrous fire razed it to the ground. Even the king ran to help damp down the flames; but only the throne, the symbol of Chakri royalty, was saved. A new audience hall, the Dusit Maha Prasad, was soon built over the ruins of the old one, and has since been remodeled several times by Ramathibodhi's successors. The new building is a real architectural jewel of the Bangkok (or Rattanakosin) period of the 18th to the 20th centuries, in which the ancient splendor and elegance of the Ayutthaya buildings were reinterpreted with an increased use of gold, lacquer and mother-of-pearl. The Dusit Maha Prasad stands on a marble terrace and is roofed with red and green enamel tiles. Above this dazzling cover rises the gilded *mongkut* supported by four *garuda*. The great black lacquered throne with mother-of-pearl inlays stands in the wide room inside, but it was rarely used by the king to receive his visitors, as he preferred to use a small silver throne that stands in a niche in the south wall. On his death in 1809, the remains of the "lord of life" were displayed in the Dusit Maha Prasad which has since then been reserved for royal funeral ceremonies and has lost its original function.

The king usually arrived at the Dusit on a throne carried on the back of an elephant; to be able to dismount, he built a small pavilion on a raised base, the Phra Thinang Aphon Phimok Prasad, to the northeast of the Dusit Maha Prasad. Here the king got down from his massive mount and briefly paused in the shade to change clothes before giving audience.

Rama I continued to build his city and in 1785 to the west of the Dusit Maha Prasad he constructed the residential complex known as the Maha Monthien or Great Residence. It is split into three buildings that are connected on a north-south axis. The first building, the Amarinda Vinichai, was the main audience room where high dignitaries and ambassadors were received. They could "park" their elephants outside by tying them to the large red poles by the entrance. The Phra Thinang Busbok Mala, a splendid throne of gilded wood in the shape of a boat with a nine-tiara canopy, stood inside the room. The king sat here, hidden from the sight of mortals by sumptuous gold curtains.

Behind the Amarinda Vinichai lies the Phra Thinang Phaisal Taksin, the room where the all

magnificent coronation ceremonies have taken place, from that of Rama II to that of the current ruler. The long ceremony still requires the king to be invested on an octagonal throne facing east; after moving to another throne facing west, he must take possession of the seven symbols of power: the crown, the sword, the rod of command, the fan, the fly-whisk, the shoes of gold and the chatra (the umbrella used during parades).

In the center between the two thrones is an altar that contains the Phra Syamadevadhiraj, the symbol of Siam and bringer of wealth to the state.

From the last building in the Maha Montien, access is had via an antechamber to what was once the true residence of the first

three kings: the Phra Thinang Chakraphat Phiman. Since the death of Rama III in 1851, the Chakraphat Phiman has not been used as a permanent residence; but every king since the first kings of the Chakri dynasty spends at least one night there, as soon as he has been crowned, to symbolize the official start to his reign.

The most striking building of all, for the visitor crossing the threshold of the Royal Palace, is the Chakri Maha Prasad, built by Rama V, King Chulalangkorn in 1876–82. This monarch is worth a paragraph or two: he and his father, Rama IV, King Mongkut (1851–1868) were the enlightened rulers, the true innovators who brought modernization to Siam. During that period, Indochina was being squeezed by

colonialism: the French were in Laos, Cambodia and Vietnam, the British were in Burma, and the Dutch were to the south in Indonesia. Siam was encircled by the great European powers, but with great effort it managed to hold onto its independence, treaty by treaty. King Mongkut realized that without an education comparable those had in Europe, the future Siamese kings would have little space to maneuver against their western counterparts. So it was that his son, Chulalangkorn, began to learn English at the age of 14. But the heir's interest in the west became engrossing. When he was only 19, Chulalangkorn had the opportunity to visit India and Java, where he was able to study the systems of administration used by the British

and Dutch colonial governments. His trips abroad and a long period of study with American and English tutors created a different sort of king; no longer a "god on earth" but an accessible regent able to speak for his country to his foreign counterparts and to carry forward a policy of development. His "Westernism" did not stop at administrative, bureaucratic and economic reforms. Chulalangkorn was fascinated and attracted by European art, architecture and taste, and while some of his many children were sent to study in the most prestigious European universities, he brought European jurists, financial and educational experts, sculptors, architects and painters to Siam.

It was while he was returning from a trip to

style with enameled ceramic tiles topped by three soaring *mondops* (four-sided structures topped by sloping roofs and a soaring spire). The king wanted a Neoclassical "Italian" roof but gave way when conservative members of his court opposed anything so "Western."

Chulalangkorn was the (happy) victim of a vogue similar to what had by then swept across all of the west: there was hardly a house in Europe that did not have at least one Oriental object on show, perhaps *chinoiserie* or a touch of Asian extravagance to encourage dreams of adventurous trips to far-off countries. Chulalangkorn indulged himself in the opposite way; like the Great Palace, all of Bangkok became affected with Western

298 center A gilded kinnara, a mythical being created by the union of a bird with a human, guards the entrance to Wat Phra Keo's Bot, the principal shrine of the temple. The kinnara is made from gilded bronze and is covered with varicolored glass tiles.

298-299 The Wat Phra Keo is surrounded by a double enclosure wall. In the center stands the Bot of the Emerald Buddha. To the left of this stands the Prasad Phra Thep Bidom. Behind the Prasad Phra Thep Bidom is the chedi Phra Si Ratana, entirely covered with gold.

The Royal Palace in Bangkok
In the City of the Angels

298 top The central section of the building is occupied by a mondop, a four-sided structure topped by sloping roofs and a soaring spire. The silver spire in late Bangkok style has a bell-shaped base crowned with lotus flowers.

Europe that Chulalangkorn decided to build the Chakri Maha Prasad, a new building with the principal function of receiving foreign diplomats, a function which it has retained. The palace was designed by an English architect, and Chulalangkorn requested a facade of pink marble in Italian Renaissance style. A double stairway leads to the main entrance, through which one enters the audience room containing a marvelous niellated silver throne. But the visitor's eyes are pulled upward by the roof, built in full Thai

architectural features, and the most important palace rooms were decorated with frescoes, paintings and sculptures in European style that had been commissioned from English, French or Italian artists, like those in the Phra Thinang Aphon Phimok Prasad, the 1909 work of Cesare Ferro.

To the south of the Chakri Maha Prasad stretches the Inner City; it is an ancient residence in the extensive women's section of the complex. The wives of the king lived here with the many children who made up the royal

299 top left The architectural style of the Phra Si Ratana chedi comes from the Indo-Singhalese stupa with a bell-shaped anda topped by a square pavilion (harmika) which, with a small colonnade, forms the base made of concentric rings.

299 top right Two pairs of symmetrical buildings (the prang) welcome pilgrims at the entrance of the Emerald Buddha's Bot. These buildings on the east side of the Bot, together with two other pairs of prang of the same type, were built in Khmer style by the first Chakri kings.

300 top left This terrifying giant wearing court military clothes comes from Ramakien mythology. He exemplifies the "Baroque" form and lively color contrast that were typical of the Rattanokosin/Bangkok style.

300 center left The heart of the Chakri dynasty and its power is kept in this room. On a throne 36 feet high, surrounded by valuable hangings and objects of worship, sits the tiny Emerald Buddha that has watched over the peace and prosperity of the Thai kingdom and the fortunes of its kings since 1784.

In the City of the Angels
The Royal Palace in Bangkok

300 bottom left King Maha Majiravudh, Rama VI, decided to house the "Pantheon" of the Chakri dynasty in the Prasad Phra Thep Bidom. Here the bronze lifesize images of all Chakri rulers can be worshiped.

300 top right One of the jewels of Wat Phra Keo is without doubt the front of the Emerald Buddha's Bot. Framed by intertwined leaves among hundreds of small reflecting tiles, a winged figure prostrates himself in the traditional and reverent Thai greeting.

300 bottom right The gentle beauty of young Thai girls shines out in this gilded bronze statue depicting a kinnari, half woman and half bird, the female equivalent of the more terrifying male kinnara.

301 Giant demons watch over the Prasad Phra Thep Bidom, the surrounding buildings and the members of the faithful who burn incense sticks as they pray. The proud and fearless nature represented by these giants are shown in the different colors of their faces.

family. From Ramathibodhi to Chulalangkorn, the Chakri kings practiced polygamy for about a century, and they each had dozens of children. The young princes could live in the women's apartments until puberty, the age of transition from childhood to adulthood. When the moment to leave the Inner City arrived, the young boy underwent the ceremony of tonsure or Chulamangkala. An Italian colonel, Gerolamo Emilio Gerini, who stayed in Siam as a military instructor in 1860–1913, left a detailed description of this ceremony. Each boy had been raised with a shaved head except for a single lock of hair on the top; at the end of the tonsure ceremony, for which he wore special clothes, a Brahmin priest ritually cut off this single lock from the boy's head.

The Sivalaya gardens lie to the north of the Dusit Maha Prasad in the eastern quarters. Here, every year on the king's birthday, the rulers would give a huge reception. In the center a small shrine was built, the Phra Buddha Ratana Sathan, in which only the queens were allowed to pray.

Still further to the east toward the city walls, Rama VI, King Vajiravudh (1910–1925) commissioned the Boromphiman Palace, a large building completely in Western style, from a group of Italian architects who were members of the Ercole/Ekarit Manfredi circle (1883–1973). From Rama VI to Rama VIII, King Ananda Mahidol (1945–46), only the hereditary princes were allowed to stay here. The center of the square dome of this building was covered with magnificent frescoes in 1917 by the Tuscan painter Carlo Rigoli (1883–1962). In one of the first rows, four important gods are shown—Indra, Yahuma, Varuna and Agni—while above them, as a warning, are shown the ten virtues that a ruler must possess to be able to govern Siam, today known as Thailand.

BIOGRAPHIES, BIBLIOGRAPHIES AND PHOTOGRAPHIC CREDITS

INTRODUCTION
Text by Marcello Morelli

Marcello Morelli is a Literature professor at the University of Siena and at Tor Vegata University in Rome. He is the author of a number of volumes and has been Secretary General of the Association of Italian Historical Houses since 1997.

Bibliography

J. S. Ackerman, *La villa de la Rome antique à Le Corbusier*, Paris, 1997.
C. Erder, *Our Architectural Heritage: From Consciousness to Conservation*, Lanham, Mass., 1987.
J. D. Hoag, *Architettura islamica*, Milan, 1989.
W. Lotz, *L'architettura del rinascimento*, Milan, 1989.
G. Mitchell, A. Martinelli, *Royal Palaces of India*, London, 1999.

Photographic creditsonio Attini/Archivio White Star: pages 11 top, 13 top; Marcello Bertinetti/Archivio White Star: page 15 left; Giulio Veggi/Archivio White Star: pages 9 top right, 9 bottom, 15 right; Stefano Amanti-ni/Atlantide: page 10 top; D. Ball/Ag. Marka: page 1; Wojtek Buss: pages 9 top left, 12 top, 12-13; Stefano Cellai: page 10 bottom; Giovanni Dagli Orti: pages 4-5, 6, 8 top; Ag. Double's: page 7; Flavio Pagani: page 14 left; Photobank: pages 14 center, 14 right, 16-17; Ripani/Sime: pages 6-7; R. Schmid/Bildarchiv Huber/Sime: pages 8-9; Giovanni Simeone/Sime: pages 2-3; Yvan Travert/Ag. Franca Speranza: pages 10-11.

SPLENDORS AND MEMORIES OF THE COURTS OF EUROPE
Text by Marcello Morelli

Bibliography

R. De Fusco, *Mille anni d'architettura in Europa*, Bari, 1999.
W. Lotz, D. Howard, *Architecture in Italy, 1500-1600*, New Haven, 1995.
C. Steenbergen, W. Reh, *Architecture and Landscape: The Design Experiment of the Great European Gardens and Landscapes*, Bethel, Conn., 1996.
W. Von Kalnein, *Architecture in France in the Eighteenth Century*, New Haven, 1995.
D. Watkin, *Storia dell'architettura occidentale*, Bologna, 1990.

Photographic credits: Antonio Attini/Archivio White Star: page 19 center left; Wojtek Buss: pages 18-19; Giovanni Dagli Orti: page 21 top right; Frank Ihlow/Ullstein: page 18 top; Photobank: page 21 left; Nicolas Rakhmanov/Ag. ANA: pages 20-21; Ripani/Sime: pages 20 top, 21 bottom right; Giovanni Simeone/Sime: page 18 bottom; The Bridgeman Art Library, London: page 19 top right.

THE ROYAL PALACE OF TURIN
Text by Maria Luisa Moncassoli Tibone

Maria Luisa Moncassoli Tibone, art historian and journalist, studies the important artistic and historical aspects of Italy's cultural heritage and is a member of various associations that aim to promote cultural awareness and preservation. Formerly a teacher of art history in the Liceo Artistico dell'Accademia Albertina di Belle Arti in Turin, she has published about 40 books focusing particularly on art in Piedmont.

Bibliography

M. Bernardi, *Il Palazzo Reale di Torino*, Turin, 1959.
U. Chierici, R. Tardito Amerio, *Palazzo Reale di Torino: Appartamento di Madama Felicita*, Turin, 1971.
M. L. Tibone, "I Savoia munifici fautori delle arti" in *Iconografia e collezionismo sabaudo*, Turin, 1982.
A. Griseri, G. Romano (editors), *Porcellane e argenti del Palazzo Reale di Torino*, exhibition catalogue, Turin, 1986.
Various authors, *I giardini a Torino. Dalle residenze sabaude ai parchi e ai giardini del '900*, Turin, 1991.
V. Comoli Mandracci, A. Griseri, *Filippo Juvarra architetto delle capitali da Torino a Madrid 1714-1736* , Turin, 1995.
Il Palazzo Reale di Torino nelle guide della città, Turin, 1995.

Photographic credits : Antonio Attini/Archivio White Star: pages 22-23; Marcello Bertinetti/Archivio White Star: pages 22 bottom left, 23 center; Archivio Attilio Boccazzi Varotto: pages 24-25, 25 top and bottom, 26 left, 26 bottom right, 27, 28 top and center, 28-29; Archivio Scala: pages 22 top, 23 top; Civica Raccolta Stampe A. Bertarelli, Castello Sforzesco, Milan: page 23 bottom; Fototeca Turismo, City of Turin: page 24 bottom; D. Donadoni/Ag. Marka: page 22 bottom right; Marco Mairani: page 26 top right; The Bridgeman Art Library, London: page 28 bottom.

THE ROYAL PALACE OF CASERTA
Text by Salvatore Ciro Nappo

Salvatore Ciro Nappo earned a degree in Classical Literature at the University of Naples with a major in archaeology, and attended the Naples Classical Archaeology College. He has taken part in numerous archaeological missions, collaborates with Italian universities and foreign institutes on Pompeiian research, and has given speeches at various congresses and seminars.

Bibliography

L. Vanvitelli, *Dichiarazione dei disegni del Real Palazzo di Caserta alle Sacre Maestà*, Naples, 1756.
M. R. Caroselli, *La Reggia di Caserta. Lavori, costi, effetti della costruzione*, Milan, 1968.
C. De Seta, *Il Real Palazzo di Caserta*, Naples, 1991.
G. M. Jacobitti, W. Ferola Frizzi, *La Reggia di Caserta*, Naples, 1993.

Photographic credits: Giulio Veggi/Archivio White Star: pages 30-31, 31 top, 34 bottom left, 35 bottom; Archivio Scala: page 35 top; Giovanni Dagli Orti: pages 30 center, 30 bottom, 31 bottom, 32 bottom, 33 bottom, 36 top left, 37 bottom, 38 top, 39 bottom, 40 bottom, 40-41, 41; Luciano Pedicini/Archivio dell'Arte: pages 34 top, 36 bottom left, 36 bottom right, 38 center; Giovanni Simeone/Ag. Marka: page 34 bottom right; Giovanni Simeone/Sime: pages 34-35, 35 center, 36-37, 38-39; Photo Sud/Realy Easy Star: pages 32-33.

THE ROYAL PALACE OF VERSAILLES
Text by Milena Ercole Pozzoli

Milena Ercole Pozzoli earned a degree in Modern Literature from the University of Turin and worked as a foreign language assistant at Grenoble University. She has worked as a freelance photographer and journalist for major travel and cooking publications for 20 years. She has written numerous travel guides and the book *Castles of the Loire*.

Bibliography

J. M. Pérouse de Montclos, R. Polidori, *Versailles*, Cologne, 1996.
S. Pincas, *Versailles:The History of the Garden and the Sculptures*, Farnborough, England, 1996.
D. L. Lebard, *Versailles, Le petit trianon*, Paris, 1989.

Photographic credits: Bowman/Ag. Double's: page 42 top left; Hervé Champollion: pages 54 bottom, 54-55, 55 bottom; Marco Cristofori/Sie: page 44 bottom right; Giovanni Dagli Orti: pages 42 bottom left, 46 bottom, 47 right, 48 left, 48 top right, 50, 50-51, 51, 52 bottom left, 52-53, 53 top left, 53 bottom, 54 center, 55 top, 56 top and center, 56-57, 57 bottom; Ag. Double's: pages 46-47, 48 center right, 52 bottom right; Mary Evans Picture Library: page 42 bottom right; Anne Gaël-Serge Chirol: page 56 bottom; HP Huber/Sime: page 44 top; M. J. Jarry/J. F. Tripelon/Ag. Top: page 54 top; Daniel Philippe: pages 42-43; Ag. Luisa Ricciarini: page 42 top right; G. Sini/Ag. Marka: page 43 top; The Bridgeman Art Library, London: pages 45 bottom, 48 bottom right, 49, 53 top right; Paul Trummer: pages 43 bottom, 44 bottom left; Sandro Vannini/Ag. Franca Speranza: page 47 left; Hans Wiesenhofer/Ag. Regina Maria Anzenberger: page 45 top; P.Wysocki-S. Frances/Hémisphères: pages 44-45.

THE CASTLE OF CHAMBORD
Text by Milena Ercole Pozzoli

Bibliography

P. Miquel, J. B. Leroux, *Les Châteaux de la Loire*, Bienne, Switzerland, 1998.
M. Melot, *Chateaux of the Loire*, 1997.

Photographic credits: Archivio Scala: page 59 top right; Wojtek Buss: pages 62-63; Hervé Champollion: pages 61 bottom, 63 top; Hervé Champollion/Ag. Top: pages 62 right, 64 bottom left; Serge Chirol: pages 60 top right, 62 bottom left; Giovanni Dagli Orti: pages 58, 59 top left, 62 top left and center, 64 top left, 64 right, 64-65, 65; Daniel Philippe: pages 60 top left, 60-61; Andrea Pistolesi: page 60 bottom; P. Wysocki-S. Frances/Hémisphères: pages 58-59.

THE CASTLE OF FONTAINEBLEAU
Text by Milena Ercole Pozzoli

Bibliography

A. Lefébvre, *Fontainebleau: guide de visite*, Paris, 1997.

Photographic credits: AKG Photo: page 67 bottom; Serge Chirol: pages 68 center, 70 top, 70 bottom left, 74-75; Marco Cristofori/Sie: pages 72-73; Marco Cristofori/Marka: 75 top; Giovanni Dagli Orti: pages 66 top right, 67 center, 68 top, 68 bottom, 69 top right, 71 top left, 72 bottom, 73 left, 73 top right, 74 left, 74 top right, 76, 77 bottom, 78, 78-79, 79; Ag. Double's: pages 73 bottom right, 76-77; Franck Lechenet/Hémisphères: pages 66-67; The Bridgeman Art Library, London: pages 70-71, 70 bottom right, 71 bottom; Sandro Vannini/Ag. Franca Speranza: pages 66 top left, 68-69, 69 top left, 71 top right.

THE ALHAMBRA
Text by Giuseppe Mazzocchi

Giuseppe Mazzocchi lecturer in Spanish culture at the University of East Piedmont in Vercelli, specializes in Castilian literature from the Middle Ages to the Baroque, and in cultural contacts between Christendom and Islam in Spanish areas. He has published books and papers about late-medieval Spanish poets and has also translated various works into Italian.

Bibliography

F. Gabrieli, *Storia della letteratura araba*, Florence-Milan, 1967.
J. D. Hoag, *Architettura islamica*, Milan, 1973.
F. Gabrieli, *Gli arabi*, Florence, 1987.
G. Goodwin, *Spagna islamica*, Milan, 1992.
A. Castro, *La Spagna nella sua realtà storica*, Milan, 1995.
P. A. Galera Andreu, "Granada," in *Enciclopedia dell'arte medievale*, Rome, 1996.

Photographic credits: Antonio Attini/Archivio White Star: pages 80 top right, 81 bottom right, 82-83, 82 bottom right, 83, 84 top left and center, 84 center and right, 86, 86-87, 87 bottom, 88 left, 90 center left, 90 right, 91, 92 top left and bottom, 92 top right, 92-93, 93 bottom; Felipe Alcoceba: page 87 top; Ag. Double's: page 81 top; Grafenhaim/Bildarchiv Huber/Sime: page 85; Johanna Huber/Sime: pages 88-89; Flavio Pagani: pages 80-81; Lorenzo Sechi/Realy Easy Star: page 80 top left; Gerard Sioen/Ag. Regina Maria Anzenberger: page 90 bottom left; Henri Stierlin: pages 81 bottom left, 82 top, 82 bottom left, 84 bottom left, 88 top, 88 right, 89 bottom, 92 center left.

THE ESCORIAL
Text by Giuseppe Mazzocchi

Bibliography

F. Chueca y Goitia, "Juan de Herrera," in *Enciclopedia Universale dell'arte*, Venice-Rome, 1958.
J. de Contreras Marqués de Lozoya, *Escorial e San Ildefonso*, Novara, 1965.
G. Parker, *Un solo re, un solo impero: Filippo II di Spagna*, Bologna, 1985.
El Escorial, biografía de una época, Madrid, 1986.
Felipe II, un monarca y su época, Madrid, 1998.

Photographic credits: AISA: page 103 top; Archivio Scala: page 94 top; Stefano Cellai: pages 94 center, 96 left, 96 top left; Giovanni Dagli Orti: page 94 bottom; Fotografias Oronoz: pages 95 top right, 96-97, 97 top, 97 bottom, 98 top, 98 center, 98 bottom, 99, 100, 101, 102; Index Fototeca: page 95 top left; Andrea Pistolesi: pages 96 top right, 102-103; Rossenbach/Zefa: pages 94-95.

THE ROYAL PALACE OF QUELUZ
Text by Giuseppe Mazzocchi

Bibliography

H. Sedlmayr, H. Bauer, "Rococò," in *Enciclopedia Universale dell'Arte*, Venice-Rome, 1963.
C. Norberg-Schulz, *Architettura tardobarocca*, Milan, 1972.
J. H. Pais da Silva, "Queluz," in *Dicionário de história de Portugal*, Porto, 1979.
J. H. Pais da Silva, "Rococó," *ibid.*
J. Saramago, *Viagem a Portugal*, Lisbon, 1981.

Photographic credits: Massimo Listri: pages 104 top, 105 top and bottom, 106, 107, 108, 109; Jean Charles Pinheira: page 105 center; Giovanni Simeone/Sime: pages 104-105; Henri Stierlin: pages 104 left, 104 bottom left; Pawel Wysocki/Hémisphères: page 104 bottom right.

BUCKINGHAM PALACE
Text by Michael Leech

Michael Leech has worked in the arts in London, New York and Canada. He has been a professional writer full time since 1969, and is the author of various guidebooks. A member of Pen and the London's Critics' Circle, he has published fiction and poetry and his articles have appeared in British Tourist Authority publications and other periodicals, most recently in *History Today* magazine.

Bibliography

J. Martin-Robinson, *Royal Palaces: Buckingham Palace*, London, 1995.
E. Heeley, *The Queen's House*, London, 1997.
Official Guide to Buckingham Palace, London, 1996.

Photographic credits: Chorley Handford: pages 110-111; Luciano Ramires/Archivio White Star: page 111 top; Ripani/Sime: page 110 center right; The Bridgeman Art Library, London: page 110 bottom left; The Royal Collection © Her Majesty Queen Elizabeth II: pages 110 top, 112, 113, 114, 115, 116, 117, 118, 119.

HAMPTON COURT
Text by Michael Leech

Bibliography

The Royal Palaces, Andover, 1991.
S. Thurley (editor), "The Privy Garden," in *Apollo Magazine*, London, 1995.
Official Guide to Hampton Court, London, 1996.

Photographic credits: Crown Copyright: Historic Royal Palaces: pages 120 center, 120-121, 121 bottom, 122 top, 123 top, 124, 125, 126, 127, 128, 129, Ripani/Sime: pages 122 bottom, 122-123, 123 bottom; The Bridgeman Art Library, London: pages 120 top, 128 bottom; The Royal Collection © Her Majesty Queen Elizabeth II: pages 120 bottom, 121 top.

THE CASTLE OF BRUSSELS
Text by Maria Longhena

Maria Longhena Bruyndonckx has a degree in Ancient History at Bologna University. She has worked for several years at the Royal Museums of Art and History in Brussels, studying the history of the city's architecture.

Bibliography
M. Wasseigen (editor), *Le quartier royal* (Collection Bruxelles ville d'Art et d'Histoire), Brussels, 1995.
Various authors, *Le palais royal de Bruxelles*, Brussels, 1993.
Photographic credits: Archives Du Palais Royal, Bruxelles: pages 130 bottom, 131 bottom, 133 top left; Bart Cloet: pages 130 center, 130-131, 132-133, 133 bottom, 134 top and bottom, 134-135; Collection Royale Belgique: page 130 top; Luc Schrobiltgen-Liste Civile Du Roi, Bruxelles: pages 132 bottom, 133 top right, 135 top.

HET LOO PALACE
Text by Adriaan Willem Vliegenthart

Adriaan Willem Vliegenthart has, since finishing his studies in History of Art at the University of Utrecht, worked at the Art Historical Institute of the Dutch Universities in Florence. Since April 1972 he has been director of Het Loo Palace; under him, the restoration of the palace took place between 1974 and 1984.
Bibliography
A. W. Vliegenthart, A.M.L.E. Erkelens, *Guide to Het Loo Palace and Gardens*, Appeldoorn, Belgium, 1995.
A. W. Vliegenthart, "Het Loo: de renaissance van een paleis," in *Architecturaal Digest*, October 1984.
Photographic credits: Giulio Veggi/Archivio White Star: pages 136 top, 137 top left; E. Boeijinga/Paleis Het Loo: pages 136 bottom right, 136-137, 138-139, 140, 140-141; A.A.W. Meine Jansen/Paleis Het Loo: page 139 top; R. Mulder/Paleis Het Loo: pages 136 bottom left, 137 center and bottom, 138, 141 bottom.

THE CASTLE OF NEUSCHWANSTEIN
Text by Paola Calore

Paola Calore has published articles and photographs in numerous travel and vacation magazines. Following various jobs in the tourism field, she has worked for the press offices of Bavaria and of the National German Tourism Agency and for the Historical German Cities association. She is the author of the book *Castles of Bavaria* .
Bibliography
A. Rauch, *Neuschwanstein*, Munich, 1997.
H. Nöhbauer, *Auf den Spuren Konig Ludwigs II*, Munich, 1995.
M. Petzet, *Ludwig und seine Schlösser*, Munich, 1995.
Bayerischer Verwaltung der staatlichen Schlösser, Gärten und Seen (editorial board), *Schloß Neuschwanstein*, Munich, 1996.
Photographic credits: Stefano Amantini/Atlantide: page 148 top; L. Botta/Ag. Marka: page 150 bottom left; Achim Bunz/Ag. Regina Maria Anzenberger: pages 144, 145 top right and center, 146 center and bottom, 146-147, 148-149, 149 center and bottom, 150 top, 150 bottom right, 151; Giovanni Dagli Orti: pages 142 bottom left, 146 top, 147 top; Photobank: page 142 right; Sergio Pitamitz/Focus Team: pages 142 top left, 149 top; Giovanni Simeone/Sime: page 143.

THE CASTLE OF CHARLOTTENBURG
Text by Paola Calore

Bibliography
T. W. Gaehtgens (editor), *Schloß Charlottenburg*, Berlin, 1995.
M. Kühn, *Schloß Charlottenburg. Die Bauwerke und Kunstdenkmäler von Berlin*, 2 vols., Berlin, 1970.
H. J. Giersberg, J. Julier (editors), *Königliche Schlösser in Berlin-Brandenburg*, 1993.
M. Sperlich, *Schloß Charlottenburg*, Berlin, 1974.
Photographic credits: Marcello Bertinetti/Archivio White Star: page 155; Giulio Veggi/Archivio White Star: pages 152 bottom left, 154 left, 154-155; AKG Photo: pages 152 top, 152 right, 154 bottom, 158-159; Klaus Frahm: pages 157 bottom, 158 bottom, 159 top left; Gregor M. Schmid: page 156 left; Johann Scheibner: page 159 right; Günter Schneider/Ullstein: pages 156-157; Stiftung Preussische Schlösser und Gärten Berlin-Brandenburg/Bildarchiv: page 159 bottom left; Lothar Willmann/Ullstein: page 153.

THE CASTLE OF SANS SOUCI
Text by Heidi Böcker

Heidi Böcker earned a degree in Art History, Classical Archaeology and Italian Literature after studies in Munich, Vienna and Florence. She has worked for the Bavarian Tourist Board and for many years as a guide in Regensburg and throughout Bavaria.
Bibliography
H. J. Giersberg, J. Julier (editors), *Königliche Schlösser in Berlin-Brandenburg*, Berlin-Potsdam, 1993.
Stiftung Preußische Schlösser und Gärten Berlin-Brandenburg (editorial board),*Schloß Sanssouci; Bildergalerie Sanssouci: Gemälde und Skulpturen; Das chinesische Haus im Park von Sanssouci; Die neuen Kammern im Park von Sanssouci,* Berlin, 1996.
Photographic credits: Marcello Bertinetti/Archivio White Star: page 160 top; AKG Photo: pages 161 top, 161 bottom; Stiftung Preussische Schlösser und Gärten Berlin-Brandenburg/Bildarchiv: pages 162 top left and center, 164 bottom, 165 top right, 165 bottom; Wojtek Buss: page 160 center; Klaus Frahm/Contur: page 173 bottom left; Cesare Gerolimetto: pages 166 bottom, 167 top; Brigitte Hiss/Ullstein: pages 170-171; Frank Ihlow/Ullstein: pages 166 center top, 167 bottom; Ansgar Koch/Ullstein: page 168 bottom left; Jurgens Ost+Europa Photos, Berlin: page 172 top left; Andrea Pistolesi: pages 166 top, 170 center, 171 top left, 171 right, 172 bottom left, 172 top right, 173 top; Rossenbach/Zefa: pages 160-161, 166-167, 170 bottom left; R. Schmid/Bildarchiv Huber/Sime: pages 166 center bottom, 172-173; Gerd Schnürer/Ullstein: page 170 top; Schulenburg/The Interior Archive: page 168 bottom right; Klaus Frahm: pages 162 bottom, 162 top right, 163, 164-165, 168-169, 169 top, 169 bottom, 173 bottom right; Lothar Willmann/Ullstein: page 160 bottom.

THE CASTLE OF SCHÖNBRUNN
Text by Andrea Affaticati

Andrea Affaticati was born in Austria. She is a freelance journalist who contributes to several Italian publications, concentrating mainly on cultural themes and travel articles regarding Austria.
Bibliography
P. Parenzan, B. Korvin, *Schloß Schönbrunn*, Vienna, 1998.
E. M. Seuhs, H. Lust, *Schönbrunn, Wege rund ums Kalserschloß*, Vienna, 1996.
Photographic credits: Giulio Veggi/Archivio White Star: page 177 top; Archivio Scala: page 175 bottom right; Wojtek Buss: page 176 top; Mary Evans Picture Library: page 175 top; Photobank: pages 174 bottom, 176-177; J. Fuste Raga/Ag. Marka: page 177 bottom; The Bridgeman Art Library, London: page 175 bottom left; Prof. Gerhard Trumler: pages 174-175, 178 top, 179 top and center, 180, 181, 182, 183; Johannes Wagner: pages 178 bottom, 178-179, 179 bottom; Hans Wiesenhofer/Ag. Regina Maria Anzenberger: page 174 top; Pawel Wysocki/Hémisphères: page 176 bottom.

THE CASTLE OF ESTERHÁZA
Text by Francesco Guida

Francesco Guida is a professor of East European History at the TRE University of Rome and a member of the Directorate of the Inter-University Center for Hungarian Studies in Italy. He is the author of various books and essays.
Bibliography
I. Haynal, *Esterhàzy Miklòs Nador Lemondàre (Székfaglalo értekezés)*, Budapest, 1929.
M. Horanyi, *The Magnificence of Eszterháza*, Budapest, 1962.
F. Guida (editor), *Dalla Liberazione di Buda all'Ungheria del Trianon. Ungheria e Italia tra età moderna e contemporanea*, Rome, 1996.
G. Motta, R. Tolomeo (editors), *Storia dell'Ungheria*, Milan, 1998.
Photographic credits Manfred Horvath/Ag. Regina Maria Anzenberger: page 184 bottom right; Roger Moulin/Ag. Top: page 189 top right; Giovanni Simeone/Sime: pages 184 center, 184-185; Szépmüvészeti Museum, Budapest: page 185 top right; Prof. Gerhard Trumler: pages 184 top, 184 bottom left, 185 top left, 185 bottom, 186, 187-188, 188-189, 189 left, 189 bottom right.

THE CASTLE OF PRAGUE
Text by Franti˘ sek Kadlec

Franti˘sek Kadlec, a historian, graduated from the Charles University in Prague. He is head of the department of tourism of the Prague Castle administration, and is the author of several articles and books including: *The State Rooms of Prague Castle* and *The Golden Lane at Prague Castle.*
Bibliography
P. Chotebor, *Guide to Prague Castle*, 1994.
Photographic credits: Miroslav and Barbara Hucek: pages 190, 191, 192, 193, 194, 195.

THE PALACE OF WILANÓW
Text by Gianfranco Giraudo

Gianfranco Giraudo earned a degree in Foreign Languages and Literature at the University of Venice and is a professor of Slavic philology. He is the author of four books and several articles on history, philology, Ukrainian studies, and the comparative lexicography of the Eastern Slavic nations.
Bibliography
J. Cydrik, *Wilanów*, Warsaw, 1975.
Fiazkowski (editor), *Artystyczane zbiory Wilanowa*, Warsaw, 1979.
Photographic credits: Archivio Scala: page 196 top; Stefano Cellai: pages 198 top, 200 top, 200-201, 201 bottom right, 201 top and bottom, 204 top right; Stefano Cellai/Sie: pages 198 center, 203 bottom right; E.T. Archive: page 199 top; Andrea Pistolesi: pages 196 bottom, 196-197, 197, 198 bottom, 202 top, 204 top left, 205; R. Schmid/Bildarchiv Huber/Sime: pages 198-199; Mark E. Smith: page 204 center right; Prof. Gerhard Trumler: pages 196 center, 201 bottom left, 202 center and bottom, 202-203, 203 bottom left, 204 bottom left, 204 bottom right.

ROSENBORG
Text by Peter Kristiansen

Peter Kristiansen earned a master's degree in Architectural History and Building Archaeology in 1988 from the Danish Royal Academy of Fine Arts. He was employed as curator at the Nationalmuseum from 1988 to 1991, and has been at the Royal Danish Collections of Rosenborg Castle since 1992.
Bibliography
Rosenborg, The Royal Danish Collections, Esbjerg, 1995.
Photographic credits: Antonio Attini/Archivio White Star: pages 206 bottom right, 207 center, 208 top, 209 right, 208-209, 209 bottom, 211 bottom; E.T. Archive: page 206 top; Massimo Listri: pages 210-211, 210 top and bottom, 211 top right; Gérard Sioen/Rapho: pages 206-207, 207 bottom; Rosenborg Slot: pages 207 top, 211 top left, 211 center; Angelo Tondini/Focus Team: page 206 bottom left.

THE ROYAL PALACE IN OSLO
Text by Thomas Thiis-Evensen

Thomas Thiis-Evensen received a Ph.D. at Oslo University. Professor of the Theory and History of Architecture at the School of Architecture in Oslo, he is the author of numerous works on architecture including a book on royal Norwegian houses. He was also responsible for the premises of the restoration of the Royal Palace of Oslo.
Bibliography
S. Tschudi-Madsen, *To Kongeslott*, Oslo, 1954.
G. Kauli, *Slottet I Oslo*, Oslo, 1996.
T. Thiis-Evensen (editor), *Kongens Hus*, Oslo, 1996.
Photographic credits: Jiri Havran: pages 212, 212-213, 213 bottom, 214, 215, 216, 217; Royal Palace, Oslo: page 213 top.

THE ROYAL PALACE IN STOCKHOLM
Text by Göran Alm

Göran Alm holds a doctorate in Philosophy and Art History and is deputy director of information of the Swedish Royal Court. Author of many books on Swedish art history, especially of the 18th and 19th centuries, he is a well known lecturer and frequently participates in television programs.
Bibliography
G. Alm, *Great Royal Palaces of Sweden*, New York, 1997.
Photographic credits: Stefano Cellai: page 218 bottom; E.T. Archive: page 218 top; Massimo Listri: pages 220-221, 221 top, 222-223; Flavio Pagani: pages 219 top left, 222 center; Schulenburg/The Interior Archive: pages 220 top, 222 top; Vittorio Sciosia/Focus Team: pages 218-219, 222 bottom; The Royal Collection, Stockholm: pages 219 top right, 219 bottom, 221 bottom, 223 top and bottom.

THE KREMLIN
Text by Gianfranco Giraudo

Bibliography
I. Ê. Grabar (editor), *Istorija russkogo iskusstva*, vol. III, 1955.
C. Rodimzeva, *Kremlin and its Treasures*, London, 1990.
Photographic credits: Marcello Bertinetti/Archivio White Star: pages 224 center, 227 top, 227 center right, 229 top, 236 top, 236-237, 237 bottom; Jürgens Ost+Europa Photo: pages 224-225, 234 bottom; AKG photo: 225 bottom left; Nicolas Rakhmanov/Ag. ANA: pages 224 top and bottom, 225 bottom right, 226 top and bottom, 226-227, 227 bottom, 228 top and center, 228-229, 229 bottom, 230 top and center, 230-231, 231 bottom, 232 left, 232 top right, 232 bottom right, 232-233, 234-235, 235 left, 235 right, 236 center and bottom, 237 bottom right, 238-239, 239; National Library of Russia, St. Petersburg: 225 top left.

KARSKOE SELO
Text by Gianfranco Giraudo

Bibliography
I.V. Semennikova (editor), *Puškin, Dvorcy i parki*, Leningrad-Moscow, 1964.
I. da Madariaga, *Caterina di Russia*, Turin, 1990.
Photographic credits: Giulio Veggi/Archivio White Star: page 241 bottom right; Archivio Scala: pages 240 top, 241 top; Benelux Press B.V.: pages 244-245; Wojtek Buss: pages 240 center and bottom, 240-241, 241 bottom left; Carlos Domenech Photography: pages 243 center right, 244 center and bottom; Hazard Publishing: pages 242-243, 243 top left, 243 bottom right, 244 top, 245 top and bottom.

PETERHOF
Text by Claudia Sugliano

Claudia Sugliano translates books from Russian for important Italian publishers, and contributes articles on Russian art and culture to various publications. She studied and worked for many years in Russia has been a lecturer on Russian language.
Bibliography
A. Benois, *Peterhof*, Saint Petersburg, 1995.
Peterhof, The Great Palace, Saint Petersburg, 1996.
Peterhof, The Fountains, Saint Petersburg, 1996.
M. di Grecia, *Palazzi Imperiali Russi*, Milan, 1992.
"Gli scultori carraresi all'Ermitage e a Peterhof," in *I marmi degli Zar*, Milan, 1996.
Vozrozdennye Iz Pepla. Petrodvorec, Puskin, Pavlosk, Leningrad, 1989.
Photographic credits: Giulio Veggi/Archivio

White Star: pages 252 center bottom, 252 right; Benelux Press B.V.: page 249 bottom; Wojtek Buss: pages 248-249; Carlos Domenech Photography: pages 246 top right, 248 bottom right, 251 top, 251 bottom, 252 top left, 252 center top, 253; Marco Mairani: page 246 center; Photobank: pages 246-247; Gregor M. Schmid: pages 246 top left, 246 bottom, 247 bottom, 248 top, 248 bottom right, 249 top, 250-251, 252 bottom left; Schulenburg/The Interior Archive: page 250 top; The Bridgeman Art Library, London: page 247 top.

MAGNIFICENCE AND POWER IN THE ORIENTAL PALACES
Text by Paola Mortari Vergara Caffarelli

Paola Mortari Vergara Caffarelli is the sole East Asian Art professor in Italy, at University of Genoa. She has completed many study programs in Asia and is the author of about eighty articles and monographs on the architecture and monuments of Tibet, Mongolia, China, Korea and Japan.
Bibliography
M. Bussagli, *Architettura orientale*, Venice, 1973.
L. G. Liu, *Chinese Architecture*, Hong Kong, 1989.
P. Mortari Vergara Caffarelli, *L'Architettura di stile tibetano dei Ch'ing. Diffusione di un linguaggio architettonico di tipo "occidentale" nell'Asia Orientale*, Rome, 1982.
P. Mortari Vergara, G. Béguin, *Dimore umane, Santuari divini. Origini, sviluppo e diffusione dell'architettura tibetana*, Rome, 1987.
C. Tadgell, *The History of Architecture in India*, London, 1990.
Photographic credits: Giulio Veggi/Archivio White Star: page 256 top; Marcello Bertinetti/Archivio White Star: page 255 right; Massimo Borchi/Archivio White Star: page 256 bottom left; Christophe Boisvieux: page 257 top left; Giovanni Dagli Orti: pages 256-257; Ag. Double's: page 257 top right; Flavio Pagani: pages 254-255; Photobank: page 255 top left; Günther Thöni/Ag. Regina Maria Anzenberger: page 254 top right.

TOPKAPI PALACE
Text by Giuseppe Mazzocchi

Bibliography
Albert Gabriel, *Ottomane scuole*, in *Enciclopedia universale dell'arte*, Venice-Rome, 1963.
G. Goodwin, *A History of Ottoman Architecture*, London, 1971.
J. D. Hoag, *Architettura islamica*, Milan, 1973.
F. Braudel, *Civiltà e imperi del mediterraneo nell'età di Filippo II*, Turin, 1986.
G. Mandel, *Mamma li turchi*, Bergamo, 1990.
P. Gennaro, *Istanbul. L'opera di Sinan*, Milan, 1992.
Photographic credits: Giulio Veggi/Archivio White Star: pages 258-259, 261 top; Cem Akkan/Ag. Regina Maria Anzenberger: pages 262 bottom, 262-263; Christophe Boisvieux: pages 260 top, 266 bottom left; Marco Casiraghi: pages 262 top and center, 263 top, 267 center; Giovanni Dagli Orti: pages 259 bottom, 261 bottom left, 264-265; Ag. Double's: page 258 top right; Namikawa Foundation, Shimane: pages 264 top, 264 bottom, 265 top, 265 bottom; A.W.C. Images/Sie: page 258 bottom; Andrea Pistolesi: pages 260 bottom, 260-261, 266 bottom right, 267 top and bottom; Ag. Luisa Ricciarini: page 259 top; R. Schmid/Huber/Sime: page 261 bottom right; Angelo Tondini/Focus Team: 266-267.

AMBER FORT
Text by Marilia Albanese

Marilia Albanese teaches Indian Studies at the Milan School of Oriental Languages and Cultures, of which she is also the director. She is the director of the Lombardy section of the Italian Institute for Africa and the East in Milan and has written a number of books and papers.
Bibliography
G. S. Ghurye, *Rajput Architecture*, Bombay, 1968.
Maharaja of Baroda, *The Palaces of India*, London, 1980.
L. Pellicani, *I Rajput: storie, leggende e tradizioni dei santuari dell'India*, Rome, 1994.
C. Tadgell, *The History of Architecture in India*, New Delhi, 1990.
G.H.R. Tillotson, *The Rajput Palaces*, New

Haven-London, 1987.
Photographic credits: Christophe Boisvieux: page 270 bottom; Thomas Dix: pages 268 top right, 268-269, 269 top right, 270-271, 271 top and bottom, 272, 272-273, 273 bottom; Patrick Frilet/Hémisphères: page 270 top; Laurent Giraudon/Ag. Regina Maria Anzenberger: pages 268 bottom left, 269 bottom; Alain Petit/Ag. Top: page 271 center; Photobank: page 269 top left Henri Stierlin: page 273 bottom; Alberto Zabert/Realy Easy Star: page 268 center left.

THE RED FORT IN DELHI
Text by Marilia Albanese

Bibliography
H. G. Behr, *Moghul, imperatori dell'India*, Milan, 1984.
V. Berinstain, *L'India dei Moghul: i fasti di un impero*, Trieste, 1997.
C. Tadgell, *The History of Architecture in India*, New Delhi, 1990.
S. C. Weich, *The Art of Mughul India*, New York, 1963.
Photographic credits: Marcello Bertinetti/Archivio White Star: page 274 center; Massimo Borchi/Archivio White Star: page 275 top left, 278-279, 279 top and center; Christophe Boisvieux: pages 277 top left, 276-277, 278 bottom left; Thomas Dix: pages 274-275, 276 top, 277 bottom left, 277 bottom right, 278 top, 279 bottom; Michel Dortes: page 274 top right, 274 bottom left, 277 top right; Index, Florence: page 274 bottom right; Henri Stierlin: page 278 bottom right; Angelo Tondini/Focus Team: page 275 top right.

THE FORBIDDEN CITY
Text by Guido Samarani

Guido Samarani is associate professor of Chinese history at Ca' Foscari University in Venice. He has written several volumes on the history of China and has published essays in historical, academic and Sinological magazines.
Bibliography
M. Sabattini, P. Santangelo, *Storia della Cina. Dalle origini alla fondazione della Repubblica*, Rome-Bari, 1996.
L. Sickman, A. Soper, *The Art and Architecture of China*, Harmondsworth, England, 1960.
Various Authors, *Daily Life in the Forbidden*

City: the Qing Dynasty, 1644-1912, New York, 1998.
R. Howard, L. Sherman, *Masterworks of Ming and Qing Paintings from the Forbidden City*, Lansdale, 1998.
Photographic credits: Marcello Bertinetti/Archivio White Star: pages 280 top right, 280 center, 280-281, 281 top right, 282-283, 282 bottom, 283 right, 284 top, 285 bottom left and right, 286 top and bottom, 287 top, 288 top and center, 288-289, 289 top, 289 bottom left, 290-291, 290 bottom, 291 bottom left, 291 top and center; AKG photo: pages 280 bottom, 281 top left; B & U: page 283 center left; Wojtek Buss: pages 282 top right, 286-287, 291 right; Flavio Pagani: pages 282 top left, 289 bottom right; Photobank: pages 284 bottom, 284-285, 287 bottom; The Bridgeman Art Library, London: page 281 bottom.

THE ROYAL PALACE IN BANGKOK
Text by Fiorella Rispoli

Fiorella Rispoli is deputy director of the Thai-Italian Lopburi Regional Archaeological Project. She contributes as archaeologist and ceramics expert to the Thai-U.S. Thailand Archaeo-metallurgy Project, and is a collaborator at the IsIAO's Asian Center for Archaeological Studies and Research and at the National Museum of Oriental Arts in Rome. She is also the author of various articles on southeast Asian archaeology.
Bibliography
S. Besso, *Siam and China*, London, n.d.
J. Blofeld, *King Maha Mongkut of Siam*, Bangkok, 1987.
L. Ferri de Lazara, P. Piazzardi, *Italiani alla Corte del Siam*, Bangkok, 1997.
D.G.E. Hall, *Storia dell'Asia sudorientale*, Milan, 1972.
Rong Syamananda, *A History of Thailand*, Bangkok, 1988.
M. C. Subhadradis Diskul, *Art in Thailand: A Brief Introduction*, Bangkok, 1991.
S. van Beek, L. Invernizzi, *An Introduction to the Arts of Thailand*, Hong Kong, 1988.
Photographic credits: Marcello Bertinetti/Archivio White Star: pages 299 top right, 300 top left, 300 top right; Photobank: pages 292, 293, 294, 295, 296, 297, 298, 298-299, 299 top left, 300 center left and bottom, 300 bottom right, 301.

The Castle of Sans Souci stands near Potsdam in Germany; the rear facade of the castle overlooks the gardens.